Ethics, Dis/Ability and Sports

Edited by Ejgil Jespersen and Mike McNamee

Routledge
Taylor & Francis Group

LONDON AND NEW YORK

First published 2009 by Routledge
2 Park Square, Milton Park, Abingdon, Oxon, OX14 4RN

Simultaneously published in the USA and Canada
by Routledge
711 Third Avenue, New York, NY 10017

Routledge is an imprint of the Taylor & Francis Group, an informa business

First issued in paperback 2011

© 2009 Edited by Ejgil Jespersen and Mike McNamee

Typeset in Myriad by Value Chain, India

British Library Cataloguing in Publication Data
A catalogue record for this book is available from the British Library

ISBN13: 978-0-415-48797-9 (hbk)
ISBN13: 978-0-415-51867-3 (pbk)

Ethics, Dis/Ability and Sports

This timely book is comprised of a range of essays by international scholars whose backgrounds embrace the philosophy and social theory of disability, medicine and sport, pedagogy and adapted physical activity. Based on an international symposium hosted by the Norwegian School of Sport Sciences, the chapters explore neglected ethical and philosophical dimensions of research, performance and professional practice across the adapted physical activity and disability sport spectrum and from an array of, sometimes competing, theoretical perspectives.

This book was published as a special issue in *Sport, Ethics and Philosophy*.

Ejgil Jespersen is former Associate Professor in the Department of Physical Education at the Norwegian School of Sport Sciences, having served as Head of Department there from 2004-2008.

Mike McNamee is a Professor of Applied Ethics at the Department of Philosophy, History and Law, School of Health Science at Swansea University. In the field of publishing, with Routledge, he is the series editor of *Ethics and Sport* and the journal editor of *Sport, Ethics and Philosophy*. He is a former President of the International Association for the Philosophy of Sport and the Founding Chair of the British Philosophy of Sport Association. He is a member of the Clinical Ethics Committee at Cardiff and Vale National Health Service Trust, UK.

Ethics and Sport
Series editors
Mike McNamee
University of Wales Swansea
Jim Parry
University of Leeds
Heather Reid
Morningside College

The Ethics and Sport series aims to encourage critical reflection on the practice of sport, and to stimulate professional evaluation and development. Each volume explores new work relating to philosophical ethics and the social and cultural study of ethical issues. Each is different in scope, appeal, focus and treatment but a balance is sought between local and international focus, perennial and contemporary issues, level of audience, teaching and research application, and variety of practical concerns.

Also available in this series:

CONTENTS

ACKNOWLEDGEMENTS

The Editors wish to sincerely thank Professor Sigmund Loland, Rektor at the Norwegian School of Sport Sciences, Oslo, for hosting the original symposium which gave birth to this volume, and Dame Tanni Grey-Thompson and Mark Shearman for their kind permission to use the great photo which serves as the cover for this book.

Introduction

PHILOSOPHY, ADAPTED PHYSICAL ACTIVITY AND DIS/ABILITY

Ejgil Jespersen and Mike McNamee

In the formation of the multi-disciplinary field that investigates the participation of disabled persons in all forms of physical activity, little ethical and philosophical work has been published. This essay serves to contextualise a range of issues emanating from adapted physical activity (APA) and disability sports. First, we offer some general historical and philosophical remarks about the field which serve to situate those issues at the crossroads between the philosophy of disability and the philosophy of sports. Secondly, we bring brief but critical attention to the contestation of key concepts such as "ability" and "normality" and the recent criticisms of polarisation of the medical and social models of disability. Finally, we show how these conceptual issues are implicated in the whole spectrum of contexts of APA and disability sports from the ethics of research with and for the disabled, to coaching, rehabilitation and teaching, and sports administration, that are predicated on key ethical concepts including empathy, entitlement and equity.

Resumen

En la formación del campo multidisciplinario que investiga la participación de personas discapacitadas en todas las variedades de actividad física se han publicado pocas obras éticas y filosóficas. Este ensayo sirve para contextualizar una panoplia de temas que surgen de la actividad física adaptada (AFA) [adapted physical activity (APA)] y los deportes de discapacitados. En primer lugar ofrecemos algunas observaciones generales históricas y filosóficas sobre este campo que sirven para situar estos asuntos en la encrucijada entre la filosofía de la discapacidad y la filosofía del deporte. En segundo lugar prestamos breve pero crítica atención a la disputa sobre conceptos tales como los de "habilidad" y "normalidad" y las críticas recientes de la polarización de los modelos de minusvalía médicos y sociales. Por último mostramos como estos temas conceptuales están involucrados en todo el espectro de contextos de AFA y deportes de discapacitados desde la ética de investigación con y para discapacitados al entrenamiento, la rehabilitación y la enseñanza, y la administración deportiva, los cuales se basan en conceptos éticos clave que incluyen la empatía, el merecimiento, y la equidad.

Zusammenfassung

Seid der Entstehung jenes mulidisziplinären Feldes, das sich der Erforschung sportlicher Aktivitäten von Behinderten widmet, sind bisher nur wenige ethische und philosophische Arbeiten publiziert worden. Dieser Essay dient der Kontextualisierung einer Reihe von Fragen und Problemen die im Feld Bewegung, Spiel und Sport in Prävention, Rehabilitation und Behinderung (APA = adapted physical activity) zum Vorschein kommen. Zunächst präsentieren wir einige allgemeine historische und philosophische Anmerkungen zu diesem Themengebiet, um die Kernprobleme an den Schnittstellen zwischen Philosophie und Behinderung, sowie der Philosophie des Sports besser verorten zu können. Des Weiteren beleuchten wir kurz die Streitigkeiten um Kernbegriffe wie „Fähigkeit" und „Normalität", sowie die neuerliche Kritik an der Polarisierung in medizinisches und gesellschaftliches Verständnis von Behinderung. Schließlich zeigen wir wie diese terminologischen Schwierigkeiten mit einer Reihe von Rahmenbedingungen von Bewegung, Spiel und Sport in Prävention, Rehabilitation und Behinderung (APA) verwoben sind. Es zeigen sich hier Verflechtungen zum einen mit der Ethik des Forschens (mit und für Behinderte), zum anderen in Bezug auf Coaching, Rehabilitation und Unterreichten, aber auch im Hinblick auf Sportadministrationen. Denn sie alle basieren auf ethischen Schlüsselbegriffen wie Empathie, Anspruchsberechtigung und Gleichheit.

摘要

在眾多各種有關失能身體活動參與的各領域研究中，很少人會用倫理及哲學的角度來發表文章。本文在於將適應身體活動(APA)及殘障運動中所產生的各種課題提出來探討。首先，我們提供一些用一般歷史及哲學觀點來討論這些課題，特別是介於殘障哲學與運動哲學的交會點上。其次，我們用一種簡單但具批判的角度來關注一些概念之間是否能被接受，如"能力" (ability) 及 "正常" (normality)，以及最近對醫藥與殘障失能社會模式兩極化的批判。最後，我們顯示這些概念在整個適應身體活動及殘障運動中，在倫理研究上是如何呈現在一些活動上，如教練、復健及教學，及運動行政上。這些關鍵課題是基於一些重要的倫理概念來探討，包括同理心、權利及公平的角度。

This book addresses a range of philosophical and ethical issues in adapted physical activity and disability sports participation more broadly. It is based upon invited papers[1] presented at a workshop at the Norwegian School of Sport Sciences from 30 August to 1 September 2007 by a range of international scholars whose backgrounds embraced different traditions of philosophy, pedagogy and adapted physical activity.[2] The principal aim of the symposium was to open up and critically explore a range of conceptual and ethical issues and perspectives that have arisen with respect to the engagement of persons with dis/abilities in a range of physical activity contexts including, but not exclusively located in, mainstream sporting activities. The symposium was a tremendous success. In such intellectual milieux there is rich potential for scholars and scientists to talk past each other in a cacophony, to assume too much of their given disciplinary or professional background, or to fail to recognise the diversity of sources that frame and attempt to solve ethically dense problems in the field. Happily, in this case, this book that has ensued bore none of the hallmarks of interdisciplinary conflict and we hope in some small way to have started a serious, polyphonic and timely debate on issues that have not hitherto been prominent in the professional and scholarly contexts of dis/abled persons' engagement with sports and other physical activities. Our aim in this introduction is to offer some general historical and philosophical remarks about the field. In this way, we hope to critically situate the essays of this volume within disability and sport studies and to better scrutinise the various forms of movement of persons with disabilities or different abilities (thus: 'dis/ability') that constitute the present field of enquiry.

Disability Sports

The sportive version of adapted physical activity has a short history. One can say that competitive sports participation for people with disabilities was initiated by Sir Ludwig Guttman at Stoke Mandeville, Great Britain. Guttman, a neurologist, used sports activities in the rehabilitation of war veterans returning home from the Second World War with spinal cord injuries. It was his belief that sport was a useful method to build strength and self-esteem during the rehabilitation process. At his hospital, Guttman began to organise competitions for the war veterans. Gradually these games began to attract international participation and the competitors came to be recognised as athletes rather than merely as patients. The general focus of sports participation for persons with disabilities thus changed from treatment to performance, which for a long time had been a focus in the deaf community. Indeed the football huddle was invented at Gallaudet University by their quarterback Paul Hubbard in 1894.[3]

The broader development of competitive sports reflected the general development in other activity settings for people with disabilities: Beginning as a tool for the treatment of disabling conditions, adapted physical activity today emphasises self-determined involvement in sports and recreational activities in a life span perspective (Reid 2003).

Adapted Physical Activity

The international body that deals with sports, physical education and movement activities for persons with disabilities, the International Federation of Adapted Physical Activity (IFAPA), characterises its focus today as 'individual differences in physical activity that require special attention'.[4] According to Sherrill and DePauw (1997) the terminology for adapted physical activity has varied considerably during the twentieth century. Even today there are—despite the politics of disability—a heterogeneity of terms to reflect the whole field within disability studies. Thus, for example, while the word 'handicapped' has fallen into disrepute in Anglo-American contexts due to its apparent negative connotations, it is still widely used in Scandinavia and some parts of Europe to describe persons with disability. Notwithstanding this, it is useful to situate the synonyms for adapted physical activity (in the USA) in a historical manner:

Until 1920s: Swedish, medical, curative, or corrective gymnastics;
1920s–1950s: Corrective or individualised physical education;
1950s: Struggle between therapeutic (rehabilitative) and educational (sport) orientations for dominance ('adapted physical education' became an official AAHPER term in 1952);
1960s, 1970s: 'Adapted physical education' challenged as term of choice by strong advocacy for 'developmental physical education' and for 'special physical education'.

Also terms from legislation such as 'physical education for the handicapped' further complicated the terminology issue;

1980s: 'Adapted physical activity' became umbrella term of choice with the 1985 merger of Therapeutics Council and Adapted Physical Education Academy into the *Adapted Physical Activity Quarterly* from 1984 onwards, and the growth of the International Federation of Adapted Physical Activity (IFAPA), founded in 1973 (Sherrill and DePauw 1997).

Partly mirrored by the key disciplines in areas such as medicine, psychology and law, adapted physical activity has historically been associated with the following nomenclature:

- *Impairment*: any disturbance of, or interferences with, the normal structure and function of the body;
- *Disability*: the loss or reduction of functional ability and/or activity;
- *Handicap*; a condition produced by societal and environmental barriers (Sherrill and DePauw 1997).

Finally, it is worth mentioning that adapted physical activity services are mostly associated with autism; blindness; deafness; emotional disturbance; mental retardation; orthopaedic impairment; specific learning disability; traumatic brain injury; and other health impairments such as asthma, diabetes and obesity.

Understanding how these different categories are utilised is a matter of intense controversy within disability studies and APA. Like all serious and seriously entrenched disputes, one necessarily does violence to their nature by placing adherents and opponents into dichotomised camps. As this is the standard, however, we (with some regret and reservation) follow the norm and lay out the broad contours of the opposing models of disability.

'The' Medical and 'the' Social Model of Disability and Dis/ability

An important trend in adapted physical activity (APA) over the past two decades has been based on the belief that it should move away from its previous commitment to the medical model of disability (cf. Sherrill 2003). The medical model of disability is predicated on the belief that there is a causal relationship between a person's impairment and their disability; it is therefore an outgrowth of the biomedical model of health. In a series of essays, widely regarded as classics in the philosophy of medicine, Christopher Boorse (1975, 1977, 1987) famously argued that health was conceptually the equivalent to 'normal functioning'. His position is a sophisticated version of what can be called a naturalistic or non-normative account of health. Health, within his theory, is understood as 'species typical functioning' that occurred normally in the absence of deformity, disease, disorder, impairment or illness. His account is deeply sympathetic to the medical professions' dominant self-understanding, techniques and ideologies. Moreover, it is positivistic in spirit. For Boorse is a matter of fact what normal functioning is. But there is a twist in the tail: the cauterisation of values from human health that is the grounding motivation only holds for so long. It is true that we can choose to see human beings as complex machines that, in their normal state, functions as they should. The next stage may be more problematic for our purposes, though. In disease, illness and of course disability, human beings display species-atypical or abnormal functioning. It is not uncommon for healthcare practitioners thus to collapse the fact-value dichotomy; in one sweep, what is normal thus becomes what is desirable and of course vice versa. Rudnick (2000, 572) puts the point in an opposing way: 'naturalism', he writes, 'does not consider the normal as in need of medical intervention'. Those that fall below a threshold of normal functioning require medical therapy or treatment to restore or develop normal functioning. Quite how such a model works when there are no obvious pathologies yet the person still displays abnormality, as in conversion gait disorder, where the patient is apparently unable to walk unaided, is a moot point (see Jordbru, Jespersen and Martinsen in this volume).

Disability activists since the 1980s and 1990s have challenged this understanding of disability in various ways, not all of which are germane to our present concern. Suffice it to say, they have claimed *inter alia* that the medical model devalues (consciously or otherwise) those who are possessed of deficient levels of functioning and seeks to normalise them (Silvers 1998). Where certain persons cannot be normalised they are left in a parlous, limbo, state of apparent abnormality. Moreover, the medical model is located within an individualistic perspective that effectively ignores disabling barriers in the social environment by focusing on statistically derived abnormalities. Many activists and scholars have argued that biomedically driven levels of normal functioning bear no necessary relation to human activities, goals or purposes. In contrast, Davis writes: 'The idea of a norm is less a condition of human nature than it is a feature of a certain kind of society' (2001, 1). Under a revisionary model, all abilities and disabilities ought to be viewed contextually or relationally and not as essential properties of the disabled person.

A standard line of criticism thus has become canonised in the idea that the medical profession had socially constructed an ideologised understanding of disability with pernicious consequences. The terrain of definition or conceptualisation has therefore shifted from the life-worlds of medicine to society at large, where conceptions of normality and abnormality, far from being scientifically (for which read 'non-normatively') based were to be contested as part of highly charged disputes. Advocates of the social model sought to shift the dispute from one of 'deficient ability' to 'different ability' and in so doing politicised the very definition of disability itself. Thus many scholars in their writing attempt to avoid the baggage of the medical model by coining new terms such 'dis/ability' or 'disAbility' (DePauw 1997).[5]

The loose collection of activists and scholars who associated themselves as opponents of the medical model are often referred to as adherents of the 'social model'. But this is no more than a conceptual convenience, for their opposition masks many kinds of differences. They have focused on social and political conditions that construct disabling features of the world and which require social and political action to address inequities in the treatment of persons labelled 'disabled'.

One might think that the legions of critiques of the medical model that have followed would have led to its downfall, yet it shows remarkable powers of endurance and indeed regeneration. Evidence of the continued ubiquity of the medical model of disability in research is not difficult to find. A cursory review of the last few years' articles in *Adapted Physical Activity Quarterly* (APAQ), the official journal of IFAPA, reveals its continued pervasiveness. Much of the research presented in APAQ is results from different forms of tests that measure some type of performance of a group of people with a specific disability and compare them to their non-disabled peers (see Bredahl, this volume). This is not to deny that this form of research might be valuable for certain medico-scientific purposes. Nevertheless, it is undeniable that it has the undesirable function of enforcing an ideal of normality, where the performances of the non-disabled body are the standard and disability is (wittingly or otherwise) characterised as a deviation from an empirical (often, but not always, statistically derived) norm.

Recently, however, philosophers of disability have challenged this dichotomy between a medical and a social model in a variety of ways (Edwards 2005; Shakespeare 2006, 29–53; Sorrell 2007, 15–25). Might there be something wrong with the demonisation of the medical profession *qua* its conceptualisation of disability, via the 'medical model'? Indeed it is not readily apparent that significant members of the medical profession ever held such a view or operated with a singular thing called '*the* medical model' (Shakespeare 2006). Is there a sense that both stances embody a crude generalisation: disability is all natural, or all social? If ability and disability are context-specific, do we need to acknowledge the centrality of certain contexts in living generally from those that are specifically chosen by sub-populations. Contrast the need to be skilled in the movement from a bed to a wheelchair (Papadimitriou, this volume*)* from the ability to pass a ball at speed and with precise anticipation of teammates and opposition in wheelchair rugby (Gard and Fitzgerald, this volume). The former seems a precondition for all wheelchair-bound persons; the latter is a 'problem' only for a select few. The new critics still focus on the same problematic: precisely how do we conceive ability and disability? how do we conceptualise autonomy and dependence in relation to disabled persons and their choices (Goodwin, this volume)? When the medical model is rejected totally, as it is with most social model adherents, do we throw the baby out with the bathwater? As Sorrell (2007) asks: is this an act of denial?

Ability, Dis/ability, and Sports/Movement Contexts

How can we come to understand disability in sports and other movement activities as something other than a deviation from 'normal' abilities? DePauw (1997) argues that a redefinition of ability and sport is required. We must come to understand how current conceptualisations of ability in sport, physical education and movement in general enable some participants and at the same time disable others (Evans 2004). If disability is not simply a result of some individual deviation from biomedical norms, but also and importantly the outcome of social processes, then the notions of *ability* and *dis/ability* stand in need of sustained philosophical attention and pedagogical application. If 'ability' is not simply to be thought of as some form of innate or latent set of characteristics, but also as a set of dynamic socio-cultural processes (Evans 2004), then philosophers and pedagogues alike will do well to consider how better to frame the various movement activities and related contexts—such as curricular design, media promotion, organisational structures, sponsorship programmes and so on—that help and hinder all persons therein.

One potential aspect of the ability–dis/ability relation might be highlighted if we considered the temporality of disabling conditions. Consider, for example, the phenomenology of athletic injuries that have recently been investigated (Allen Collinson, 2003). Here we attempt to understand our experience of the moving body in pain, not at-one with itself, arrhythmic, ruptured or disjointed or discontinuous in its flow. Is this not for most of 'us'[6] a real and present identification with our *apparently* able bodies? Shining a light on these kinds of articulated awarenesses might lead 'us' to (i) question how closely the experience of able-bodied athletes can usefully be compared to disability populations; or (ii) more radically, to question whether able-bodied scholars should view abilities and disabilities as more transient rather than substantive properties of persons.

Philosophy, Ethics and Equity in Dis/ability Sports

There is a dearth of research applying philosophical, and particularly ethical, analyses within adapted physical activity. When the term 'philosophy' is used in the APA context, it merely designates a personal orientation or set of professional convictions towards one's reflective engagement in or upon practice. Rarely are there any references to philosophy as a scholarly discipline that can challenge as well as inform professional self-conceptions and practices in APA, such as whether and to what extent professionals can be guided by the evidence-based reasoning model of medical professionalism or the wise and open-textured judgement that pedagogues are possessed of (Standal, this volume). Yet, in terms of APA or disability sports more generally, the field is saturated with dense epistemological and ethical issues.

As Reid (2000, 370) points out, this research lacuna in APA is troubling, since 'a careful study of ethics will assist adapted physical activity to critically evaluate accepted rules and practices'. Jones and Howe's essay (2007) is, therefore, a relatively rare careful analytical critique of the classification systems that structure sports for the disabled. They illustrates how (often unintentionally) the classification systems of Paralympic sport can serve to problematise the notion of winning fairly. Given the potential randomness of such classifications, they point to the inevitable (and potentially undesirable) heightening of chance or luck in athletic contexts, especially at elite levels.

The recent and very public debates regarding the eligibility of Oscar Pistorius, the South African Paralympic gold medallist, to run in the Beijing Olympics, have raised to a more general awareness in sports studies and sports science certain issues of justice, merit and ability within disability populations (see Edwards, this volume, and Van Hilvoorde and Landeweerd, this volume). Despite the quantity of ink spilt on Pistorius's case, the issue is not new. DePauw cites many earlier instances before Pistorius came along to awaken general sensibilities to athletes with disabilities: 'Athletes with an impairment, or "disability", have competed in the Olympic Games but these athletes were considered Olympians and not considered athletes with a disability. Their "disability" was erased and was little more than a footnote in the history books.' (DePauw 1997, 423).

As examples, she cites Liz Hartel (post-polio), who won a silver medal in the equestrian dressage at the 1952 Olympics, and Jeff Float, a deaf swimmer, who won a gold medal in swimming at the 1984 Los Angeles games. Similarly, a wheelchair archer, Neroli Fairhall, also competed in the 1984 Olympic Games; however, her disability became an issue as her alleged stability advantage was questioned by traditional upright archers. A similar, though more high-profile, case arose when professional American golfer Casey Martin won the right to play on the highly lucrative US Professional Golf Association tour (Pickering Francis 2007). Martin required the use of a buggy (motorised cart) to move between shots. The USPGA, in a move similar to the IOC's first response to Oscar Pistorius, argued that this gave him an unfair advantage. It was argued that Martin did not have to undergo the same physical test as able-bodied golfers and therefore would be less fatigued, thus gaining an unfair advantage. In 2001 the Supreme Court in the USA held, by seven votes to two, Casey's legal right to use the golf cart between shots.[7]

These cases, highlighted by various high-profile media, have raised the awareness of issues of ability and disability as their norms collide or coalesce respectively in the context. Yet they represent for many a double-edged sword. They shine a light on disabled athletes' struggles for acceptance, status and even (sexualised) adulation (see Gard and Fitzgerald, this volume) but they can also have the effect of localising public attention on the rarefied elite level of participation and reduce an ethically complex array of issues to just one: fair eligibility or entitlement. Ironically, then, one potential problem associated with Pistorius's high-profile test case is that it can narrow the lens of ethical debate to issues of eligibility and lead to a continued disavowal, once that particular issue is settled. This is of course an unjustifiable reduction of myriad and complex issues (for a catalogue of which see Hutzler, this volume) across APA more generally.

Phenomenology, Pedagogy and Dis/ability Sports

While the phenomenology of sports is only gaining attention in mainstream philosophical and sociological thought in more recent years,[8] it is perhaps ironic that one potential exception to the general neglect of philosophy within APA can be seen in the growing interest in phenomenologically oriented research in APA. It can be argued, however, that these studies rely more on phenomenology as a methodological device to gain access to the first-person perspective than on insights from philosophers in the phenomenological tradition. Connolly, in her entry on Physical Education in the *Encyclopedia of Phenomenology* wrote that 'The phenomenological character of physical education seems to manifest itself in three loose categories: work that acknowledges phenomenology as relevant and useful; work that involves using phenomenological methods; and work that is based in doing phenomenology in an applied and/or heuristic fashion.' (Connolly 1997, 536).

Notable examples of practitioners *doing* phenomenology can be found in the work of Connolly (1995) and Connolly and Craig (2002) and can be seen to drive curricular and pedagogical choices at the most practical level (see Connolly, this volume). Phenomenological studies can be of particular relevance for APA, because their characteristic modes of enquiry place such importance upon the living, moving, sensing body that is intertwined with the world (Edwards 1998). Phenomenology thus provides insight to the first-person perspective in a way that is often frowned upon in analytical philosophy as *mere* subjectivism. Yet, properly utilised, it can serve as a critical lens to open out the lived experiences of abilities and dis/abilities. Kay Toombs's (1995) account of the lived experience of multiple sclerosis offers a paradigmatic example of the fruitfulness of this philosophical approach to our corporeality in ways that have been mysterious to much Western philosophy that is indebted to Plato and Descartes. Whether this should be characterised as affording empathy to the non-disabled researcher is a moot point. Indeed it might be argued that this apparent empathising (Smith, this volume) with the relevant populations by 'outsiders' may be a form of symbolic violence itself.

Conclusion

DePauw writes that 'To be able to "see" individuals with disabilities as athletes (regardless of the impairment) requires us to redefine athleticism and our view of the body (DePauw 1997, 423). The essays of this volume attempt to address this call in a

- Amputees;
- Athletes with total or partial loss of sight;
- Athletes with intellectual disability and learning difficulties; and
- 'Les autres' disabilities (a complex 'all the rest category')

Both the concept of 'sport' and 'disability' have their own specific distinctions and internal differentiations, such that a combination of both gives rise to all sorts of complexities and new issues, in particular regarding definition and fairness. The distinction between different disabilities listed above is only relevant for disability sports. There is no medical categorisation of disabilities that fits smoothly and logically into the context of sport. What is considered a disability in 'regular life' may even become an advantage in the context of elite sports. In basketball, extreme height is considered to be an advantage rather than a disability, while possibly posing a disability, albeit slight, in daily life. A huge sumo wrestler may have problems travelling on a bus, but at the same time be celebrated as a Japanese sport hero. A genetic mutation that corresponds to extreme muscle growth can be classified in one case as a high-risk potential for disablement and in another as a precondition of being exceptionally talented. It appears that in many ways the scales on which one ranks human traits are not value-neutral, or are at least established from a very specific (albeit hidden) perspective. This poses the question whether one can neutrally or objectively define what should count as a disability (or impairment), what as a trait within a normal variance and what as a super-ability.

Several authors have shed light on the philosophical dimensions of classification, categorisation, merit and justice related to disability sports (cf. Bowen 2002; Wheeler 2004; Pickering 2005; Jones and Howe 2005). Categorisation and classification are ongoing processes and discussions need to be continued, not least because our views on disabilities change and evolve, as does the technology to compensate for certain disabilities. From an egalitarian perspective one can strive for the neutralisation of luck and reward specific talents (cf. Bailey 2007). On the other hand, specific distinctions between (severity of) disabilities can be drawn in such a way that extreme efforts are awarded in order to compensate for a lack of talent. Categorisations within disability sports appear to be the site of an 'ongoing struggle' to find the right balance between a good competition based on differences in talent on the one hand and the demonstration of excellence within a group with relevant similar skills on the other. We will try to show that this tension eventually also bears relevance for the distinction between elite sports and disability sports.

Defining Disability: Normative or Neutral

The concept of disease and disability was heavily debated in the 1970s and 1980s by Christopher Boorse (1975, 1976, 1977) and H. Tristam Engelhardt and S.F. Spicker (1974). Boorse looked upon the difference between health and diseases as a natural given, basing his stance on a statistically derived definition of normal and abnormal function. Health was therefore defined as 'the ability to perform all typical physiological functions with at least typical efficiency level' (Boorse 1977, 542). Correspondingly, disease is any state that interferes with this normal functioning. In Boorse's words:

> An organism is healthy at any moment in proportion as it is not diseased; and a disease is a type of internal state of the organism which (i) interferes with the performance of some

natural function—i.e., some species-typical contribution to survival and reproduction—characteristic of the organism's age; and (ii) is not simply in the nature of the species, i.e., is either atypical of the species or, if typical, mainly due to environmental causes. (Boorse 1976, 62)

This means that Boorse's account of the concepts of health and disease is heavily dependent of an objective image of 'nature', 'natural' or 'normal functioning'.

Among others, Tristam Engelhardt criticises this naturalist approach to the conceptualisation of diseases. In his opinion, one cannot analyse concepts of health and disease solely on the basis of the biological nature of the organism and its functioning. The social context needs to be taken into account as well. In this normative approach diseases are normative constructions with a specific socio-cultural background, rather than natural givens within a bio-statistical framework. In the words of Toulmin, supporting Engelhardt's view,

The nature of health is, at one and the same time, a matter for empirical discovery and a matter of evaluative decision. We refine our sense of how the human body ought to work, and ought to be helped to work, in the course of and in the light of our empirical studies of how it does in fact work. (Toulmin 1975, 51)

So, according to the normativists, what counts as a disability and what not is as much dependent on socio-cultural values and decisions as on medical standards. Essentially, within this perspective, the latter are even to be seen as a subcategory of the former. The discussion between the bio-statistical and the normative or contextual definition of diseases and disabilities has continued up to now. As has been put forward by Moser (2006, 374), 'Being disabled is not something one is by definition, but something one becomes in relation to specific environments. Disability is enacted and ordered in situated and quite specific ways.' People can become disabled by the environment or by specific (lack of) technologies. A person with an average intellectual ability may 'become' disabled in an environment with just highly gifted people. An elite athlete who chooses not to use performance-enhancing substances may become dis-abled in a context in which the use of doping is 'normalised'. In these cases (and in many similar cases) one can argue that one is free to choose the 'right' environment in which specific qualities can be shown and compared to 'relevant others'. The person that one wants to be cannot be detached from the financial rewards that are attached to specific practices, as well as the status and meanings that are intrinsically related to the community of superior athletic performances. The valuation of human performances cannot be effected irrespective of a social-cultural hierarchy, ranking specific talents and making differences between highly valued talents (e.g. the ability to throw a ball in a basket) and less valued talents (e.g. running on prostheses).

New technologies such as prostheses apparently help to turn disabled people into 'normal' subjects. This may explain the urgent wish of Oscar Pistorius, an athlete who usually competes in races for disabled athletes, to become part of the 'normal Olympic Games'. What may be considered 'normalisation' in the context of daily life is at least ambivalent in the context of elite sport. Running on prostheses may be defined as crucial for the specific talent that is tested in a competition against 'relevant others': athletes who have the ability to show a similar talent. The wish of a disabled person to become part of 'normal' elite sport may be framed as a way of 'inclusion' or 'integration', but this at the same time reproduces new inequalities and asymmetries between performances of able and dis-abled bodied.

If one is to enhance the traits needed to function optimally in society, one takes that society as a universal standard against which the functioning of people is measured, while one could also say that within a just society people should not be made to follow the dictations of a larger ideal. When one defines what counts as a disability in a normative rather than a descriptive fashion the notion of a disability also becomes political. In contemporary (Western) democracies, each citizen is presupposed to be self-reliant within a competitive capitalist environment. Therefore, society is set up to deal primarily with an idealised version of the 'average person' (Taylor and Mykitiuk 2001, 1). Anything that falls below this picture of the ideal citizen is treated as abnormal. In many respects, however, the ideal of the elite sportsman has all characteristics of abnormality as well. But in contrast to the disabled, the elite sportsman is not considered a political and medical burden. So on the one hand society invests quite willingly in the 'abnormal' super-abilities of the elite sportsman, while on the other it does this only reluctantly, and from a ethics of inclusion, with respect to the disabled. In the case of disabilities, one wants to eradicate abnormalities by equalising on the basis of 'sameness' (Taylor and Mykitiuk 2001, 1), while in the case of super-abilities we support abnormalities. This 'selective investment in the abnormal' and the admiration for the 'genetically superior' could be seen as a token of a society that cannot meet up with the criteria for justice (cf. Tännsjö 2000). On the other hand, sport is a competitive practice, whose internal logic consists of the display of an unequal distribution of abilities. These internal goods are considered worth striving for, for their own sake (cf. MacIntyre 1985; Brown 1990; McNamee 1995). Sport consists of an internal logic that may conflict with more societal ideals (for example concerning justice or equality). These internal goods cannot be brought in agreement with the ideal, for example, to create as many sport categories as possible with the aim of producing as many sport stars as possible. It may be that everyone has certain abilities and disabilities; we cannot however freely choose the practice in which our own specific abilities are admired by people around the world.

Rawls and a Just Distribution of Disabilities

In the 1970s, Rawls, among others, gave rise to a revival of liberal political philosophy. Next to his general influence on political and ethical philosophy, Rawls also had an extensive influence on bioethics and sport ethics. Rawls most important contribution to juridical and political philosophy was his publication in 1971 of *a Theory of Justice*. In *a Theory of Justice*, John Rawls set out to find a more rational basis for the contractualist tradition in political and ethical theory. He tried to find general principles of justice that would function as basic rules for justice in society. These principles would, as is typical for contractualism, be supported by a *social* agreement. However, Rawls combined this with a stronger notion of justice which he derived from Kantian philosophy, and with the utilitarian notion of costs and benefit calculus to find the best overall balance for individual and collective well-being or happiness. Rational agreement was to be the basis of this philosophical system. For Rawls, principles of justice

> are the principles that free and rational persons concerned to further their own interests would accept in an initial position of equality as defining the fundamental terms of their

association. These principles are to regulate all further agreements; they specify the kinds of social cooperation that can be entered into and the forms of government that can be established. (Rawls 1971, 11)

So, in Rawlsian philosophy, the basic principles of justice should balance individual liberty with an equal distribution of liberty. This should be combined with a provision of the greatest benefit for the least advantaged. People should come to this agreement through rational reflection, unaware of their specific individual place, talents or background in society. This is what Rawls called 'original position'. Rawls's conception of an 'original position' forms the rationale behind these basic principles of justice. It stems from the contractarian tradition in political theory. The original position was usually posed as the beginning position from which the social contract was formulated, from within a 'state of nature'. In Rawls's work, this construction of an original position should be regarded as a hypothetical position rather than a true historical occurrence. It functions as a maxim rule; it is the basic position one should take to come to the principles for a just society. In Rawls's original position, one is supposed to wear a 'veil of ignorance'. With this construction, Rawls tried to find a tool that can balance freedom or liberty and equality and leave out any prejudices stemming from one's class or one's ethnic, linguistic, religious or cultural background.

In Rawls's vision, those who are at the same level of talent and ability, and have the same willingness to use them, should have the same prospects of success regardless of their initial place in the social system. Social class, gender or any other contingency should have no influence on the liberty individuals are to enjoy in the pursuance of his or her goals in life. Moreover, social and economic inequalities should be distributed in such a way that they can reasonably be expected to be advantageous to all those who are the worst off in the first place. Rawls aimed at a distributive justice to compensate for the differences in fortune that we come across. Justice is seen as being independent of luck and favouring more equal distribution.

This position, although dominant in our current theoretical framework of justice, is on a par with the notions of both talent and disability. Our world is primarily designed for the average human being. People with a disability cannot partake in it as fully as they should according to the principles of distributive justice. By redesigning the world around us, however, we can make this world more accessible for the disabled. The question remains what obstacles can and should be taken away in order for the disabled to become part of other spheres of life. Making a building accessible is not the same thing as trying to become (a successful) part of one of the most competitive practices on earth. Following Rawls, we should adjust the person rather than the environment. Therefore, a defence of plurality is often not the outcome of a Rawlsian approach to justice. Our dominant understanding of elite sport cannot be brought in agreement with the right to become an elite athlete, similar to the right for example to receive good education. It may be difficult to justify the difference in admiration for the elite athlete and the disabled athlete just based upon concepts as 'talent' or 'effort'. Some talents are more valued in a society than others in spite of a (changing) terminology, one that sometimes even seems to suggest that being disabled is the norm for each human being.

paraplegia, say, is able to do the things which are most important to him/her, he/she is not disabled. Adoption of a definition such as Nordenfelt's would in fact support OP's contention that he is not disabled. What this response highlights is that were this to be the main ground for exclusion of OP from the Olympics, it would have to be shown that the WHO definition of disability is superior to that offered by Nordenfelt (for example). We will not pursue this here but now move on to the second response to this first argument.

The second response is that to deny OP the opportunity to compete in the Olympics is to violate principles of fair opportunity. This is because competing in the games is plausibly regarded as a 'good' for those who wish to participate in it. And to deny someone the opportunity to participate solely on the grounds that they have a disability may constitute unfair discrimination. It would be morally on a par with excluding potential competitors on grounds such as their having too many teeth, or being bald or having the wrong eye colour. What is morally relevant in the assessment of eligibility to compete is the athleticism of the athlete; not what colour their eyes are or how many teeth they have and so on. The determination of what characteristics are and are not relevant should take into account only those 'talents and skills relevant to the position being sought' as Daniels expresses it (Daniels 1985, 40).

A similar appeal can be advanced in support of the case for OP's participation in the Olympics. What is most relevant is his athletic ability, not his physical constitution. For, as well as overcoming considerable levels of prejudice and disadvantage due to his disability, OP is as dedicated and trains as hard as any top athlete. The blades are mere means that make it possible for him to manifest his athletic prowess in his chosen events; they compensate for his lack of legs.

(b) OP Has an Impairment

Turn now to a second argument against OP's eligibility to compete. According to this, since he has an *impairment* (his atypical morphology) he should be denied access to competition. This objection exploits the distinction between impairment and disability. While there is a dispute concerning the concept of disability, this is not so in relation to that of impairment. The WHO definitions of this have remained constant between the period 1980–2001 and Nordenfelt's definition, for example, coheres with that developed by WHO.

Response. In response to this, the definition of impairment present in the International Classification of Functioning, Disability and Health refers (among other things) to 'a loss or abnormality in body structure'; where the idea of normality presumed is a statistical one— as stated: 'Abnormality here is used strictly to refer to a significant variation from established statistical norms' (WHO 2001, 190). And if all competitors with impairments were excluded this would entail the exclusion of athletes with conditions such as fused toes or extremely tall or small athletes. Presumably this would not be regarded as acceptable practice, so if OP is to be excluded from eligibility some other ground must be sought. Also, the success of some athletes can be attributed, if only in part, to their having physical anomalies which bring some advantages in competition. For example the Finnish skier Eero Mantyranta and also the cyclist Miguel Indurain. Each of these sportsmen had impairments, strictly speaking. Mantyranta's physical constitution was such that he naturally had higher than normal levels of haemoglobin in his blood chemistry. Indurain's lungs were significantly larger than normal male adult lungs. Yet they were each allowed to compete and were each extremely successful. So the mere presence within OP of an impairment does not look like sufficient grounds to exclude OP. Also, the same kinds of consideration rehearsed in response to the first objection, appealing to a certain construal of 'equality of opportunity', can again be appealed to here. To exclude OP solely on grounds of his having an impairment would transgress rules of equality of opportunity.

(c) OP Has an Unfair Advantage

Consider now the objection mentioned in the early part of the paper, namely that the blades give OP an unfair advantage. For mechanical reasons, there may be advantages to OP due to the special properties of the blades. They may be lighter than natural legs, more aerodynamic, and have reduced contact area with the ground when compared with natural legs. They may also give greater 'spring' than natural legs, thus leading to a longer stride. All these properties, it may be claimed, give OP an unfair advantage over athletes with natural legs.

Response. So if this unfair advantage exists, does it provide sufficient grounds to exclude OP from the Olympics?

A first way of responding is to contest the claim that the blades do in fact provide OP with an advantage. This might be done by pointing to the fact that OP's blades bring some disadvantages. The disadvantages include slower initial acceleration compared with natural legs, and decreased stability/balance compared to natural legs. In addition, at least one medical expert, Robert Gailey, has suggested that the blades confer a disadvantage, compared with normal legs, in terms of energy efficiency: 'A prosthetic leg returns only about 80 per cent of the energy absorbed in each stride, while a natural leg returns up to 240 per cent, providing much more spring'.[4]

So, arguably, far from its being the case that OP is competing with an unfair advantage, it appears that he is running at a disadvantage when compared to runners with natural legs.

Suppose, for the sake of argument then, that the blades do indeed confer an advantage; if this were so, would that be sufficient grounds upon which to exclude him? It is plain that advantages abound in sport. Current rules of competition do not exclude competitions in which some athletes have an advantage over others. For example, there are advantages which stem from the natural and social lotteries. These are not 'deserved' in that they are not earned. They are matters of historical accident. Thus an athlete brought up in the high plains in Ethiopia might have an advantage over other athletes raised at sea level. An athlete raised in the wealthy USA might be said to have an advantage over athletes raised in much poorer countries.

So some athletes are advantaged in relation to others because of factors over which they have no control—for example the geography and economic conditions which prevail in their birthplaces.

This conception of advantage can be illustrated in the following schema: A has an advantage, compared with B, since A had access to a resource, R, which was unavailable to B, and this resource enhanced A's capacity to achieve a goal shared by both A and B. In the examples just given, if A is a long-distance runner born and raised at high altitude he has access to a resource—the natural environment at that height—which B, an athlete raised at sea level, did not have access to.

So given that advantages abound in athletics, what is distinctive about that allegedly possessed by OP? Suppose it is argued that the advantage that OP is said to have is an unfair one—i.e. not just an advantage, but an *unfair* advantage. How could such a claim be made to stick? One way would be by consideration of a definition of unfair advantage such as the following:

> A has an advantage, compared with B, since A had access to a resource, R, which was unavailable to B, and this resource enhanced A's capacity to achieve a goal shared by both A and B. This is 'unfair' since A had access to R and B did not. Principles of equality of opportunity are violated.

The relevant opportunity here being access to whatever means enhanced A's capacity to achieve the goal in question.

However, an argument of the kind just given will not succeed since it does not distinguish the kind of advantage (allegedly) possessed by OP from the advantages possessed by other athletes and regarded as unproblematic—such as those regarding athletes from the high plains of Africa, or from the USA. For just as the blades might not be available to other athletes, so being born and brought up in the USA or some other country is not available to other athletes. And of course, strictly speaking, the blades could be available to other athletes, were they prepared to have their lower legs amputated.

Thus far, then, it has not proved possible to distinguish advantages that are fair (such as those involving natural origin) from those that are unfair. What could be the basis for the distinction?

Recall the examples given above of the Finnish skier Mantyranta and Miguel Indurain. It is accepted that their impairments gave them advantages over other competitors in their respective sports. What is the difference between the advantage they enjoyed and that (allegedly) enjoyed by OP? Clearly the relevant difference cannot consist exclusively in the *effects* that the blades have on OP's performance. For, as we have seen, it is accepted that athletes can be constituted differently physically in ways such that the differences enhance their performances, but this is not considered problematic. So the main objection to the blades must lie in the fact that they are synthetic—they are made by humans and not by nature. In other words, what makes an advantage unfair is that it is a consequence of science and not of nature.

But of course many developments in athletics result from scientific research relating to diet, responses to injury and the construction of implements such as javelins and pole-vault poles, for example. Perhaps what is being pointed to in the distinction is the fact that the actual blades themselves are products of science. And so science—the sphere of the 'artificial' as opposed to sphere of the 'natural'—is more obviously present in the performance of OP than in the performance of an athlete whose recovery from injury has been helped by developments in medicine (though what of the javelin thrower or pole vaulter?).

Anyway, in spite of apparent problems with the attempt to base the distinction between fair and unfair advantages on that between the synthetic and the natural, let us accept the distinction for the sake of argument. Can it bear the moral weight being placed upon it?

I think there are at least two grounds for being sceptical about it. The first one consists in a reminder that the advantages enjoyed by Indurain and Mantyranta stem from accidents of nature. The advantages they bring about stem from the natural lottery, they are not deserved. Moreover, recall Daniels's point regarding the principle of fair opportunity. According to this, the relevant considerations are those relating to 'talents and skills relevant to the position being sought' (Daniels 1985, 40).

So it seems reasonable to query the priority attached to the completely contingent, random events in nature that generated the advantage enjoyed by athletes such as Indurain and Mantyranta in comparison with the effort and athleticism of OP. Surely the latter are more morally relevant than the former in assessing entitlement to perform; they are grounded in non-arbitrary considerations relevant to justice, in contrast to natural constitution which is bestowed arbitrarily.

A further problem in resting so much on the natural/synthetic distinction is that these are difficult to disentangle in ways other than those described above (in relation to scientific developments which have an impact in sport). To illustrate this point consider the following hypothetical scenario. Suppose Indurain would like a son to continue his own cycling legacy. To ensure the son has the same genetically bestowed advantage that he has benefited from, Indurain requests genetic manipulation of the embryo to ensure that this happens. Or he simply selects the embryo with that hereditary advantage to be implanted in the womb of his wife. The child grows up to be a great cyclist like his father. Yet this has been brought about by science. So should Indurain's son be barred from competition? I doubt that he would be, since he is so genetically similar to his father. (One might raise the quibble that Indurain was not an Olympic athlete, but the example can easily be made in relation to Mantyranta, so this is not a serious objection.)

So in this section we have been tackling the most pressing of the grounds in favour of OP's exclusion from the Olympics. From what has been said here, first it is not at all clear that the blades generate an advantage for OP. More likely, the opposite is the case. Second, even if they do confer an advantage, these abound in sport. And if a claimed distinction between the natural and the synthetic is to be the basis of a decision to exclude OP, I have tried to show how weak a ground this is to sustain the distinction between fair and unfair advantages. Turn now to some other objections.

(d) OP Might Harm Other Athletes

The fear here is that due to the instability caused to OP by the blades , he is at an increased risk of falling over. Given this, he seems to generate an additional risk to other athletes if he falls close to them—possibly injuring them or impugning their performance at best.

In response to this, if this is so, then he should not be permitted to run in the Paralympics either. Yet he is permitted to compete in these, of course. So the additional risk must be judged to be negligible. To deny this would be to concede that it is thought acceptable to expose disabled athletes to higher levels of risk than those to which non-disabled athletes can be exposed.

Also, what risks there are can be minimised by placing him in the outside lane (albeit with subsequent disadvantage for OP).

(e) Permitting Blades Opens the Door to All Performance-enhancing Measures

The fear here is that if it is allowed that use of the blades does not confer an unfair advantage to OP, will that then permit the employment of other any additional performance enhancing measures. Indeed an IAAF official, Elio Locatelli, is quoted as saying: 'Next it will be another device where people can fly with something on their back.'[5]. So the fear is that if OP is allowed to compete with his blades it will be difficult to remain consistent and yet to disallow other performance-enhancing measures.

Response. Divide such measures into two broad kinds, internal and external ones. By external ones is meant means comparable to OP's blades, and by internal ones is meant means that involve ingestion of performance-enhancing substances, or so-called gene doping. An example of the kind of 'external' measures might be some kind of extra-springy sole designed to maximise the stride of the athlete.

To show that permitting competitors to use prostheses differs from permitting competitors to use any 'external' items, consider this definition of a prosthesis: 'An artificial replacement for a missing or diseased part of the body, for example artificial limbs' (BMA 2002, 467). It is plain that the 'springy sole' is not a prosthesis since it doesn't replace a body part. So permitting OP to use a prosthesis need not entail the permissibility of 'springy soles' or other measures such as flying devices.

Regarding the 'internal' performance enhancers. There is a clear difference between OP's prosthesis and these in that the latter are ingested or otherwise incorporated into the fabric of the body and the former not. (This includes an 'internal' prosthesis such as a silicon-coated hip joint.)

Moreover, the possibility of OP running at all depends upon his using a prosthesis. That is not the case for athletes who want to enhance their performance by use of illegal performance-enhancing drugs or by gene-doping measures. Even without the drugs or gene doping, they can still run (if not as fast as they would like). But OP cannot run at all without the prosthesis.

(f) Purity

Some have observed that preserving the purity of the Olympics is an important ideal.[6] In support of this one might point to aesthetic ideals that lie behind some conceptions of Olympic sport concerning the human body. (Indeed, an early version of this paper was presented at the Norwegian School of Sports Science, in the grounds of which one finds striking statues of beautifully formed athletes in various athletic poses.) Permitting impaired humans to participate seems to run against the emphasis on aesthetic ideals. Indeed, Engelhardt remarks that 'deformity and dysfunction are ugly' (1996, 206).

Response. However, it seems fair to point out that determining eligibility to compete by reference to aesthetic ideals is a dubious practice to embrace. It is too subjective, and too vulnerable to ideological influence, to be a reliable guide to eligibility to compete. Moreover, to repeat an earlier point, what is relevant primarily to questions of eligibility to compete is athleticism and talent, not aesthetic appearance.

natural lottery.[8] Suppose there are two applicants for a place at a prestigious university. The applicants are equally qualified but one is able-bodied and the other has a severe visual impairment. According to the kind of conception of equality of opportunity being referred to by Kymlicka, the place should go to the visually impaired person, even though the candidates are equally qualified and equally suited to the place. This is to compensate for the disadvantages that the visually impaired student has overcome. It is highly probable that he has had to do much more than the other candidate to obtain the qualifications to get to the position in which he could credibly apply for the university place. This initial disadvantage should be compensated for.[9]

Back to Pistorius

Apply some of these views to the case of OP. The minimal application of fair equality of opportunity implies that OP should not be denied access to competitions on morally irrelevant grounds. Morally relevant ones would include those 'talents and skills relevant to the position ... being sought' (Daniels 1985, 40). So, as argued in (b) above, it is implausible that the impairment in itself should be sufficient to exclude him from consideration for competition.

Consider further the extension of the idea of fair equality of opportunity as presented in its broader, stronger application (i.e. the brute luck view). According to this, recall, some compensatory measures are obliged by the proper application of fair equality of opportunity where there are relevant 'undeserved' characteristics—such as those which result from the natural lottery.

Application of the idea of fair equality of opportunity might now be considered in two phases of competition, so to speak. There is a first phase where eligibility to compete is considered. Here, minimally, equality of opportunity obliges consideration of the eligibility of OP in relation to other applicants. And this is to be assessed in terms of those 'talents and skills' that he possesses which are relevant to his being considered eligible to compete.

Consider now a second phase of application of fair equality of opportunity: in the race itself.[10]

The stronger application of the FEO (the brute luck view) would seem to entail that some form of 'handicapping' system be introduced. This would be to provide a 'level playing field' for the competitors. Thus we should find differing starting lines: one for those athletes brought up in geographical regions congenial to the development of performance-enhancing capacities. They would be alongside those others who benefited from 'undeserved' advantages. Further up, towards the finishing line, one would expect to find another starting line, this one being for those athletes who have had to overcome undeserved disadvantages stemming from the poor deal they got from the natural lottery. Due to the disadvantages that the natural lottery has bestowed on OP, and the obligation to compensate for these, it could be expected both that he would be eligible to compete in the Olympics (even with a slower qualifying time) and that he would start closer to the finish line than other athletes who have not had to overcome comparable disadvantages.

Having pointed out this application of the idea of fair equality of opportunity as it would apply in the context of competitions themselves, I take it that this illustrates the implausibility of applying such principles in the context of competitions such as a race. Any attempt to 'equalise' the competitors to ensure a fair competition seems doomed to failure. They will not be physically identical. Even if they are genetic twins, they may have eaten differently, trained differently and had different coaching. Also, if a handicapping system is introduced, this seems to lead to a possibly absurd situation. Those best equipped to finish the 'race' quickly would start further from the finish line than those less well equipped. Perhaps a metre or less from the finish line there are those athletes who are least well equipped to finish the event. This seems to me a *reductio ad absurdum* of the idea that sporting events themselves should be constrained by fair equality of opportunity when this is taken in its strong form.

Having undertaken this slight detour into the application of the fair equality of opportunity in the context of sporting events themselves, we now move to the final section, which reviews the current situation at the time of writing (September 2007).

Present Situation Regarding OP and the IAAF

In June 2007 the IAAF declared a ban on 'any technical device that incorporates springs, wheels or any other element that provides a user with an advantage over another athlete not using such a device'.[11]

As I understand it, the IAAF intend to study OP's running action to try to determine whether or not the blades give him an unfair advantage. For reasons given in (c) above I take this to be beside the point. The central issue concerns whether or not what OP does counts as running.

However, the intention of the IAAF is to determine the length of OP's stride and compare that with the angle of his thighs while running. Apparently, calculation of that angle can be used to determine what the 'natural' length of his stride would be. Presumably, then, OP could be barred from competition if his stride is judged to be 'too long' according to biological norms. So the main objection to refusing him the chance to compete would be this unfair advantage. It is unfair since it is unavailable to those with naturally complete and properly 'angled' legs and thighs.

But, as explained above, it is far from clear that the blades do in fact bring any advantage to OP, given the numerous disadvantages of using the blades. Also, suppose that an athlete was born with the kind of stride length that the IAAF judges to be unnaturally long. Perhaps the person has a genetic anomaly which affects stride length. If possession of this 'greater than normal' stride length is the criterion determining eligibility to compete, such a person would be barred from performing. This sets a precedent such that athletes with the kinds of performance-aiding genetic advantage possessed (for instance) by Mantyranta and Indurain would similarly be excluded from competition. Of course it could be claimed that it is not solely the extra stride length that is the problem in OP's case but that this is engineered artificially; but we saw in (c) above the difficulties with this strategy.

Lastly, one wonders that if OP is barred from the Olympics surely it follows that he should be barred from the Paralympics. If he has an advantage on 'able-bodied' runners, then this is surely true in relation to the Paralympics too—at least in those races in which he is the sole competitor using two blades.

Conclusion

This paper considered the predicament of Oscar Pistorius. Following a description of the situation, some of the main arguments against allowing him to compete in the 2008 Olympics were set out and responded to. It was concluded that none of the arguments is compelling. The best hope to exclude OP from the Olympics would be to try to argue that his actions do not count as running. Arguments that appeal to his having an unfair advantage are implausible, as it seems more likely that the blades bring more disadvantages than advantages, and are anyway beside the point. Following a discussion of the application of fair equality of opportunity in the context of competitions themselves, it was concluded that to do so would lead to absurd consequences. Lastly, a review of the situation at the time of writing reasserted that the strategy of the official bodies is largely beside the point since its aim is to establish whether or not OP's blades provide him with an unfair advantage.

NOTES

1. See the Wikipedia entry on Oscar Pistorius at http://en.wikipedia.org/wiki/Oscar.Pistorius, accessed 31 August 2007.
2. J. Longman, 'An amputee sprinter: Is he disabled or too-abled?' *New York Times*, 15 May 2007, available at http://www.nytimes.com/2007/05/15/sports/othersports/, accessed 16 June 2007.
3. Quoted in ibid.
4. Reported in ibid.
5. Ibid.
6. Ibid.
7. This question is attributed to George Dvorsky in Longman, 'An amputee sprinter'.
8. For one that illustrates its application in the context of the social lottery, see Rachels (1993, 189); it should be said that the natural/social distinction is especially muddy in the context of disability issues, since the former impact upon the latter too.
9. More strongly, some suggest that in the event of the blind person's qualifications being less good than the other candidate, he should still get the place (see Rachels 1993, 189).
10. This line of thought has been developed meticulously in Loland (2002).
11. IAAF, Rule 144.2, available at http://www.enews20.com/news_IAAF_Pistorius_Not_Eligible_to_Compete_in_Bejing_Olympics_Update_05137.html, accessed 26 June 2008.

REFERENCES

BMA (BRITISH MEDICAL ASSOCIATION). 2002. *Illustrated Medical Dictionary*. London: Dorling Kindersley.

BUCHANAN, A., D.W. BROCK, N. DANIELS and D. WIKLER. 2000. *From Chance to Choice: Genetics and Justice*. Cambridge: Cambridge University Press.

DANIELS, N. 1985. *Just Health Care*. Cambridge. Cambridge University Press.

ENGELHARDT, H.T. 1996. *The Foundations of Bioethics,* 2nd edn. Oxford: Oxford University Press.

HARRIS, J. 2000. Is there a coherent social conception of disability? *Journal of Medical Ethics* 26: 95–100.

IPC (INTERNATIONAL PARALYMPIC COMMITTEE). 2007. IPC Classification code glossary, version 26, March 2007. Available at http://www.paralympic.org/release/Summer_Sports/Athletics/ About_the_sport/Rules/IPC_Athletics_Classification_Handbook_2006.pdf

KYMLICKA, W. 1990. *Contemporary Political Philosophy*. Oxford: Clarendon Press.

LOLAND, S. 2002. *Fair Play in Sport, a Moral Norm System*. London: Routledge.

NORDENFELT, L. 1993. On the notions of disability and handicap. *Social Welfare* 2: 17–24.

RACHELS, J. 1993. *The Elements of Moral Philosophy*. New York: McGraw-Hill.

WHO (WORLD HEALTH ORGANISATION). 1980. *International Classification of Impairments, Disabilities and Handicaps*. Geneva: WHO.

———. 2001. *International Classification of Functioning, Disability and Health*. Geneva: WHO.

S.D. Edwards, Centre for Philosophy, Humanities and Law in Healthcare, School of Health Science, Swansea University, Swansea SA2 8PP, UK.
E-mail: s.d.edwards@swansea.ac.uk

TACKLING *MURDERBALL*: MASCULINITY, DISABILITY AND THE BIG SCREEN

Michael Gard and Hayley Fitzgerald

The sport of wheelchair rugby is the subject of a recent film Murderball, *which tells the story of the apparently intense rivalry between the Canadian and United States men's teams. In part, the story is told through the lives of some of the game's leading players and coaches.* Murderball *deals with a series of ethical and political questions concerned with conceptions of disability, articulations of sporting bodies, and the value attached to sporting performance. In this paper we offer a critique of* Murderball *and explore a number of themes including: (1) What can disabled bodies do?; (2) This is not the Special Olympics; and (3) 'Hot' and disabled. We conclude that these themes offer us new intellectual challenges for thinking about the physical education experiences of young disabled people and progression in disability sport. Indeed, we argue that* Murderball *moves disability issues into new intellectual terrain, thus increasing the ways in which people who work with young people and sport might need to take account of disability.*

Resumen

El deporte de rugby sobre silla de ruedas es el tema de un film reciente, Murderball, *que cuenta la historia de la aparentemente intensa rivalidad entre los equipos masculinos de Canada y de los Estados Unidos. En parte la historia se cuenta por medio de las vidas de algunos de los principales jugadores y entrenadores.* Murderball *maneja una serie de preguntas éticas y políticas centradas sobre las concepciones de la discapacidad, las articulaciones de los cuerpos deportivos y el valor atribuído a la actuación deportiva. En este artículo ofrecemos una crítica de* Murderball, *y exploramos un número de temas, incluyendo: (1) ¿Qué son capaces de hacer los cuerpos discapacitados? (2) Esto no son los Special Olympics (Programas físicos para disminuídos psíquicos), y (3) "tios buenos" y discapacitados. Concluímos que estos temas nos ofrecen desafíos intelectuales nuevos para pensar acerca de las experiencias educativas físicas de la gente joven disminuída y la progresión de la minusvalía en el deporte. De hecho, argumentamos que* Murderball *lleva los asuntos sobre la discapacidad a un terreno intelectual nuevo, y de esta manera multiplica las maneras en las que la gente que trabaja con gente joven y el deporte podría tomar en cuenta a la discapacidad.*

Zusammenfassung

Rollstuhl-Rugby war kürzlich Gegenstand des Filmes Murderball. *Hier wird die Geschichte der offenen Rivalität zwischen dem kanadischen und dem US-amerikanischen Herrenteam erzählt.*

Zum Teil wird die Geschichte aus der Perspektive einiger Schlüssel-Spieler und der Trainer dargestellt. Murderball *behandelt eine Reihe ethischer und politischer Fragen, die sich mit Vorstellungen von Behinderung, athletischen Körpern sowie dem Wert der sportlichen Leistung auseinandersetzen. Dieser Aufsatz beinhaltet eine Besprechung von* Murderball, *in der unter anderem folgende Themen zur Sprache kommen: (1) Wozu ist ein behinderter Körper in der Lage? (2) Das sind nicht die Special Olympics und (3) 'Heiß' und behindert. Wir nehmen an, dass uns diese Themen neue Anstöße zum Nachdenken über die Erfahrungen von jungen Behinderten im Sportunterricht und zur Entwicklung des Behindertensports eröffnen. Wir behaupten in der Tat, dass* Murderball *Behindertenfragen auf ein neues intellektuelles Terrain führt, daher sollten Menschen, die mit jungen Leuten im Sport arbeiten, vermehrt das Thema Behinderung zur Kenntnis nehmen.*

摘要

輪椅橄欖球最近成為一部電影『謀殺球』的題材，主要是有關美國與加拿大男子代表隊之間的激烈競爭，同時包含了幾位重要球員與教練的生活故事。『謀殺球』討論了一系列與殘障的概念、運動身體的發聲、運動表現的價值等，所體現出和倫理和政治相關的議題。本研究主題包含：(1)失能的身體能做些什麼？(2)這不是特殊奧運以及(3)成為「熱門」與殘障。總結這些研究議題，為我們在思考年輕殘障者的體育課程和殘障運動的發展，帶來新的思維挑戰。『謀殺球』這部電影的確將我們帶入新的知識領域，將使得人們在教導年輕人和運動時，會將殘障、失能納入考量。

Introduction: *Murderball* and Wheelchair Rugby

The sport of wheelchair rugby (sometimes called 'quad rugby') is the subject of Henry Alex Rubin and Adam Shapiro's 2005 documentary *Murderball*. The film tells the story of the apparently intense rivalry over a number of years between the Canadian and United States men's national teams. In part, the story is told through the lives and personalities of some of the game's leading players and coaches. Although we use the word 'documentary' as shorthand, the film could be interpreted as many other things. For example, the commercial-release DVD of the film includes a range of extra material, including an episode of *The Larry King Show* in which the host interviews the players mostly prominently featured in *Murderball*, takes live phone-in questions from viewers and generally promotes the (then) upcoming cinematic release of the film. Throughout the interview both King and the players talk about the value of *Murderball* in advertising the sport of wheelchair rugby and, in fact, canvass the idea of wheelchair rugby becoming a big-money, high-profile sport. So, although we use the word 'documentary', it is clear that some of *Murderball's* proponents also see it as a piece of commercial sports promotion. In addition, both the film itself and the *Larry King* interview explicitly deal with a series of ethical and political questions. For example, how *should* disabled people be represented? What do non-disabled people know about disabled people? To what extent are non-disabled people's fears of disabled bodies a product of their wilful ignorance or the victim mentality of disabled people? And perhaps even more controversially, how should disabled people (particularly those who have recently acquired a disability) deal with their disability and what role might sport play in their 'empowerment'. The on-screen participants in *Murderball* all offer answers to these questions and, at least for this reason, the film deserves thoughtful consideration.

At the same time, the on-screen narrative of *Murderball* appears to be highly contrived (even choreographed) such that there are at least arguments against describing it as a documentary at all. In short, we argue that *Murderball* is a groundbreaking film and in some (if not all) respects a daring and complex piece of social activism.

With these preliminary points in mind, in this paper we offer a thematic critique of *Murderball*. We do so in the knowledge that a mean-spirited 'trashing' of the film is possible but that this is an approach we firmly reject. We hold some of the explicit and implicit arguments made in *Murderball* 'up to the light' and consider their origins, efficacy and implications. We examine some of the questions and issues raised by *Murderball* and attempt to analyse the *techniques* used to address them. Furthermore, we are aware that *Murderball* has aroused lively discussion in the print and electronic media. Our purpose, therefore, is to make a scholarly contribution to this discussion and, in particular, to consider the implications of this film for physical education (PE) contexts. We want to make a connection with PE because we believe *Murderball* has the potential to raise important questions about the relationship between disability, PE and sport.

Before moving to our critique of *Murderball* we examine the broader literature focusing on sport, media and disability. First, we discuss participation in sport by disabled people and highlight the tensions that can arise when dominant understandings of sport and disability attempt to coexist. We then focus on media and disability and briefly explore the different ways in which disability has been represented in films. Next, we identify the methodological approach we used to develop our critique of the film. Finally, we present our critique of *Murderball* under three thematic headings. The first of these, 'What can disabled bodies do?', centres on the film's use of representations of the players' lifestyles and a hyper-masculine physicality and sexuality. Within our second theme, 'This is not the Special Olympics', we describe the way the sport of wheelchair rugby and its athletes are actively and explicitly distanced from people with intellectual disabilities and the sports they play. *Murderball* leaves us in little doubt that its stars see this form of disability sport as superior to the sports we might see at events like the Special Olympics. Our last theme, 'Hot and disabled', shows how the film's makers seem (from our point of view) to prosecute an agenda that sees wheelchair rugby as a viable, media friendly, big-money sport. A specific model of sport has been chosen in *Murderball*, a model that uses music, the manipulation of video footage and a set narrative set pieces to produce not just a sport, but a *media* sport. Taken together, we conclude that these three themes offer us new intellectual challenges for thinking about such issues as the PE experiences of young disabled people and their progression in disability sport. That is, we do not presume to know how young disabled people will respond to or 'read' *Murderball*. Rather, we argue that *Murderball* moves disability issues into new intellectual terrain, thus increasing the ways in which people who work with young people and sport might need to take account of disability.

Physical Education, Sport and Disability

Historically, the development of sport and PE for disabled people has been influenced by medical understandings of disability (Sherrill and DePauw 1997). Medicalisation is particularly evident in the United States and United Kingdom, where rehabilitation centres and therapeutic recreation programmes attempt to use sport as a means of remedying or adjusting patients to the 'limitations' of their disability. Internationally, legislation and policy developments in recent years have explicitly sought to address issues relating to inclusion generally within education. Within PE this has led to the development of numerous resources and guidelines and the publication of a number of syllabuses that address, to differing degrees, issues of inclusion (DfEE/QCA 1999; Ministry of Education 1999; Downs 1995). The purported goal of these developments is to contribute to more positive and inclusive PE and sporting experiences for students, including those who happen to be disabled. Articulating precisely what 'inclusive' PE looks like, however, has been problematic and is a source of confusion and debate among physical educators (Vickerman 2002). Recent research in this era of apparent inclusion suggests that the realities of disabled students' broader school experiences remain complex and reflect practices that reinforce oppression, while at the same time supporting conditions that can enable disabled students to be agents of change (Davis and Watson 2002). In addition to using PE and sport for rehabilitative and educative means, disability sport has also emerged as an avenue for disabled people to engage in competitive pursuits.

Pathways have been developed that enable disability sports to be played from recreational to competitive levels. Some disability sports, such as wheelchair rugby, wheelchair basketball, seated volleyball and table cricket, are adaptations of what could be considered 'mainstream sports' played by non-disabled people. Other disability sports such as goalball and boccia have been developed with specific impairment groups in mind.[1] The *need* for adaptation or the creation of new sports signal as least some level of tension between sport and disability (DePauw 1997).

To clarify this point, a significant dimension of competitive sport is its concern with developing, refining and performing athletic techniques while adhering to rules (Coakley 2007). Typically, and especially (but not only) for boys and men, this practice is associated with aggression, competition and masculinity (Connell 1995; Light and Kirk 2000; Wellard 2002). In contrast, disability often signifies deficiency and impaired bodies are frequently viewed in negative ways. In this context, non-conforming disabled bodies are commonly perceived as 'spoilt' (Goffman 1968) and 'flawed' (Hevey 1992). The tension, then, arises when disabled bodies are expected to conform to the accepted and normalised practices dominating PE and sports discourse (Barton 1993). Even though adapted and disability sports serve to provide an alternative means of participation, the same kind of status or recognition as their non-disabled counterparts has not yet been achieved by its best proponents (Barton 1993; Fitzgerald 2005).

Some significant developments have taken place and are undoubtedly intended to promote the *value* of disability sport. These include closer alignment of the Paralympics to the Olympics, the organisation of disability sport world championships and an increasing commitment by mainstream sporting organisations to player development pathways for disabled people. One of the purposes of these developments seems to be to legitimise what Siedentop (2002) describes as the 'elite development goal'. According to Siedentop, a central feature of the elite development goal concerns the need for members of the sporting practice to work towards established standards of excellence. The development of player pathways within disability sport would seem to signal the possibilities that elite disability sport will achieve greater recognition. Yet the standards of excellence aspired to in relation to the elite development goal remain predominantly aligned to normalised understandings of ability and sporting performance.

With this as a background, we now turn to the ways in which the tensions between sport and disability have been interpreted and negotiated in popular media.

Media, Disability and Sport

It has long been recognised that the media are a key arena in which society's attitudes and values are shaped and reinforced. There is no reason to see this as any less true for disability (Norden 1994; Swain et al. 2005). According to Darke (1998, 181), 'images matter; for the disabled, images of themselves are especially important as they are presumed by virtually all critics and audiences to be essentially self-evident in the truths they reveal about impairment, the "human condition" and, as such, disability'. A critical question to ask here is: What images and discourses of disability dominate the mass media? Mitchell and Snyder (2006) suggest tragic news stories highlight accidents that result in disability and then focus on how individuals learn to manage, regain normal life or miraculously recover. Similarly, it has been argued that telethon events and other charity promotion organisers seek to secure public donations by portraying disabled people as needy and pitiful. Furthermore, the printed media have been accused of misrepresenting imagery of disability (Swain et al. 2005) and in particular coverage of disability sport has been marginalised (Thomas and Smith 2003). In relation to these 'deficit' understandings of disability it has been suggested that 'With so little exposure to contrary messages, this reinforces a straightforward "hypodermic syringe" model in which the "naturalness" of disability is seen to be confirmed to the media' (Barnes et al. 1999, 197).

Issues relating to disability and disabled characters have featured in many films (Norden 1994). For example, Hayes and Black (2003) contend that understandings of disability often emphasise a discourse of pity and this is articulated through storylines and characters that encourage audiences to associate disability with (1) confinement, (2) hope for rehabilitation, (3) denial of rehabilitation and (4) reconciliation of confinement. Confinement is concerned with spatial, physical or social forms of restriction and limits participation in social life. *Elephant Man* (1980) illustrates this with the main character initially restricted to a dark cellar and later isolated in hospital. Storylines focusing on rehabilitation and denial of rehabilitation highlight hope, often with the support of other non-disabled people, for overcoming disability. Lenny, in *Of Mice and Men* (1992), dreams of raising rabbits with his friend George. In this way the film depicts aspirations that will lead to a normal life. Nevertheless, this film and others also reinforce a view that rehabilitation may not always be achieved—Lenny kills the farmer's wife and is subsequently killed himself. Some films emphasise a reconciliation of confinement and in this way re-articulate confinement in a manner that transforms this from intolerable to an accepted benevolence. Lenny is killed by a friend so that he does not have to experience punishment and ridicule from others within his community. Within these different understandings of disability, disabled characters are regularly depicted at different ends of a continuum—either 'villains' (violent, evil and repulsive) or 'saints' (courageous, innocent and thankful) (Norden 1994). As a consequence of these kinds of representations, disabled people are often positioned as 'other' and 'isolated' in a similar manner to experiences encountered in wider society.

A number of film storylines have focused, in differing ways, on sport and disability including: *The Other Side of the Mountain* (1975), *Ice Castles* (1979) and *Million Dollar Baby* (2004). *Ice Castles* tells the story of an 'up and coming' ice skater who becomes visually impaired. Following a period of depression, she begins to skate again and gains competitive success. Although the film conveys an important message that if you become disabled you can still do sport, it also has heroic undertones that emphasise the incredible feat of the visually impaired skater. Dahl (1993, 141) describes the film as featuring 'two dimensional characters who "learn to cope" and "live happily ever after"'. In contrast, *Million Dollar Baby* is the story of a female professional boxer who, following a world championship fight, becomes a quadriplegic. After acquiring a disability the boxer loses the will to live and her trainer supports her request to end her life. In the USA the film evoked considerable criticism with Duncan (2007) describing it as 'bleak and depressing'. Disability activists were particularly critical of the film and outspoken about the way in which euthanasia was presented (Haller 2006). According to Boyle et al. (2006) *Million Dollar Baby* perpetuates 'able-centric' notions of normality and reinforces negative perceptions of disability—such that it is better to die than live with a disability.

In the selective context of this paper's discussion of *Murderball*, two general points emerge from this brief account of popular media and disability. First, there is the obvious conclusion that popular media encourage their consumers to see disabled bodies as grotesquely 'other' and therefore objects of pity. Secondly, because its assumed consumers are non-disabled people, the popular media offer a tragic/heroic account of disabled lives and the subjectivities of disabled people. While readers may have their own views about whether this is a fair or helpful state of affairs, what these representations consistently leave out is much sense that a disabled life can be, in many respects, just like a non-disabled life. In popular media disabled lives are very rarely playfully enjoyable (as opposed to heroically triumphant), sexually active or curious, hip or in tune with modern fashions and cultural trends. They are, instead, a ghetto.

Constructing a Thematic Critique

We want to stress that the 'research' we present below is not, in any straightforward sense, empirical. Two points can be made by way of initial justification for this claim. First, our intention was not to offer a definitive analysis of what *Murderball* is 'really' about or what its effects in the world might be. Secondly, we attempted to connect with, and develop upon, existing conversations about disability. For example, we are aware that *Murderball*'s release occasioned a great deal of spirited online debate. This debate centred on whether or not *Murderball* was good for disabled people and, as a result, was played out through quite predictable ideological positions. That is, *Murderball* was either seen as a bit of high-spirited fun which offered disabled people another way of being in the world or, on the other hand, as crude, sexist and out of touch with the realities of the majority of disabled people who will never be elite athletes.

By contrast, we sought to bring a range of academic perspectives to bear on *Murderball*. However, we wanted to work through the film in a comparatively systematic way but to do so without the pressure of being sure that we had 'captured' its apparent essence.

Both authors viewed the film separately and then met informally to discuss their impressions of it. We then independently compiled and later compared lists of questions and issues that we felt the film was trying to answer or address. Through discussion, we settled on a shortlist of specific questions/issues that we agreed were central to the composition of the film. We then watched the film again (and the extra material contained on the commercial-release DVD) and wrote our separate reflections about *how* these questions and issues are dealt with. Once again, we brought these reflections together with a view to doing two things. First, we wanted to decide whether we still felt our shortlist of questions/issues needed to be collapsed or expanded. Secondly, we looked for similarities and differences in the techniques that the two of us perceived operating in the film to answer or at least address these questions and issues. For example, we agreed that the film's makers appeared to want to educate viewers and to address misconceptions about disabled bodies. So when we re-watched the film we did so with an eye on this issue. As indicated above, however, we did not do this in order to simply describe the issue and to report on the film's content. Rather, we analysed what we took to be the film's explicit arguments, what we call its discursive techniques: what did we understand to be the film's explicit intentions and how does it try to communicate these intentions. What discursive techniques appear (to us) to have been used and which were ignored? For example, we would argue that the film's makers chose to construct disabled bodies as not so different from non-disabled bodies and, in fact, to draw on fairly mainstream ideas about heterosexual masculinity to do so. That is, *Murderball* tells its audience that disabled male bodies can be beautiful, muscular and sexually active. Is this a 'good' use of the educative potential of documentary film? For this paper we mostly suspended judgement on this kind of question and, instead, discuss the potential consequences of the choices that appear (to us) to have been made in the making of *Murderball*.

In short, our analysis begins by engaging with *Murderball* on what we might provisionally call 'its own terms'. We are, of course, aware that such a claim invites the criticism of essentialism. We take for granted the possibility that our analysis totally misrepresents the actual intentions of the film's makers. More to the point, we accept the possibility that no single coherent statement of intention could capture the disparate agendas and aspirations of the many people who, no doubt, participated in the film's construction. Our use of the phrase 'its own terms' indicates our focus on what we took to be the film's most important content. We treated the film, as it were, like an interviewee; we listened and then tried to interpret what it said. Whether our interpretations are justified is for others to judge. On the other hand, however, we also wanted to emphasise that we were not concerned with what the film might have said or should have said. We focused on what the film actually said. We wanted to engage in dialogue with the film, not lecture to it.

Finally, having arrived at a determinate list of questions/issues and a summary of our discussions about them, we watched the film together to test our tentative conclusions. We bore in mind questions such as whether we had missed anything important or whether we had made too much of particular question or issue, or been too harsh in our reactions to them. In the following section we offer a summary of our analysis.

Tackling *Murderball*

Three major themes emerged from our critical analysis of *Murderball*. They are (1) What can disabled bodies do? (2) 'This is not the Special Olympics' and (3) 'Hot' and disabled.

(1) What Can Disabled Bodies Do?

The narrative of *Murderball* tells a story of the rivalry between the Canadian and USA wheelchair rugby teams. It spans a period from the 2002 World Championships in Göteborg, where the Canadians took first place by upsetting the traditionally dominant USA team, to the 2004 Athens Paralympics in which Canada again defeated the USA but were themselves beaten by New Zealand for the gold medal. Wheelchair rugby is a game played between two squads of players. The aim of the game, played on a standard basketball court, is for teams (a maximum of four players are allowed on court at any one time) to advance the ball downfield by either passing it among themselves or by players rolling with the ball in their possession. A point is scored when a player wheels over their scoring line at the end of the court with the ball in their possession.

The purpose and techniques of the game are significant because it is not actually clear why the sport should be called wheelchair rugby at all. Wheelchair rugby has many dissimilarities to mainstream rugby; forward passes are allowed in wheelchair rugby, players must bounce or pass the ball once every ten seconds, a round ball instead of an oval ball is used and there is only one way of scoring points. Wheelchair rugby and mainstream rugby are far less similar than the disability sport and mainstream versions of other sports such as tennis, volleyball, basketball, track and field or cricket, and it is at least debatable whether many first-time viewers would actually recognise wheelchair rugby as a form of rugby. In fact, the two sports arguably share only two significant similarities: both games involve passing a ball (a feature of many other sports) and points are scored when a ball carrier crosses a line at one end of the field.[2]

Although the naming of the sport preceded the making of *Murderball*, our argument here is that the choice of the name wheelchair rugby suggests an obvious desire to be linked with mainstream rugby and other heavy contact sports. Early in the film we see the New Zealand team doing a wheelchair 'Haka', the Maori ceremonial dance made famous by the New Zealand men's rugby team. Likewise, *Murderball* spends much of its time linking its main characters to a series of sporting and, in particular, masculine sporting stereotypes. Indeed, whatever else might be said about *Murderball*, it is, first and foremost, a story about the performance of masculinity. And as a generation of scholarship has shown, rugby and other forms of football such as American football are sports that in many Western countries signify 'normal', hegemonic and heterosexual masculinity. In short, *Murderball* is a film about a sport that has *already* tried to draw on the masculine cachet of mainstream men's rugby and contact sport. Specifically, the film appears to imagine a non-disabled audience asking 'How is it possible for disabled people to play a rough game like rugby?' Having posed the question, *Murderball* constructs an answer. Unlike the disabled men interviewed in a Sparkes and Brett's study (2002), the wheelchair rugby players in *Murderball* emphasise, in a positive way, how the similarities between the sports they played prior to acquiring their disability attracted them to wheelchair rugby. The action of the film constantly reiterates the physical toughness of the players and, moreover, the way the players relish the sport's alleged brutality. One of the USA players featured in the film, Bob Lujano, gleefully announces that basic aim of the sport is to 'kill the man with the ball'. During the *Larry King* interview Lujano says 'I'm a huge football fan, Dallas Cowboys fan, so I definitely love the physical contact'. Andy Cohn, another USA player, emphasises his desire to play physical contact sport: 'It's not that I wanted to play despite all the contact, I wanted to play because of all the contact. I played high school football. As soon as I saw you could totally hit someone as hard as you can … I'd found the perfect sport for me.'

It would be perhaps churlish to note that nobody actually 'hits' anybody in wheelchair rugby, at least not in the games featured in *Murderball*. What *is* emphasised is the collisions between wheelchairs. The opening sequences of the film have Marty, a member of the USA team's 'pit crew', describing the wheelchairs used. The wheelchairs themselves are a mass of roughly welded metal, the wheel hubs resemble barbarian warrior shields, while the overall effect is the stylised ultra-violent grunge of the Australian film *Mad Max*. Marty sees the resemblance as well, calling the wheelchair a 'gladiator, battling machine, a Mad Max wheelchair that can stand knocking the living daylights out of each other'. Wheelchair collisions, which sometimes result in the chair and player toppling on their side, accompanied by heavy death-metal guitars, are a mainstay of the movie's action.

The jock-ish masculinity that we see as a central discursive ingredient in *Murderball* is most obviously prosecuted through the personality of the USA player Mark Zupan. Zupan appears to have become the public face of wheelchair rugby and his macho attitudes, goatee beard, large tattoos and bodily muscularity are proudly and repeatedly displayed in the film. For example, the film presents Zupan visiting a spinal injury rehabilitation centre and promoting wheelchair rugby to patients. During this scene Mark takes a 'question and answer' session:

> STAFF MEMBER: Do you wear helmets?
> ZUPAN: No Mam.
> STAFF MEMBER: And why not?
> ZUPAN: You don't to do it, wearing helmets, elbow pads, shin pads, a helmet or whatever. but that may just be a macho man thing.

What is interesting here is the self-conscious use of 'macho' masculinity. It is as though it were not enough for the film to leave viewers with a strong sense of the macho behaviours of the players. Rather, the film wants you to know that the players *see themselves* as macho men. Early in the film the featured players talk about their aggressive rejection of condescending comments while drinking in pubs or doing the shopping. Zupan recalls daring another man to hit him and promising to hit him back. All this is accompanied with a regular stream of swearing.

In attempting to show what disabled bodies can do, *Murderball* does not simply present the central figures doing remarkable things like play a heavy contact sport; this is not just a story about 'supercrips'. For example, large sections of the film are spent showing that these disabled men are capable of doing 'normal' everyday things like driving, cooking, having sex and being a father to their children. In the case of sex, the film tells the viewer that lots of people, particularly young women, are curious about the sexual functioning of disabled men and, therefore, seeks to answer this curiosity. All the central characters in the film are presented as keen to articulate their sexual abilities. Here Andy Cohn proudly reflects upon his first sexual encounter after acquiring his disability: 'My first full-on sex after being in a wheelchair was a very great moment in my life. Just knowing that I could still, not just the physical act but the, you know, you could still go out, meet a girl and get lucky.'

Another player describes his use of 'modified doggy style' while Zupan claims that 'when you're in a chair you usually like to eat pussy'. The part of the film that explicitly deals with the players heterosexual functioning appears early in the film when the personalities of the main characters are being established. But unlike other aspects of the film's narrative (such as the physicality of wheelchair rugby or the intensity of the rivalry between the Canadian and USA teams), the sexual functioning of these disabled bodies appears in a short, clearly self-contained section, almost like a commercial break. It is as if the film makers decided that this topic needed to be dealt with and, once dealt with, the film could move on. We think this raises an obvious question: why is it there? After all, there is no particularly obvious reason why *Murderball* needed to spend time 'educating' its audience about the sexual capacities and predilections of its male stars.

It is possible that this section is included simply to titillate and attract viewers. Sex sells, after all. And yet we would argue that it is precisely because *Murderball* is a film about *sport*, with its historic and symbolic relationship to heterosexual masculinity (Connell 1995; Light and Kirk 2000; Wellard 2002) that a connection to sexuality can be made in the minds of the film's makers. While to us this section seems a gratuitous and somewhat clumsy insertion, it makes more sense if the intention of the film is to establish its characters as 'real sporting men'. That is, addressing the question of heterosexual functioning makes symbolic sense alongside the claim that these men are tough, cool, masculine men. Our claim would be, then, that given the film's intended mainstream audience, the claim that these men are 'normal', 'typical' sporting jocks was understood (consciously or unconsciously) as less convincing if there was suspicion that they were either gay or sexually impotent. Although one of the USA players, Scott Hogsett, mentions that sexual function depends on the kind of injury sustained, all the stars of *Murderball* claim to be sexually active. The one exception is Bob Lujano, about whose sexual life we learn nothing.

In short, rather than saying nothing about the sexual lives of these men (a perfectly reasonable choice, given that it is predominantly a film about sport), *Murderball's* makers included a short, sharp statement that links wheelchair rugby players to symbols of hegemonic, straight, non-disabled masculinity—sports-loving, physically tough and 'horny'.

(2) 'This is Not the Special Olympics'

Perhaps a more surprising aspect of *Murderball* is its assertive repudiation of other areas of disability sport. For its participants, wheelchair rugby is presented as an extremely competitive sport requiring the same aggressive outlook and physical excellence of non-disabled elite sport performers. However, as with the displays of heterosexual masculinity discussed in the previous section, there is a sense of 'protesting too much' in that the film appears to have consciously chosen to *prove* its *bona fide* nature through exaggeration. For example, *Murderball* offers viewers a window into a world of almost apocalyptic competitive intensity. Team huddles involve red-faced, screaming team chants while coaches 'candidly' claim 'we're going to kick the shit out of them'.

Although non-disabled elite sports cultures are diverse, the modern discourse of coaches and players in the heavy body-contact sports (such as rugby and American football) tends, at least when communicating with the media, to obscure or downplay inherent violence. Instead, talk of 'process', 'accountability', 'controlled aggression', 'discipline' and 'minimising errors' dominates. In this respect, the hyper-aggressive banter in *Murderball* is a kind of throwback; there is virtually no mention of tactical subtlety throughout the entire film. At the end, viewers are none the wiser about *how* a game wheelchair rugby is won or about how the Canadian and USA teams differ in their styles of play. All we are told is that they hate each other.

For example, the film makes much of the fact that Joe Soares, the Canadian coach, is an American and ex-USA star player who defected to Canada in order to prolong his career. A number of times during the film Joe is accused by USA players of 'betraying his country'. Of Soares, Zupan says: 'If Joe was on the side of the road on fire I wouldn't piss on him to put it out'. When Joe comes face to face with ex-teammates they trade obscenities in an almost pantomime demonstration of mutual antipathy. In the two of the medal presentations captured in the film, losing players cry inconsolably while winners sing national anthems at the top of their voices, seeming almost to take pleasure in taunting their defeated opposition.

For his part, Soares is portrayed as a brooding, intense and manically competitive individual who is determined to take revenge on the USA for trying to finish his sporting career. In a television story about the lead up the Athens Paralympics, a sports reporter says that 'Joe's one of the most competitive men I've ever been around'. Soares's family life and, in particular, his relationship with his 'nerdy' violin-playing son is framed as a test of whether he can curtail his competitive sporting nature and be a 'good father'. The resolution of this subplot, in which Soares and his son are finally able to communicate their affection for each other, is achieved only once Soares's sporting intensity is portrayed as an all-consuming threat to his health (during the film he suffers a heart attack) and family life.

In our view, these displays of hatred are included in order to distance wheelchair rugby from other disability sports. That is, they are designed to distance the sport from the participatory 'feel-good' ethos of other disability sport and position it closer to the competitive seriousness of elite mainstream sport. For example, the USA coach comments that 'there is a perception that everyone can play this game' and then goes on to describe how the final 12 players in the USA squad are ruthlessly culled from a much larger field of participants.

This distancing finds full voice in the film's climax, the build-up to the Athens Paralympics. In a collage of short sections of footage accompanied by the obligatory heavy metal music, fans are shown with national emblems tattooed on their face; the Olympic flame burns; lycra-clad athletes carry a USA flag in victory, while others celebrate deliriously. The message is clear: this is *real* sport. There is no 'feel-good' here. This is about winning.

In a hotel room prior to the Paralympics, Hogsett and Zupan drive the no-feel-good point home. Hogsett is talking about his wedding day where a relative came to him and said that she had heard he was going to the Special Olympics.

HOGSETT: And all of a sudden I went from being the man at the wedding, to a fucking retard. And it was the worst feeling. The Special Olympics are something that happens once a year and it's for people who are mentally challenged. What they do in the Special Olympics is very honourable. It's amazing what they can do. But this is something that's totally different.

ZUPAN (with irony): It's a little different. We're not going for this feel good 'please, pat me on the back. Thank you. Thank you for participating.' No, no, no, no.

HOGSETT: We're not going for a hug. We're going for a fucking gold medal.

Whatever else we might think about this section of dialogue, we can say that a choice has been made to include it. Therefore, we might justifiably ask why this kind of distancing work seemed necessary or desirable to the film's makers. Once again, *Murderball* seems in a time-warp, back to the 1970s catch-cry 'winning isn't the main thing, it's the only thing'. Today, it is almost impossible to imagine non-disabled elite athletes talking openly and publicly about disabled athletes in this way and escaping public censure. In fact, the archetypal modern non-disabled sports star works hard to cultivate a more wholesome image that will be attractive to sponsors. This is not to pass particular moral judgement on Hogsett and Zupan. Rather, it is to simply note that *Murderball* seems to be saying that entry to the club of 'real sport' means, in part, defining itself by reference to what it is not. In the previous section, we saw how *Murderball* explicitly links wheelchair rugby to the conventions of heterosexual sexuality and aggressive, male dominated mainstream sports.

(3) 'Hot' and Disabled

The final theme that we discuss follows closely on from the previous theme. However, while we have just discussed the way *Murderball* attempts to assert its sporting credentials, in this section we see how the film tries to position wheelchair rugby as an exciting, media-friendly sport with the potential to attract greater media exposure, fans and sponsors.

This point is made explicitly and repeatedly during the *Larry King Show* interview. At the beginning of the show, King invites his audience to stay watching by presenting the players as 'must watch' stars and athletes. King announces: 'Tonight! They're handsome, sexy, world class athletes and they're quadriplegics in wheelchairs.' Later, discussion turns to the potential and future possibilities for wheelchair rugby.

KING: Does the sport, does it draw people Scott?

HOGSETT: Yeah, especially with this movie out it's going to get bigger. Next year we're really excited for it.

KING: Where are you playing, what sort of gyms?

HOGSETT: We'll play in high schools, we'll play arenas, we'll play in community centres.

KING: Do you think you'll play one day at Madison Square Gardens?

HOGSETT: We'd like that.

ZUPAN: That's the biggest stage.

KING: I know the people there. Why wouldn't they be interested in this? Especially, they could put on a two-day tournament.

ZUPAN: What we've been talking about is incorporating it into the X-Games.

Murderball says to its viewers: 'With the right marketing, disabled people can be sports megastars too.' This point is implicitly reiterated by emphasising the media build-up prior to the Athens Paralympics. A video collage shows TV anchors talking to cameras, television crews going about their business and a series of press conferences. The message is that this sport is 'hot' and people really are excited about it. In one of these press conferences

Zupan answers a question about wheelchair rugby: 'It used to be called "Murderball", but you can't really market "Murderball" to corporate sponsors.'

Murderball swings between framing wheelchair rugby in a *WWF*-style hyper-theatricality—heavy metal music, lighting effects, rapid-fire editing and fast camera zooming—and, in the final section of the film, presenting it as a poignant and serious sporting contest: the final moments of the Athens match between USA and Canada unfolds in agonising slow-motion, string accompaniment and, later, the defeated and distraught USA players are greeted post-match by tearful friends and family.

Our argument here is that *Murderball* is much more than a conventional piece of film-making that strives for roughly equal measures of human pathos and sporting spectacle; it is not simply that the film's makers wanted to make it entertaining for a mainstream audience. There are, after all, many ways to make a film entertaining. Rather, *Murderball* employs an eclectic set of tools to chart a discursive course towards (to paraphrase Kuhn) 'normal sport'. Sex, masculinity, hyper-aggressive competition and media stardom come together to construct a disabled athlete who claims both elements of elite sport's macho past and a popular-culture future for disability sport. This is interesting for many reasons but particularly because there is also a clear agenda within the film to connect with other disabled people. Zupan's outreach work in hospital spinal units makes it clear that *Murderball* sees itself as reaching up—to sporting stardom—and down—to other disabled people. This raises a tension to which, in conclusion, we now turn.

Pleasure, Disability and Physical Education

There is a moment in *Murderball* during Zupan's visit to the spinal injury clinic where he meets Keith, a young man recently injured in a motorcycle accident. Keith is clearly excited by what he hears about wheelchair rugby and sees on the video that Zupan plays. He is captivated by the metallic wheelchair Zupan has brought with him and pleads with his nurse to let him try running into something in the chair. Eventually she reluctantly relents and, using Zupan's chair, Keith gently bumps, to and fro, into Zupan who is now in a standard wheelchair. There is no music, just the soft bumping sound of metal on metal. The scene ends.

It is as if we have just witnessed an awakening moment. Keith's tiny collisions are miniaturised version of the fierce wheelchair impacts that litter the action of *Murderball*. Although the film's makers may not put it this way, they seem to be saying that disabled boys and men have the same drives and impulses as other boys and men. We are not inclined, here, to buy into an implied biological determinism about masculinity, but *Murderball* is a plea for more fully embodied physical experiences for disabled boys and men. In this respect, the film is simply part of a long-established movement to push through one more sporting barrier while, at the same time, pushing through one more socio-cultural barrier—legitimate access to a macho, sporting, hyper-heterosexual masculinity that is celebrated in the wider culture. It is difficult to see how *Murderball* could be criticised for this, just as it is difficult to see how (putting to one side the thorny question of legal liability) physical educators could deny these kinds of desires, pleasures and identities to young disabled people. There will, one day, be female 'murderballers' too and physical educators have to begin to think about how the desires of students who want to 'get more physical' will be managed and supported.

In exactly the same way, there may be some viewers of *Murderball* and readers of this article who are concerned about the 'corrupting' influence of corporatised sport on disability sport. The stars of *Murderball* make it clear that they will have no patience for those who are queasy at the sight of disabled athletes behaving badly or, indeed, ultra-competitively. They say 'not all disabled people will want to be like us, but those who do, come along for the ride!' In this sense, they pre-empt those who might wonder about how young disabled people, who will never have the capacity to be assertive, aggressive elite athletes, will 'read' *Murderball*. The answer is that they will read it in the same way non-disabled young people 'read' non-disabled athletes: in a variety of ways and without the sky falling in. Once again, what *Murderball* does is unveil a set of desires which both are legitimate but potentially unsettling to some viewers simply because they are being felt by disabled bodies. But desires are always scary to somebody and physical educators are now faced with potentially new answers to questions about disabled identities and what disabled young people want.

In the end, the question for us is not whether *Murderball* is an accurate or positive symbol for all disabled young people; of course it is not and could never be. As we tried to stress in the methodology section above, we did not see a fair-minded critique of *Murderball* harping on about the female or gay or old athletes or black athletes not being depicted. These depictions are for another day. The question that we *would* raise about *Murderball* is the way it both tries to build certain bridges but, in the process, seems intent on destroying others. The victims of *Murderball* are those that are explicitly marginalised in the film, particularly intellectually disabled people. *Murderball* argues that in order for some disabled people to be lifted up, others have to be pushed down. It does this over and over again by *selectively* using non-disabled stereotypes—about masculinity, sport, and sexuality—that the film's stars can measure up to. In the world of *Murderball* the film, sexual incapacitation, being a 'retard' and being a happy and gracious loser are the ways you let the side down.

We should not forget that *Murderball* is, among other things, a commentary on, even a parody of, non-disabled mainstream sports culture. And yet, drawing on our thematic critique, in order to establish wheelchair rugby's sporting legitimacy, certain dominant ideas about sport are not so much rehearsed in *Murderball* as amplified. This leaves physical educators with a new set of questions about the hierarchies that might exist between different forms of disability and the formation of new disabled sporting cultures. *Murderball* wants to tell us that certain forms of disability sport are more legitimate than others. This should prompt us to think about the application of Siedentop's 'elite development goal': who is it for and why?

NOTES

1.   For further information about these disability sports see http://www.paralympic.org
2.   Though in rugby the ball must be grounded on or over the line.

REFERENCES

BARNES, COLIN, GEOF MERCER and TOM SHAKESPEARE. 1999. *Exploring Disability A Sociological Introduction*. Cambridge: Polity Press.
BARTON, LEN. 1993. Disability, empowerment and physical education. In *Equality, Education and Physical Education*, edited by J. Evans. London: Falmer Press: 43–54.

BOYLE, ELLEXIS, BRAD MILLINGTON and PATRICIA VERTINSKY. 2006. Representing the female pugilist: Narratives of race, gender, and disability in *Million Dollar Baby*. *Sociology of Sport Journal* 23: 99–116.

COAKLEY, JAY J. 2007. *Sport in Society: Issues and Controversies*. London: McGraw-Hill Higher Education.

CONNELL, ROBERT, W. 1995. *Masculinities*. Sydney: Allen & Unwin.

DAHL, MARILYN. 1993. The role of the media in promoting images of disability – disability as metaphor. The evil crip. *Canadian Journal of Communication* 18 (1), available at http://www.cjc-online.ca/viewarticle.php?id=141, accessed 15 March 2006.

DARKE, PAUL. 1988. Understanding cinematic representations of disability. In *The Disability Reader: Social Science Perspectives*, edited by T. Shakespeare. London: Cassell: 181–200.

DAVIS, JOHN and NICK WATSON. 2002. Countering stereotypes of disability: Disabled children and resistance. In *Embodying Disability Theory, Disability/postmodernity*, edited by M. Corker and T. Shakespeare. London: Continuum: 159–74.

DEPAUW, KAREN P. 1997. The (in)visability of disAbility: Cultural contexts and 'sporting bodies'. *Quest* 49 (4), 416–30.

DFEE/QCA (DEPARTMENT FOR EDUCATION AND EMPLOYMENT/QUALIFICATIONS AND CURRICULUM AUTHOR-ITY). 1999. *Physical Education: The National Curriculum for England*. London: HMSO.

DOWNS, PETER. 1995. *An Introduction to Inclusion Practice*. Canberra: Australian Sports Commission.

DUNCAN, BARBARA. 2007. Disability in the US media—notes on 2006, available at http://www.disabilityworld.org/01_07/media.shtml, accessed 12 Feb. 2008.

EVANS, JOHN and BRIAN DAVIES. 2002. Theoretical background. In *The Sociology of Sport and Physical Education*, edited by A. Laker. London: Routledge/Falmer: 15–35.

FITZGERALD, HAYLEY. 2005. Still feeling like a spare piece of luggage? Embodied experiences of (dis)ability in physical education and school sport. *Physical Education & Sport Pedagogy* 10 (1), 71–89.

GOFFMAN, ERVING. 1968. *Stigma*. Harmondsworth: Pelican.

HALLER, BETH. 2006. Thoughts on Million Dollar Baby. *Journal of Research in Special Educational Needs* 6 (2), 112–14.

HARDING, MARIE M. and BRENT HARDING. 2004. The 'Supercrip' in sport media: Wheelchair athletes discuss hegemony's disabled hero. *Sociology of Sport Outline* 7 (1), available at http://physed.otago.ac.nz/sosol/v7i1/v7i1_1.html, accessed 27 July 2006.

HAYES, MICHAEL T. and RHONDA S. BLACK. 2003. Troubling signs: Disability, Hollywood movies and the construction of a discourse of pity. *Disability Studies Quarterly* 23 (2), 114–32.

HEVEY, DAVID. 1992. *The Creatures That Time Forgot: Photography and Disability Imagery*. London: Routledge.

LIGHT, RICHARD and DAVID KIRK. 2000. High school rugby, the body and the reproduction of 'hegemonic' masculinity. *Sport, Education and Society* 5 (2), 163–76.

MITCHELL, DAVID and SHARON SNYDER. 2006. Narrative prosthesis and the materiality of metaphor. In *The Disability Studies Reader*, edited by L.J. Davis. London: Routledge: 205–27.

MINISTRY OF EDUCATION. 1999. *Health and Physical Education in New Zealand Curriculum*. Wellington: Learning Media.

NORDEN, MARTIN F. 1994. *The Cinema of Isolation*. New Brunswick, NJ: Rutgers University Press.

POINTON, ANNE, ed. 1997. *Framed Interrogating Disability in the Media*. London: British Film Institute.

PRIESTLEY, MARK. 1999. Discourse and identity: disabled children in mainstream high schools. In *Disability Discourse*, edited by M. Corker and S. French. Buckingham: Open University Press: 92–102.

SHAKESPEARE, TOM. 1994. Cultural representation of disabled people: Dustbins for disavowal? *Disability and Society* 9 (3), 283–99.

SHERRILL, CLAUDINE and KAREN P. DEPAUW. 1997. Adapted physical activity and education. In *The History of Exercise and Sport Science*, edited by J.D. Massengale and Richard A. Swanson. Champaign, IL: Human Kinetics.

SIEDENTOP, DARYL. 2002. Junior sport and the evaluation of sport cultures. *Journal of Teaching in Physical Education* 21: 392–401.

SMART, JULIE F. 2001. *Disability, Society, and the Individual*. Gaithersburg, MD: Aspen Publishers.

SPARKES, ANDREW C. and BRETT SMITH. 2002. Sport, spinal core injury, embodied masculinities, and the dilemmas of narrative identity. *Men and Masculinities* 4 (3): 258–85.

SPORT ENGLAND. 2001. *Disability Survey 2000 Young People with a Disability and Sport, Headline Findings*. London: Sport England.

SWAIN, JOHN, SALLY FRENCH, COLIN BARNES and CAROL THOMAS. 2005. *Disabling Barriers – Enabling Environments*. London: Sage.

THOMAS, NIGEL and ANDREW SMITH. 2003. Pre-occupied with able-bodiedness? An analysis of the British media coverage of the 2000 Paralympic games *Adapted Physical Activity Quarterly* 20 (2): 166–81.

VICKERMAN, PHILIP. 2002. Perspectives on the training of physical education teachers for the inclusion of children with special educational needs – Is there an official line view? *The Bulletin of Physical Education* 38 (2): 79–98.

WELLARD, IAN. 2002. Men, sport, body performance and the maintenance of exclusive masculinity. *Leisure Studies* 21 (3 & 4): 235–47.

Michael Gard, School of Human Movement Sciences, Charles Sturt University, Bathurst, New South Wales, Australia

Hayley Fitzgerald (corresponding author), Leeds Metropolitan University, Carnegie Faculty of Sport and Education, Headingley Campus, Leeds, W Yorkshire.
E-mail: H.Fitzgerald@leedsmet.ac.uk

IMAGINING BEING DISABLED THROUGH PLAYING SPORT: THE BODY AND ALTERITY AS LIMITS TO IMAGINING OTHERS' LIVES

Brett Smith

Qualitative research methods in sport often advocate that to understand others, obtain significant knowledge and do ethically admirable research we should empathise with our participants by imagining being them. In philosophy, it is likewise often assumed that we can overcome differences between people through moral imagination: putting ourselves in the place of others, we can share their points of view, merge with them, and enter into their embodied worlds. Drawing partly on the view that imagination is embodied and the philosophy of Bakhtin and Levinas, along with research on people's experiences of becoming disabled through playing sport, this paper problematises the assumption that we can imagine ourselves differently situated or being another person. It argues that our imagination and ability to put ourselves in the place of others is constrained partly by embodied experience and otherness. Some reflections on what this might mean for disability and sport research are then offered.

Resumen

Los métodos de investigación qualitativa en el deporte a menudo defienden que para comprender a los demás, conseguir un conocimiento significativo, y llevar a cabo una investigación ética admirable deberíamos empatizar con nuestros participantes imaginándonos que somos ellos. En filosofía a menudo se asume similarmente que podemos superar las diferencias entre las personas a través de la imaginación moral. Metiéndonos en la piel de otros podemos compartir sus puntos de vista, combinarlos y entrar en sus mundos corporales. Basándonos parcialmente en la posición de que la imaginación es corporal y la filosofía de Bakhtin y Levinas, además de en la investigación sobre las experiencias de gente que se vuelve discapacitada al hacer deporte, este artículo problematiza la presunción de que podemos imaginarnos a nosotros mismos situados de otra manera diferente o siendo otra persona. Argumenta que nuestra imaginación y la habilidad de ponerrnos en lugar de otras personas se encuentran limitadas en parte por la experiencia corporal y la alteridad. Se ofrecen algunas reflexiones sobre lo que esto puede significar para la investigación sobre la discapacidad y el deporte.

Zusammenfassung

Qualitative Forschungsmethoden im Sport erfordern oftmals sich in die Teilnehmer hineinzu-versetzen, um andere verstehen zu können, signifikante Erkenntnisse zu erhalten und um ethisch korrekte Forschung zu betreiben. In der Philosophie wird in gleicher Weise oftmals angenommen, die Unterschiede zwischen Menschen durch moralische Vorstellungskraft überwinden zu können, das heißt, uns an die Stelle der anderen zu versetzen, ihre Perspektive teilen, mit ihnen verschmelzen und in ihre körperliche Welt eintreten. Dieser Artikel problematisiert die Annahme, dass wir uns in die Lage anderer denken oder gar eine andere Person sein können. Dies geschieht zum Teil unter Rückgriff auf die Sichtweise, dass unsere Vorstellungskraft körpergebunden ist, auf die Philosophie von Bakhtin und Levinas sowie auf die Forschungsergebnisse zu den Erfahrungen von Menschen, die durch Sport zu einer Behinderung kamen. Es wird behauptet, dass unsere Vorstellungskraft und die Fähigkeit, uns in andere hineinzuversetzen, begrenzt ist, zum Teil durch körpergebundene Erfahrungen und dadurch, anders geartet zu sein. Einige Überlegungen zur potenziellen Bedeutung dieser Aspekte für die Forschung im Bereich Behinderung und Sport werden anschließend präsentiert.

摘要

運動的質性研究提到，我們想要瞭解他人、獲得重要知識，以及做出倫理上值得讚揚的研究，需要設身處地想像作為他們的感受。哲學上我們也假設，透過精神的想像，可以克服人之間的許多不同，設身處地的思考，可以分享相同的視角，和他們合而為一，並進入他們所體現的世界。著眼於想像是體現的，以及巴赫汀與列維那斯的哲學，意即研究透過運動體驗殘障的經驗，本研究嘗試提出，我們可以想像成為他人或是不同的狀況。並且認為當我們進行設身處地思考的想像和能力時，部份的限制來自於體現經驗和他者性。這些反省也提供了殘障與運動研究的意義。

Within qualitative sport research it is often presupposed that to understand others, to attain knowledge and to do so ethically we should empathise with our participants by imaginatively putting ourselves in the place of the other. Amis (2006), Bondi (2003), Duquin and Schroeder-Braun (1996), Krane and Baird (2005) and Ortiz (2005) all suggest that through imaginatively entering into the experiential world of the people they study, qualitative researchers may increase their ability to better understand another person, engender rapport, reduce emotional harm and thereby help them obtain significant knowledge of the human situation in ethically admirable, or at least ethically defensible, ways. For Andrews (2007, 489), 'if we wish to access the frameworks of meaning for others, we must be willing and able to imagine a world other than the one we know'. This may be enabled, she suggests, through narrative imagination:

> Our narrative imagination is our most valuable tool in our exploration of others' worlds, for it assists us in seeing beyond the immediately visible. It is our ability to imagine other 'possible lives'—our own and others—that creates our bond with 'diverse social and

historical worlds'. Without this imagination, we are forever restricted to the world as we know it, which is a very limited place to be. (Andrews 2007, 510)

Within qualitative studies in disability research specifically, the importance of imaginatively projecting oneself into another has also been noted. Michalko (2002), Toombs (2001), and Coles (2004) suggest that through the process of imagining the lives of disabled people we can come to know and better understand the experiences and points of view of other people. We may also engage with them in an empathetic manner and thus act in ethically approvable ways.

In addition to qualitative research and disability studies, the idea of imaginatively putting oneself in the place of the other has found expression in philosophical work. Thus in the philosophy of mind and consciousness, Depraz (2001) and Thompson (2001) argue that through empathically trying to imagine what it might be like to be the other person from the perspective of that other we can experience another person as a unified whole, as *their* whole. There is an imaginative transposal of myself to the place of the other person. For Finlay (2006, 6), 'Having imaginatively projected ourselves into the Other's situation and identified with it—and proved we stay focused on the Other's experience— we are able to experience empathy'. The idea that of imaginatively putting ourselves in the place of different others is also central in the political philosophy of Goodin (2003) and also in the account given by simulation theory of how we come to understand other minds (Heal 1998). Furthermore, Mackenzie and Scully (2007) point out that in moral and political philosophy, as well as bioethics, it is often assumed that we can overcome epistemic gaps through the exercise of moral imagination: 'By imaginatively "putting ourselves in the place of others", it is argued, we can come to understand the experiences and points of view of others whose lives are quite different from our own' (ibid., 337).

Finally, and autobiographically, in recent years I have been enmeshed in the dynamics of what might be termed research-imagination.[1] This has come about due to my life history of research with a small group of men who have suffered spinal cord injury (SCI) and become disabled through playing the sport of rugby union football (see Smith and Sparkes 2005, 2008a). These men graciously shared their stories with me, and I aspired to imaginatively put myself 'inside' their self-narratives as sporting men who were propelled across the border from the world of the able-bodied into the world of disability. One central reason for doing this was due to my being presently able-bodied. Furthermore, my aspiration to imagine their lives was strongly shaped by my readings of qualitative research along with work within disability studies and philosophy. This literature taken together, as noted above, suggests that when exploring disabled people's lives qualitative sport researchers should empathise with them to develop our understandings and for ethical reasons. This can be achieved, so the story goes, by imaginatively putting oneself into their worlds—imaginative projection. The following extract from my reflexive diary, in which I reflected upon an interview with one man (Max) who suffered a SCI and became disabled through playing rugby union, provides a flavour of this aspiration in action.

I've just finished interviewing Max, a 35-year-old man who seven years ago while playing rugby broke his neck and became disabled. Lots of things stick in my mind about the interview. But one thing keeps gnawing away at me. During the interview, I tried putting myself in his place. I tried and tried and tried to imagine being disabled through playing sport and to feel what it's like to live in and as an impaired body. This isn't new. Many times over the last year of this project I've tried before, during and after interviews to imagine being an athlete and then disabled. I'd like to say that I've really got under the skin and inside the mind of the participants interviewed. But, no matter how hard I try, I struggle to put myself in the place of a disabled person. What am I doing wrong? Why can't I overcome this? Am I lacking empathic capabilities? Is my imagination so impoverished that I can't imagine being another person? I was taught in my qualitative research classes and through the texts I've read to project myself into the lives of people I'm working with and to try to empathically imagine the other. So, why can't I imagine being another and put myself in the shoes of a disabled person? Why can't I overcome this?

Against this backdrop, I became interested in the role of imagination in research and began to reflexively explore the role of putting oneself in the place of others. In what follows, drawing on various scholars, including Bakhtin (1984) and Levinas (2001), I try to problematise this sense of imaginative projection. It must be recognised that I am not suggesting that we should abandon trying to engage imaginatively with the perspectives of others. Our capacity for imaginative projection can play an important part in understanding others and thus expanding our ethical horizons. It should also be made clear, lest a dualism is created, that imagining other lives is not in principle impossible. Nevertheless, there are barriers and challenges to imagining oneself 'in the other's shoes' and empathic imagination. Two such constraints are to be located in the body, so to speak, and in the idea of otherness. These are important to highlight since the problems of imaginatively putting oneself in the other's place are often underestimated, glossed over or overlooked all together. As a result, there is the danger of creating and perpetuating an over-optimistic and romantic conception of the role of imagining others' lives. Thus, without offering final answers, my modest aspiration is to offer a caution against overstating the power of imagination within sport and disability research.

Embodied Limits to Imagination: Bringing the Body In

Disability is experienced in, on and through the body, just as impairment is experienced in terms of the personal and cultural narratives that help to constitute its meaning.... Most importantly, the (impaired) body is not just experienced: It is also the very basis of experience...Disability is, therefore, experienced from the perspective of impairment. One's body is one's window on the world. (Hughes and Paterson 1997, 334–5)

In my mind, a non-reductionist materialist ontology of the body should neither deny the 'realness' of bodies and their flesh-bound variations nor concede ground to the idea that any acknowledgement of the material reality of 'the body' is tantamount to naturalising, medicalising or biologising it. It should be possible to understand the 'impaired body' as simultaneously biological, material and social – in short, as bio-social in character. (Thomas 2007, 135).

Imagination is traditionally considered to be purely a mental capacity and a cognitive act (Mackenzie and Scully 2007). However, as various scholars have more recently suggested (Lakoff and Johnson 1999; Mackenzie and Scully 2007), imagination is *embodied*. Imagination can be considered an embodied capacity because the mind is itself embodied. Indeed, there is no mental activity without a physical body, and we all have, are and experience a body within a social milieu. Accordingly, as is suggested in what follows, the body is bio-social, and this body one has, is and experiences places constraints on our capacities to imagine ourselves otherwise or to imagine ourselves being another person.

The body that one has, is and experiences is a material, biological entity. As an obdurate fact, we depend on our body as a corporeal entity to activate and use our imagination. In this regard, the physical matter of the body is a pre-condition for imagining others' lives and can as such be viewed as a source of, a location for and a means by which imagination is shaped and constrained. So for example, imagining oneself to be differently situated, or imagining being another *in* pain (for example, as a result of becoming disabled through playing sport) is constrained. This is not to say I cannot use my imagination. It is to suggest, however, that no matter how far the imagination reaches, my fleshy physicality, as a source of, location for and means through which imagination and pain partly operate, limits what and how I can imagine. I cannot, in other words, transcend my flesh and bones to entirely imaginatively put myself in another's embodied place and experience *their* pain. Thus our capacities for imaginative projection depend in very concrete ways on features of our specific embodiment. These may constrain our abilities to imagine other persons, whether, for instance, in the mode of imagining oneself 'in the other's shoes' or imagining being another.

Complicating the matter is not only the fact that having and being an able-body means that one has no physical or experiential knowledge of the bodily pain involved if one becomes disabled through playing sport, but also that pain has the ability to resist and destroy language (Scarry 1985). This ensures that the communication of personal meaning and experience is difficult to share, thereby placing further constraints on one's ability to imagine oneself differently situated, or to imagine being another in pain. This is suggested in the following interview-based dialogue between myself and one man (Doug) who suffered a spinal cord injury through playing rugby union football:

> BRETT: I'm trying to understand the pain you felt, get a sense of it. Can you describe it some more?
> DOUG: It's actually difficult to describe. Not because I can't remember it. I can, and I'm shuddering thinking about it. I just can't though get how it felt across to you. Imagine being in my body and feeling the pain.
> BRETT: Okay [15 seconds silence]
> DOUG: Do you feel it, the pain?
> BRETT: [five seconds silence] Honestly, no, I'm struggling. I want to get inside your world, though.
> DOUG: I just don't have the words, though, to truly express to you how I felt in pain now, or then.... I spoke to the doctor about the pain, and my friends asked me if I was in pain. I couldn't express what I felt, though, there weren't the words, and it hurt so much.... Being in pain is a lonely time, very frustrating as well, because you can't share it with anyone, and you are stuck staring at the ceiling day in day out. You're falling apart....If I'm really pushed, the pain felt like, like an electric shock. An electric shock going all the way through my body.

Accordingly, as suggested above, there are real difficulties of imagining oneself differently situated or imagining being another person arising, in part, from the way imagination is constrained by the biological body and the body's ability to share its experiences in a mirror- or correspondence-like manner. This constraint is augmented when one considers the body and bodily experience is also social. While bodily pain initially resists language, over time, and under specific conditions, as Scarry (1985) points out, physical pain can find a voice and, when it does, it begins to tell a story to someone. This naming and making sense of pain, as part of the 'storying' process, is *not* an act that provides unmediated access to the body in pain, a transparent window into lived experience, or a mirror into being another body. This is partly because the act of naming pain, creating meaning and making bodily experience intelligible to others is strongly shaped by the cultural and narrative resources the individual has access to. So for instance, Doug's use of an electric metaphor in the above quotation to describe and make intelligible his pain to others clearly draws upon a taken-for-granted feature of his life within a Western technological society. Likewise, words such as 'sharp', 'shooting' and 'burning' call upon a limited range of words accessible within our society for describing pain. Therefore, while a reported biographical event may be unique to the individual, its linguistic expression is shaped and structured according to socially shared conventions of reporting. Thus, however far the imagination reaches, our ability to imagine oneself differently situated, or being another disabled body in pain, is constrained by one's access to wider cultural frameworks of meaning. This is particularly so when one does not even share the conventions of reporting or have any access to the other's narrative resources to help make sense of another's bodily experiences.

The idea of the body as bio-social, however, is not simply a body shaped by society. It may also shape society. Possessed of such agential capacities, for various reasons a person may therefore seek to resist imagining another's life. For example, imaginative resistance (Gendler 2000) may arise when a sport researcher who exclusively locks into and advocates a social model of disability actively chooses to resist imaginatively entering into the mindset of athletes or fellow disabled sport researchers who think the social model is outdated and should be abandoned. Thus, here we arrive at another possible barrier to imagining others' lives. Our bodies as a source and means for shaping society may be unwilling and resistant to empathetically imagine putting oneself in the other's disabled body, thereby placing constraints on our imaginative capacities.

In a similar fashion, Mackenzie and Scully (2007) also note difficulties of imagining oneself differently situated, or imagining being another person, arising from the way imagination is constrained by embodied experience and the social possibilities foreclosed by a person's specific embodiment. As they suggest, 'imaginative projection is founded in personal experience, and therefore it is dependent on and constrained by the body, because the experiences of persons are themselves dependent on the body, in a number of ways' (ibid., 342). First, according to Mackenzie and Scully, embodiment is a precondition of experience, at pre-social levels of perception and cognition. Secondly, experience is shaped and constrained by the specificities of embodiment. Here, Mackenzie and Scully (2007) note, the bodily constraints are both biological (the experience of pregnancy is biologically restricted to women in the human species) and social (in many societies it is mostly men who suffer a spinal cord injury through playing sport). Third, bodily experience is shaped and constrained by cultural meanings. Thus

This constraint operates at the level of the socially held meanings in terms of which we make sense of our experience. In any society, for instance, the meaning given to a sexual assault can vary markedly depending on whether the act is perpetrated against a woman or a man, a child or an adult, or a person with a disability. Also, the bodies we are/have determine to some extent the social worlds that it is possible for us to inhabit during our lives, which in turn affects the social space that we can imagine inhabiting. (Mackenzie and Scully 2007, 343)

It would appear, therefore, that there are difficulties of imagining oneself differently situated, or imagining being another person. These, in part, arise from the way the imagination is constrained by embodied experience and by the social possibilities foreclosed or made available by a person's specific embodiment and their access to narratives. In this sense, constraints seem to depend on attributes, such as the bio-social nature of the body. That recognised, thinking about the difficulties of imagination requires a concept of otherness that transcends—or precedes—such attributes. This noncontingent otherness brings us to the notion of alterity.

The Other as Other: Otherness as a Barrier to Imagining Others' Lives

Alterity, as described by Levinas (1998, 2001), can be characterised as a person's *otherness* that precedes any attributes. As Levinas puts it, the other, as other, is not only an alter ego. It is what I myself am not. Installing ethics as first philosophy, before the ontology of Being, Levinas thus calls upon the relation with the other as, in part, absolute distance. He maintains that, in order to encounter the other as the other, we must encounter the other on his or her terms rather than ours. Otherness must be absolute, that is, other with an alterity constitutive of the very content of the other. Alterity in this sense is a relation that does not comprise the selfhood of the other. It describes a difference that precedes what are generally thought of as differences. Alterity does not depend of the contingency of when and where someone is born or what life choices they make. Alterity is an intrinsic quality of being human; for Levinas it may be the intrinsic human quality. Moreover, it precedes such specific differences as gender, age, ethnicity, state of health or dis/ableness. As Levinas (2001, 49) comments:

It is not because your hair is unlike mine or because you occupy another place than me – this would only be a difference of properties or dispositions in space, a difference of attributes. But before any attribute, you are other than I, other otherwise, absolutely other! And it is this alterity, different from the one which is linked to attributes, that is your alterity.

Therefore, on Levinas's account, imagining putting ourselves in the place of another person is problematic because the other *is* other: absolutely and completely other to me. So for example, just as the other is fundamentally *not* me, fundamentally irreducible *to* me, so too are his or her feelings of being and having a disabled body and the suffering they *may* experience after acquiring a spinal cord injury through playing sport. That is, the disabled person is other to me. 'An individual is other to the other. A formal alterity: one is not the other, whatever its content. Each is other to other' (Levinas 1998, 162). This means that any attempt to grasp the other's suffering or lived experiences, to place oneself in his or her shoes or to imagine ourselves being another person, is problematic and elusive. Worse, because this seeks to make the other's experience comprehensible only through my own, Levinas (1998, 2001) suggests that it is unethical: it attempts to reduce, often even efface, the alterity of the other's suffering. A fortiori, not only is imagining ourselves otherwise or imagining ourselves being another person constrained by alterity, it infringes and even violates the other. For Levinas, the way out of this predicament is to encounter the other as other rather than on our own terms, thereby respecting and preserving alterity.

Respecting and valuing alterity should not, however, be confused with a desire to avoid the other. Nor should it be viewed as a justification to be unresponsive or irresponsible to disabled people. This is because, for Levinas (2001), we should both respect the difference of the other as other and be responsibility for the other. In other words, with regard to the lives of disabled people and their sporting worlds, being human means not only respecting the other as other, but also being responsible for the other. We desire to simultaneously honour otherness and be there for the other: 'here I am' we say, and in so doing offer ourselves as a compassionate witness. Thus Levinas calls upon the relation with the other as absolute distance and absolute proximity. The way he accounts for this apparently paradoxical relation, or balance, is opened on the basis of the human face. By 'face' Levinas does not mean some arrangement of our eyes, nose, and mouth (Frank 2004). To see the other's face is to recognise the other as needing me and to feel chosen in the primacy of my obligation to meet that need. As Levinas explains:

> I define the face precisely by these traits beyond vision or confusion with the vision of the face. One can say once more: the face ... is like a being's exposure to death; the without-defence, the nudity and the misery of the other. It is also the commandment to take the other upon oneself, not to let him alone; you hear the word of God. If you conceive of the face as the object of a photographer, of course you are dealing with an object like any other object. But if you encounter the face, responsibility arises in the strangeness of the other and in his [or her] misery. The face offers itself to your compassion and to your obligation. (Levinas 2001, 48)

Despite his radical originality, Levinas's thought is not without precedent in the philosophical tradition, nor does it lack confederates in its concern for the other person. One such ally is Bakhtin (1984, 1986) who also hears the call of the other and wishes to respect the other as an other. Thus while recognising that there are differences that prevent an easy or simple alliance between their philosophies, points of contact do exist.

For Bakhtin (1984), like Levinas, no person is self-sufficient.[2] This is partly because a person realises his or her self initially through others: from them we receive words, forms and tonalities for the formation of our initial idea of ourselves. Just 'as the body is formed initially in the mother's womb (body), a person's consciousness awakens wrapped in another's consciousness' (Bakhtin 1984, 138). Thus, as symbolic interactionists also suggest, no matter how personally authentic anyone desires to be or desires to allow others to be, and no matter how separate from others we feel we might be, we are always connected and exist in relation to other people. We are, as Frank (2004) puts it, non-self-sufficient rather than self-sufficient. One implication of all this is that we have no internal sovereignty as individuals and are, as Levinas stresses (2001), responsible for the other.

In tension with non-self-sufficiency, Bakhtin (1984, 1986) makes a clear demand that one consciousness not lapse into merging with others. For Bakhtin this demand is particularly important since it sustains difference and therefore otherness. Clark and Holquist summarise this requirement to sustain difference.

> The way in which I create myself is by means of a quest: I go out to the other in order to come back with a self. I 'live into' an other's consciousness; I see the world through the other's eyes. But I must never completely meld with that version of things, for the more successfully I do, the more I will fall pray to the limits of the other's horizon. A complete fusion...even if it were possible, would preclude the difference required for dialogue. (Clark and Holquist 1984, 78)

Therefore Bakhtin (1984, 1990), like Levinas (1998, 2001), suggests a balance between recognising each person's non-self-sufficiency, which people have to recognise to remain human, and rejecting the dangerous fantasy of merging consciousness with the other, which would violate their 'otherness'. In recognising this we arrive back at the argument that seeking to imagine oneself differently situated or imagining being another person is problematic because it risks violating what makes them other. Accordingly, for example, to think that one as a qualitative researcher can put oneself in the shoes of a disabled athlete, to think that one can merge with them in order to better understand and empathise with them, is limited and risks forestalling dialogue as the other's side is infringed on: otherness is violated.

Some Reflections

In this article, I have argued that putting ourselves in the place of others is constrained and limited, in part, by our body and the nature of alterity. This, however, is not to advocate that we jettison empathy and imagination. Nor is it to say, and thereby risk producing a dualism, that imagining another's life is not in principle impossible. On the contrary, it is simply to call attention to the *difficulties* of imagining other lives so that we might better understand some of the complexities involved in this process. Equally, it is to contest any normative claims that we *should* or *ought* to *always* imagine ourselves otherwise or empathically imagine another person's life. In doing so, it is hoped that any exaggerated or romantic notion of imagining other lives is unsettled and I have disturbed the 'warm fuzzy pursuit of empathy in which we assume a union of two or more selves in a mirroring relationship' (Lather 2000, 19). These intentions may be of further value since overlooking the limitations of our abilities and willingness to imaginatively engage with others, and assuming that imagination is simply and always good, may result in an over-optimistic and perhaps misleading conception of the role that imaginative engagement with the lives of others can play in understanding and being empathetic. Researchers exploring disability and sport, therefore, might best proceed with caution against overstating the power of imagination, be wary of such dangerous assumptions and perhaps adopt an attitude of humility towards thinking we can put ourselves in another's place and understand the other's experiences of disability. This is particularly so given the potential dangers involved in projecting one's own perspective onto the other by imagining oneself differently situated, or even imagining oneself in the other's shoes.

According to Young (1997) and Mackenzie (2006), one danger of these kinds of projection is that we simply project onto the other our own beliefs and attitudes, values and priorities, fears and hopes, and desires and aversions. Equally, we may misrepresent the others views, needs and concerns, and arrive at moral judgments that are inappropriate or paternalistic. Another danger is that one can violate and infringe on the other person's alterity, thereby committing symbolic violence. As Frank (2004, 115) emphasises, 'to infringe on the other person's alterity—their otherness that precedes any attributes—is to commit violence against the other. Symbolic violence comprises the often subtle ways that alterity is challenged and violated'. For instance, a person who became disabled through playing sport may tell a tragedy story and a restitution story in which their hope is to restore their former body-self relationships and walk again (Frank 1995). For some disability scholars, while this storyline is in certain circumstances potentially problematic (see Smith and Sparkes 2005), wanting to walk again is viewed as the disabled others' choice and they are respected for who they already are. Symbolic violence can occur, however, if a disability sports scholar says to the teller of a restitution story that they are wrong to tell this kind of story, that disability has nothing to do with their impaired body, and they do not understand that the problems they experience have nothing to do with them but are due simply to structural barriers out there in society that restrict activity and oppress them.

Likewise, alterity may be violated and in so doing symbolic violence risked by projecting one's preferences in terms of telling the other how to feel better following, for example, becoming disabled through playing sport. As Frank (2004, 116) says, empathetically imagining how the other feels can be useful, 'but empathy risks the symbolic violence of telling the other how to feel better'. A further way symbolic violence can be committed in relation to imagining others' lives is by projecting one's preference for a certain type of story over others and telling people which story to live by after becoming disabled. It may also occur when one says to the other 'I *know* how you feel'. Consider, for instance, the following extract from my reflexive journal in which I aspired to emphatically imagine being another person.

> Just finished interviewing Doug, a 38-year-old man who during play rugby broke his neck nine years ago. Lots of interesting things about him came up during the interview – his unwavering desire to walk again, his lack of desire to participate in disabled sport, and his fear of living in a disabled body. He also does not want help from others, and claims this is okay. But one thing keeps pricking at me, and I can't let it go. Near the end of the interview we were talking about his experiences of depression and how he feels living in his disabled body. I wanted to know what it felt like; I wanted to enter into his bodily world. I suddenly felt his bodily world of depression. I said to him, 'Doug, I understand. I've lived with depression, and struggle with it. Partly as a result of sporting injuries, depression has me too. I know how you feel. I know the future looks bad, but you will get better' [interview transcripts confirm this]. A moment later, with tearing welling up in both our eyes, I leaned across gently squeezed his hand, holding it for a moment. He smiled and turned his palm to embrace my hand. An instant later, I felt inside my body the distance between us close further. Our bodies briefly connected. Our damp palms were attached. I entered his sadness, and felt we became one.

As the above example suggests, because I had previously experienced depression (see Smith 1999) I felt I could imagine and know the disabled other's depression and their suffering. In imagining this there is, however, a danger. Empathy can easily turn into projection, or sometimes introjection, which is an illusion that one can truly put oneself in the place of another person and unify or merge with them. This symbolic violence of empathetic projection claims that you are as I am, and I *know* how you feel. In projecting oneself onto the other through imagination and telling them how they should feel or writing that they not be who they are denies difference between self and other. In denying that difference, one denies the other and his/her alterity. Alterity, it should be underscored, is not opposed to empathy. But, as Frank (2004) reminds us, empathic imagination as an end in itself can be dangerous to alterity. Empathy tends towards unification: either projecting my fears and what would make me feel better onto you, or my fusing with your suffering. Alterity is the opposite of unification with others and thinking that one can put one's self in the place of others.

Another potential danger involved in projecting one's own perspective onto the other by imagining oneself differently situated, or even imagining oneself in the other's shoes, is that one may *finalise* the other. According to Bakhtin (1984), finalisation occurs when a person claims the last, the definitive, finalising word, about who the other is and what he or she can become. So for example, in the context of sport, one difficulty of truly imagining another's life as a disabled person is that it requires us to know and predict what he or she would think and feel and do in the myriad situations he or she might encounter, and to reproduce and anticipate their emotional responses as the imaginative process unfolds. Yet this is difficult and may be problematic because it can suggest that people's views are ossified in time instead of having the capacity to grow and change. As a consequence, there is the danger of finalising the other. This is particularly problematic, Bakhtin suggests, since to finalise another person is not only an empirically inadequate description of the human condition, but it may leave the imaginer believing they have privileged knowledge, that there is nothing more to be said about the other, and there are no other prospects to be someone different. This line of argument brings Bakhtin to the view that is, for him, a principle of ethics and empirically adequate research: 'As long as a person is alive he [*sic*] lives by the fact that he is not yet finalised, that he has not yet uttered his ultimate word' (1984, 59).

Some Implications for Sport and Disability

With all this in mind, the question still remains: what might be the implications of these issues—attractive as they might be—for sport and disability practice, research and theory? I suggest there are three interrelated points worthy of consideration. First, given such dangers attendant upon trying to imagine oneself in the other's place, and if genuine empathetic imagining of the lives of others is as difficult as is suggested above, where then does this leave us? Does imaginative engagement with the perspectives of others have any role to play in empathising, moral judgment and understanding sport and the lives of disabled people? As already noted, like others (e.g. Coles 2004; Mackenzie and Scully, 2007), I think it does. Irrespective of how, its role may be conceptualised not as a matter of enabling us to adopt the other's embodied standpoint or to understand the other 'from the inside'. Rather, to start with, its role in relation to disability and sport could be to expand the scope of our *compassion*.

Clearly, there are many ways compassion can be described and interpreted. I have found the work of several scholars, including Levinas and Bakhtin, useful in opening up this complex virtue (for another constructive account, see Nussbaum 2001). According to Levinas (1998), compassion is the 'nexus of human subjectivity' and the 'supreme ethical principle'. That is to say, more than a warm feeling in the gut, it's the self's responsibility *for* the other. This responsibility is non-reciprocal. I neither calculate nor expect reciprocity. Self-interest is subsumed by my obligation to the other. Thus, for Levinas, ethics is the compassionate exposure to and responsibility for the other without waiting for reciprocity. Compassion is asymmetrical (see also Young 1997). It begins by giving ourselves to the face. If 'you *encounter* the face,' Levinas (2001, 48) insists, 'responsibility arises in the strangeness of the other and in his [or her] misery. The face offers itself to your compassion and to your obligation.' Levinas's insistence (1985, 97) that the work of compassion is 'to do something for the other' can, however, be misleading. For example, it is not the gift of food or disabled sporting equipment that actually constitutes the ethical relation. Rather, the opening and exposure of ourselves to the other *is* the generosity of ethics. In so doing, the work of compassion becomes about being there for and with the other. It is saying, verbally or non-verbally, 'here I am': I am here for and with you. That is, the response of the ethical person to someone is 'here I am'. This encounter, this 'here I am' opening and welcoming of the person, therefore is an act of compassion as we bear witness and practice responsibility for others.

Compassion is thus respect for alterity. This is not, however, to say that we can act compassionately without at least some understanding of the other's situation. At the very least we often need some (Nussbaum 2001). But, being compassionate means valuing that we cannot understand the other totally through efforts to imagine being the other from the inside or oneself in the other's shoes. Compassion is then, somewhat paradoxically, not only the self's responsibility for the other but also respect for another. Here, I am called upon to respond to the other. At the same time the other person stands apart from me. I embrace the other person but also leave the other intact, countering the totalising tendency to possess the other. In this regard, compassion also begins by recognising the fundamental difference between people whose lives have been shaped by disability and those like myself and most readers. The other is the other, and this difference is respected.

Not only does cultivating compassion require being responsible and respecting otherness, it also includes respecting that we are never isolated or autonomous beings but exist in relation to each other: 'I exist through the other and for the other' (Levinas 1981, 114). This sense of compassion, then, is another version of the balance between what Bakhtin (1984) called recognising each person's non-self-sufficiency—the dependence of each other on dialogue with the other—and rejecting the dangerous fantasy of merging consciousness with the other. Compassion in this sense is the recognition that although there may be similarities and common understandings between us, there is also much that I do not understand about the other person's experience and perspective.

Furthermore, compassion may begin in, and is renewed through, respecting the unfinalisability of others; refusing to imagine and talk about the other in ways that are finalising. Practicing compassion, asymmetrical empathy and generosity can also include imaginatively thinking and speaking *with* their stories rather than *about* them. According to Frank (1995, 158–9):

> Thinking with stories means joining with them, allowing one's own thoughts to adopt the story's immanent logic of causality, its temporality, and its narrative tensions. Narrative ethics seeks to remain with the story, even when it can no longer remain inside

the story. The goal is empathy, not as internalising the feelings of the other, but as what Halpern calls 'resonance' with the other. The other's self-story does not become my own, but I develop sufficient resonance with that story so that I can feel its nuances and anticipate changes in the plot.... The first lesson of thinking with stories is not to move on once the story has been heard, but to continue to live in the story, *becoming* in it, reflecting on who one is becoming, and gradually modifying the story. The problem is truly to *listen* to one's own story, just as the problem is truly to listen to others' stories.

It would seem, therefore, that when doing sport research or applied work with disabled people as ways to act compassionately, empathetically, and generously we might think with stories, respect alterity, not finalise another, and be responsible for the other and see their face. This may also have implications for sporting disability policy and practice. For example, as a way to improve the life and sporting opportunities for disabled people, able-bodied people may aspire to imaginatively enter into the perspectives of disabled people within sporting contexts. However genuinely well-intentioned the project is it risks committing symbolic violence. Further, if we are formulating or enacting a sporting policy we may misrepresent the needs and concerns of those whose difficulties we are attempting to address and come up with solutions that don't fit their lives. Thus, to confirm what many people within the disabled rights movement advocate but still feel is lacking (Thomas 2007), polices arising out of consultation with disabled people rather than devised on their behalf are needed, and difference respected.

Secondly, theoretical entries into the possibilities and limits of imagination invite us to explore what Thomas (2007) identified as the contested terrain in disability theory. For example, as she notes, in recent years the focal point of attention within disability studies has been on the social model of disability and the oppressive structural barriers 'out there' in society. As a consequence, the lived, biological and social character of the body has been marginalised and neglected. By highlighting the embodied character of imagination and the consequences this can have on our understandings of disability and sport, however, weight is given to recent calls to attend not only to socio-structural factors, but also the disabled body, the effects of impairment and the lived experiences of disability in relation to, for example, the psycho-emotional dimensions of life (Smith and Sparkes 2008a). Equally, when imagining others' lives, and with the dangers of this in mind, attention is drawn to the view that the global experience of disabled people and sport is perhaps too diverse and complex to be rendered within one unitary model or set of imaginative ideas. This, then, has implications for identity politics. For instance, given the difficulties of articulating *the* disability perspective, the differences between people may need to be honored rather than eradicated. This, however, then opens us up to question whether the disability rights movement or a disability sporting governing body can represent the diversity of disabled people. It also begs further issues in identity politics, which can be as much of an obstacle as a solution (see Shakespeare 2006; Thomas 2007).

A third point arising from this exploration of imagining others' lives relates to understanding the other. According to Bakhtin (1990, 102), 'the word "understanding", in its usual, naively realistic interpretation, is always misleading'. This is because it often leads to believing in 'the exact, passive mirroring or duplication of another's experience within myself' (ibid.). As both Bakhtin and Levinas suggest, this is problematic as it denies and even violates the other as other. It confuses one into thinking that one is able to imagine and see life *as*, for example, a person suffering following becoming disabled through playing sport. To continue with the theme of suffering, Bakhtin uses suffering as his specific example to propose a different way to comprehend how people, such as sport researchers and disabled participants, might understand each other. He begins by reiterating, like Levinas, the distance of otherness: 'The *other's* suffering as co-experienced by me is in principle different...from the other's suffering as *he* [sic] experiences it' (Bakhtin 1990, 102). This distance remains unbridged. But there can develop between us, Bakhtin suggests, what may be called 'a completely new *ontic* formation [a thing or being] that I alone actualise *inwardly* from my unique place *outside* another's life' (ibid., 103). Thus, in relation to disability and sport research, there can be 'co-experienced suffering' with a disabled person that is not the same as what either person experiences— consciousnesses do not merge and otherness is not violated—but exists as a new formation that is available; as a space of consolation and compassion, between self and other.

Conclusion

In this article, the popular assumption that we can imagine being the other and imagine oneself in his/her shoes has been problematised. It has been argued that our imagination is constrained partly by one's embodied experience and alterity. For some, such considerations may be flights of fantasy. Critics may also bemoan that all this talk about imagining others' lives is no big deal; and why should we as people interested in disability and sport be concerned with imaginative projection? For me, imaginatively putting oneself in the other's place and violating alterity might not be a sound basis on which to do ethically admirable research with sports disability populations. Yet the literature often suggests that to understand the other, empathise with him/her and be ethical – this is actually what we should strive to do. I therefore add my voice to those who share a caution and anxiety about the modes of research engagement (e.g. Mackenzie and Scully 2007), and make a plea for alternative ways to capture the imagination of some other disability and sport scholars. At the very least, I hope it may nudge those of us who engage in sport disability research from taking the role of imagining disabled unproblematically and to generate a dialogue cognisant of the complexities involved.

ACKNOWLEDGEMENTS

I wish to thank the following for the contribution they have made to this article: Doug and Max, and the other participants who became disabled through playing rugby union football, for graciously sharing their stories with me; Andrew Sparkes for our continuing dialogue; and a huge thanks also to Mike McNamee for his encouragement and erudite comments on a draft of this article. The confusions that remain are entirely my own.

NOTES

1.   There are different kinds of imaginative research activities and these should be kept in mind throughout this article. These include imagining oneself otherwise, imagining oneself in another's shoes, and imagining being another (see Goldie 2000; Mackenzie 2006). In imagining *oneself* differently situated we are just imagining ourselves and we simply draw on our own experience. In imagining oneself 'in the other's shoes' we try to

enter into the other person's perspective, imagining ourselves from the inside *as* that person. In imagining *being* another, that is empathetic imagining, we leave our own perspectives behind altogether and imagine from the inside the thoughts, feelings and emotions of another person.

2.   The term self-sufficiency may be considered unhelpful as it is loaded with economic connotations. It should not be confused with this, however. The point here is that, as for symbolic interactionists like Mead, it attempts to signal that as humans we exist and make ourselves intelligible in relation to other lives. As relational beings we are socially interdependent and our selves are social in their construction and performance (see Smith and Sparkes 2008b).

REFERENCES

AMIS, J. 2006. Interviewing for case study research. In *Qualitative Research Methods in Sports Studies*, edited by D. Andrews, D. Mason and M. Silk. Oxford: Berg.

ANDREWS, M. 2007. Exploring cross-cultural boundaries. In *Handbook of Narrative Nquiry*, edited by D.J. Clandinin. London: Sage.

BAKHTIN, M. 1984. *Problems of Dostoevsky's Poetics*, translated and edited by C. Emerson. Minneapolis, MN: University of Minnesota Press.

———. 1986. *Speech Genres and Other Late Essays*, translated by V. McGee and edited by C. Emerson and M. Holquist. Austin, TX: University of Texas Press.

———. 1990. *Art and Answerability*, translated and edited by M. Holquist and V. Liapunov. Austin, TX: University of Texas Press.

BONDI, L. 2003. Empathy and identification: Conceptual resources for feminist fieldwork. *ACME: International Journal of Critical Geography* 2: 64–76.

CLARK, K. and M. HOLQUIST. 1984. *Mikhail Bakhtin*. Cambridge, MA: Harvard University Press.

COLES, J. 2004. *Still Lives*. MIT Press.

DEPRAZ, N. 2001. The Husserlain theory of intersubjectivity as alterity. *Journal of Consciousness Studies* 8 (5–7): 169–78.

DUQUIN, M. and K. SCHROEDER-BRAUN. 1996. Power, empathy, and moral conflict in sport. *Peace and Conflict: Journal of Peace Psychology* 2 (4): 351–67.

FINLAY, L. 2006. Dancing between embodied empathy and phenomenological reflection. *Indo-Pacific Journal of Phenomenology* 6: 1–11.

FRANK, A. 1995. *The Wounded Storyteller*. Chicago: University of Chicago Press.

———. 2004. *The Renewal of Generosity*. Chicago: University of Chicago Press.

GENDLER, T. 2000. The puzzle of imaginative resistance. *Journal of Philosophy* 97: 55–81.

GOLDIE, P. 2000. *The Emotions: A Philosophical Exploration*. Oxford: Oxford University Press.

GOODIN, R. 2003. *Reflexive Democracy*. Oxford: Oxford University Press.

HEAL, J. 1998. Understanding other minds from the inside. In *Current Issues in Philosophy of Mind*, edited by A. O'Hear. Cambridge: Cambridge University Press.

HUGHES, B. and K. PATERSON. 1997. The social model of disability and the disappearing body: Toward a sociology of impairment. *Disability & Society* 12 (3): 325–40.

KRANE, V. and S. BAIRD. 2005. Using ethnography in applied sport psychology. *Journal of Applied Sport Psychology* 17: 1–21.

LAKOFF, G. and M. JOHNSON. 1999. *Philosophy in the Flesh: The Embodied Mind and its Challenge to Western Thought*. New York: Basic Books.

LATHER, P. 2000. Against empathy voice and authenticity. *Kvinder, Køn and Forskning* 9 (4): 16–25.

LEVINAS, E. 1981. *Otherwise than Being, or, Beyond Essence*, translated by A. Lingis. Pittsburgh, PA: Duquesne University Press.

———. 1985. *Ethics and Infinity: Conversations with Philippe Nemo*, translated by R. Cohen. Pittsburgh, PA: Duquesne University Press.

———. 1998. *Entre Nous: Thinking-of-the-Other*, translated by M. Smith and B. Harshav. London: Continuum.

———. 2001. *Is It Righteous To Be?: Interviews with Emmanuel Levinas*, edited by J. Robbins. Stanford, CA: Stanford University Press.

MACKENZIE, C. 2006. Imagining other lives. *Philosophical Papers* 35 (1), 293–325.

MACKENZIE, C. and J. SCULLY. 2007. Moral imagination, disability and embodiment. *Journal of Applied Philosophy* 24: 335–51.

MICHALKO, R. 2002. *The Difference that Disability Makes*. Philadelphia, PA: Temple University Press.

NUSSBAUM, M. 2001. *Upheavals of Thought: The Intelligence of Emotions*. Cambridge: Cambridge University Press.

ORTIZ, S. 2005. The ethnographic process of gender management: Doing the 'right' masculinity with wives of professional athletes. *Qualitative Inquiry* 11 (2), 265–90.

SCARRY, E. 1985. *The Body in Pain*. Oxford: Oxford University Press.

SHAKESPEARE, T. 2006. *Disability Right and Wrongs*. London: Routledge.

SMITH, B. 1999. The abyss: Exploring depression through a narrative of the self. *Qualitative Inquiry* 5: 264–79.

SMITH, B. and A. SPARKES. 2005. Men, sport, spinal cord injury, and narratives of hope. *Social Science and Medicine* 61: 1095–1105.

———. 2008a. Changing bodies, changing narratives and the consequences of tellability: A case study of becoming disabled through sport. *Sociology of Health and Illness* 30 (2): 217–36.

———. 2008b. Contrasting perspectives on narrating selves and identities: An invitation to dialogue. *Qualitative Research* 8 (1): 5–35.

THOMAS, C. 2007. *Sociologies of Disability and Illness*. London: Palgrave Macmillan.

THOMPSON, E. 2001. Between ourselves. *Journal of Consciousness Studies* 8 (5–7): 197–314.

TOOMBS, K. 2001. The role of empathy in clinical practice. *Journal of Consciousness Studies* 8 (5–7):

YOUNG, I. 1997. *Intersecting Voices: Dilemmas of Gender, Political Philosophy and* Policy. Princeton, NJ: Princeton University Press.

Brett Smith, Qualitative Research Unit, School of Sport & Health Sciences, University of Exeter, St Luke's Campus, Heavitree Road, Exeter, Devon, EX1 2LU. UK.
E-mail: B.M.Smith@exeter.ac.uk

ETHICAL CONSIDERATIONS IN ADAPTED PHYSICAL ACTIVITY PRACTICES

Yeshayahu Hutzler

This article focuses on ethical concerns about modifying physical activities within a variety of education, recreation, rehabilitation and competition contexts. An ecological frame of reference common within current educational and rehabilitation theories is utilised for reflecting upon adapted physical activity practices. Ethical principles challenged in the article are (a) the utilitarian consequence to all participants; (b) professional paternalism; and (c) empowerment of individuals with a disability. Concerns arising with respect to these ethical principles in adapted physical activity practices are discussed across modifications in terms of (i) the tasks involved; (ii) the environmental conditions; (iii) the equipment used; (iv) the game rules; and (v) the instruction methods.

Resumen

El artículo enfoca los asuntos éticos a la hora de modificar actividades físicas dentro de una variedad de contextos educativos, recreativos, de rehabilitación y competitivos. Un marco de referencia ecológica común dentro de las teorías actuales educativas y de rehabilitación se utiliza para ponderar sobre prácticas de actividad física adaptada. Principios éticos que se desafían en este artículo son (a) las repercusiones utilitarias para todos lo participantes, (b) el paternalismo professional, y (c) el fortalecimiento de los individuos con una minusvalía. Asuntos que surgen con respecto a estos principios éticos son discutidos por medio de modificaciones de (a) las tareas involucradas, (c) el equipamiento utilizado, (d) las reglas de juego, y (e) los métodos de instrucción.

Zusammenfassung

Dieser Artikel richtet den Blick auf ethische Bedenken in Bezug auf Veränderungen von körperlichen Aktivitäten im Kontext von Erziehung, Freizeit, Rehabilitation und Wettkämpfen. Es wird ein ökologischer Bezugsrahmen gemeinsam mit aktuellen Erziehungs- und Rehabilitationstheorien verwendet, um auf Praktiken in Bewegung, Spiel und Sport in Prävention, Rehabilitation und Behinderung (APA = adapted physical activity) zu reflektieren. Die ethischen Prinzipien, die in diesem Artikel untersucht werden, sind (a) die utilitaristischen Folgen für alle Teilnehmer, (b) professioneller Paternalismus und (c) Stärkung von Menschen mit Behinderung. Bedenken, die in Zusammenhang mit diesen ethischen Prinzipien in Bewegung, Spiel und Sport in Prävention, Rehabilitation und Behinderung (APA) auftauchen, werden im Hinblick auf

Modifikationen von (a) Aufgaben, (b) Umweltbedingungen, (c) Material, (d) Regelwerk und (e) Vermittlungsmethode besprochen.

摘要

本文討論的重點是在改良式的身體活動實踐中在教育、休閒、復健及比賽環境中之倫理考量。本文也運用到一種在現行教育及復健之生態學結構理論來反省適應身體活動實踐的一些情況。在本文中所挑戰到的倫理原則有 (a) 有關對所有人有益之效益論結果主義, (b) 專業的父權主義, 及 (c) 身障者之個別影響能力之範圍。 有關適應體育活動中, 倫理課題逐漸受到重視的有 (a) 所牽涉到之任務, (b) 環境條件, (c) 所使用之設備, (d) 遊戲規則, 及 (e) 教學指導方法等。

Introduction

Ability may be defined as the quality permitting or facilitating performance achievement and accomplishment (The American Heritage 2003). Physical activity textbooks typically consider physical and motor abilities as the underlying basis of motor behaviour (e.g. Schmidt and Lee 2005; Schmidt and Wrisberg 2004; Singer 1980). The term disability, by contrast, expresses a condition which is essentially opposed to ability. Examples for common definitions of disability are 'a substantial and long-term adverse effect on personal ability to carry out normal day-to-day activities due to physical or mental impairment' (Disability Discrimination Act 1995); and 'any restriction or lack (resulting from an impairment) of ability to perform an activity in the manner or within the range of activity considered normal for a human being' (World Health Organisation 1980).

The relationships of disability and physical activity have always been emotionally charged and suffused with contrasting social-political perspectives. For example, disability sociologists such as Shakespeare (1996) often perceive sporting activities of individuals with disability as a form of denial in their seeking to 'overcome' their impairment, which seems to involve a refusal to submit to reality and an attempt to regain 'normal' identity through superhuman activity. In contrast, the motto of Paralympic athletes and organisations such as the Dallas Wheelchair Mavericks, one of the USA's most successful wheelchair basketball champions, 'ability not disability counts' suggests persons with disabilities are competent and equal-status residents and athletes.[1] Stafford (1939), one of the first American writers on 'sports for the handicapped', and Guttmann (1976), the 'father' of the 'Paralympic' movement, have strongly acknowledged the social value of participation in sports and physical activity. Later scholarly contributions further establish the view of disability as a disruption between personal resources and environmental challenges (Norman et al. 2004) and exercise and sports as means for bridging this gap (Hutzler 1990; Hutzler and Bar-Eli 1993).

The scholarly field of study and practice coping with the opportunities and conflicts of modifying, adjusting and accommodating physical activity and enabling participation opportunities to individuals with varying (dis)ability conditions is called adapted physical activity (APA). Contemporaneously, APA is understood as a body of knowledge and practice encompassing (a) individual differences in physical activities, mostly performed by individuals with disabilities; (b) service delivery systems developed for ensuring participation of these individuals; (c) professional responsibilities of practitioners; and (d) an academic field of study (Hutzler and Sherrill 2007; Reid 2003; Sherrill 2004). A major contribution to the construction of adaptation as a core concept in APA was provided by Sherrill (1998; 2004), who paved the way for the construction of *adaptation theory*, which emphasises modification aspects of physical activity across the entire lifespan of participant groups including children through to ageing individuals, and in a variety of activity contexts including therapeutic, pedagogical, recreational and competitive sport settings.

The main aim of this article is to apply ethical reasoning for critical discourse concerning decision-making in APA practices. After a short synopsis of essential theoretical frameworks, a model underlying adaptation within a variety of physical activity contexts will be described and selected ethical concerns with regard to adapting physical activity critically discussed.

Theoretical Framework for Adaptation

Adaptation is defined as the adjustments that occur in animals in respect of their environments (Allaby 1999). In humans, adaptation can be linked to ability, suggesting that being able to adapt increases the power to resist environmental stresses and pressures and to accomplish goals. Thus recent APA texts appreciate adaptation within an ecological context of person and environment (Davis and Broadhead 2007; Steadward et al. 2003). In the section that follows, essential attributes of the ecological system view will be described.

Ecological Reasoning of Adaptation

From an ecological perspective, the action system can be represented as a triangular space,composed of the individual, the environment and the task (Kiphard 1983; Newell 1986; Reed 1988). Accordingly, individuals possess resources enabling them to cope with environmental challenges. Task accomplishments result from specific relations between an individual and the environment such as changing a position from one point in space to another, crossing a distance or catching flying objects. The goal of a task may be purposefully determined by the individual or imposed by environmental stimuli such as teaching, instruction or therapeutic treatment. Movement patterns emerge according to this view, due to the utility of an object or an environment for an individual with certain capabilities (Gibson 1977). For example, water in a pool at chin depth is 'swim-able', but at knee depth 'walk-able'.

The concept that specific relations between the individual and environment may enhance or limit learning is important for the practice of APA, since it suggests a rationale for individually tailored explorations within the participation context. From the 1990s on, this concept has increasingly been transferred into the APA practice, using the model called ecological task analysis (ETA) (Davis and Burton 1991; Davis and Broadhead 2007). This is a structured system enabling choices and constraints to initiate adaptation for exploration and the self-construction of movement patterns.

The same major components underlying action system theory (individual, environment and task) have also been addressed by the widely accepted International Classification of Functioning, Disability and Health (ICF) (WHO 2001; Ústún 2003). This taxonomy provides criteria for classification, assessment and interventions within health, function and disability sciences and thus provides an established and broadly acknowledged frame of reference that could be easily applied to APA. The ICF addresses three major terms describing the range of potential capacities and boundaries within the interactions of an individual with his or her environment, including (a) body structures (e.g., lungs joints, brain) and functions (e.g. respiration, range of movement, muscular strength); (b) activities performed in daily, vocational and recreational life; and (c) participation in socially appropriate activities (e.g. training and competition in sporting events). Individual predispositions and environmental factors are contextually related to these functions, activities and participation, relate to the health condition and either facilitate or restrict the degree of performance (WHO 2001; Hutzler and Sherrill 2007). One of the most appealing differences embraced in the ICF over previous models of disability is the increased awareness of rehabilitation professionals with regard to social activity as a desirable outcome of rehabilitation practices. Similarly, empowerment and self-determination are the current preferred outcomes of APA for participants with disability (Bouffard and Stream 2003: Kydman and Davis 2007; Reid 2003; Sørensen 2003).

Empowerment and Self-determination

Empowerment has been defined as 'a process by which people, organisations and communities gain mastery over their affairs' (Rappaport 1987, 122). In psychological terms, empowerment includes people's self-efficacy and capability of assuming control in their lives (Zimmerman and Rappaport 1998) The concept of empowerment was linked to physical activity and individuals with disability for the first time by Hutzler (1990), making explicit the impact of physical activity on psychological well-being, social control and self-determination. Empowerment was part of the code of ethics for disability sport—'that involvement in sport should empower the athlete in his or her decision-making processes and his or her actions. The athlete should be empowered to take autonomous decisions and to further his or her development through the means of sport' (International Paralympic Committee Sport Science Committee 1995, 16). Within an interesting contribution to the philosophy of sport, Neal (1972, 38) poses that 'what the athlete becomes is dependent upon his choices. He moulds his own life according to what he chooses to be through his actions. Freedom of choice is a necessity if one is to "become". Where there is limited freedom, there is also limited fulfillment.'

Freedom of choice is often restricted in the pedagogical and social environments of physical education, recreation and sports; it is even more so within rehabilitation settings, due to liability, attitude and knowledge-base constraints. Also, medical and pedagogical interactions are overloaded with asymmetric, top-down relationships. Thus the behaviours of teachers, coaches and medical personnel often limit participants' degree of choice. Therefore it is not likely that medical and pedagogical systems assist empowerment and self-determination unless this approach is systematically promoted. Freire's (1970) problem-posing concept of 'education as an instrument for liberation' was among pioneering strategies directed towards self-control and determination through education. Yet the methodology of APA as an empowering and socially liberating agent is to be disclosed. A great example for the process of empowerment and self-determination through participation in recreation and sport activities is provided by Linda Hamilton, a young woman with an acquired disability who participates in a variety of summer and winter sports:

> In general, my participation in recreation activities has helped me to know my needs and to make informed choices about activities in which I want to take part. Through my activities, I have continued to learn more about myself and my capabilities. I have set goals and worked hard to achieve these goals. Slowly I have felt that I have more control over my life and have gained greater self-esteem. These activities have given me greater opportunities to be part of the community again. I have made more social contacts and developed relationships. As my confidence increased, I have taken on leadership roles as a Board member in a sport and recreation organisation for people with disabilities and a community health care facility (Hamilton 1997, 15).

As reflected in Hamilton's detailed narrative, needs and choices are enhanced through coping with both the adverse and the pleasant events in sports and enable the participant to select the resources he or she needs and to mould his or her own life. This can be understood as the essence of empowerment and a desirable aspect of APA.

Development of the Systematic Ecological Modification Approach

Following the experimental work of Davis and Burton (1991) and Burton et al. (1993), it has been suggested that if parameters controlling change from non-effective to effective movement patterns are recognised, they could be systematically modified to produce functional and behavioural pattern shifts (Hutzler 2007a; 2007b). The practice model, called the Systematic Ecological Modification Approach (SEMA), includes five main modification criteria (task, environment, equipment, rules and instruction) and provides a generic frame of reference for practice in physical activity and sports for participants with disability.

Ethical Consideration of Activity Modification in APA

While the author is not a trained philosopher, the frame of reference concerning ethical conduct in the discussion that follows is established on the following eclectic philosophical assumptions:

1. Based on *Utilitarian-Consequentialist Theory,* an action is morally right if the consequences of that action are more favourable and pleasurable than unfavourable and unpleasant for all participants involved (Darwall 2002). Thus the ethical concerns to be explored are of the utility provided to all participants in APA practices rather than to only a selected group;
2. Based on Kantian duty-based theory and the categorical imperative of *not treating other people as a means to an end dictated by others, but as means for themselves* (McNamee et al. 2007), the professional paternalism of practitioners, particularly coaches, administrators and teachers, should be ruled out; and

3. Based on the fundamental values of *empowerment* and *self-determination* within an APA frame of reference, practitioners are expected to encourage self-determined and self-regulated action through the provision of choices and behavioural alternatives.

For increasing transparency of the ethical discourse from a practitioner's perspective, it will follow the five modification areas embraced within the SEMA model and some other current APA textbooks (van Lent 2006; Liebermann and Houston-Wilson 2002).

Task Modifications

In APA most task modifications follow the rehabilitation principles of activity *compensation*—that is, using an alternative skill for accomplishing the same task (e.g. wheeling a wheelchair instead of running for fast locomotion)—and *restoration*—that is, changing specific technical criteria of the skill in order to accomplish the task (e.g. walking down the heel sideward for a person with an above-the-knee leg prosthesis).

All types of ethical concerns appear with respect to modifying tasks. The first group follows the utilitarian principle and argues that tasks modified to accommodate for the functional gap between normative and an individual function, i.e. for improving the state of those who are in disadvantage, provide the person with disability an unfair advantage. For example, in competitive tasks such as school final examinations, it could be argued, that completing an oral examination instead of a written essay may increase the probability of a person with a learning disability achieving a higher final score than his or her peer without a disability, thus violating fair competition and utilitarian principles. This type of claim gets publicity from time to time as they are discussed by courts mostly in response to individuals suing sport governing bodies for violating laws that have been passed towards reducing discrimination. One such law is the Americans with Disabilities Act (Federal Register 1992). Silvers and Wasserman (1998) have discussed the ethical conflicts with respect to this law in respect of some publicly widespread cases of the 1990s. The authors have outlined the major ethical criteria in question for deciding upon the legal cases. These include: (a) whether the fundamental nature of the activity (or service or goods) is being kept; (b) whether the person in question is assuming competence to accomplishing the activity otherwise not disabled; and (c) whether there is no undue burden to the other participants or organising bodies. One of the cases, which have attracted public attention, is that of Casey Martin, a talented golfer with serious leg impairment, who successfully claimed the right to use a powered golf cart during professional tournaments. The judges of this case were convinced that this person was indeed sufficiently talented for professional golf and his leg impairment could be accommodated by using the powered cart without seriously harming the other competitors or the organisers.

Another violation of the *utilitarian principle* is the harm or undue burden forced upon athletes *without* disabilities, often claimed for opposing the use of compensatory tasks by participants with disability, complaining that their presence puts the normative majority in danger due to the equipment they use. For example, after the first wheelchair athletes back in 1975 were dismissed from the Boston Marathon competition, by now wheelchair marathoners are welcome and compete in different categories such as different age and gender classes. This is a common adaptation for increasing equity and quality of competition, which became a necessity as competition gained popularity across ages from the very young to the very old and included females as well rather than being exclusive among young male participants, as in ancient times.

The second group of ethical concerns fall under the label *paternalism*—that is, taking decisions over a person without his or her will even though they are regarded for his or her own good. Paternalism may be exercised either by the practitioners such as activity counsellors and instructors, or by the participant's guardian. Paternalistic decision-making is witnessed in all contexts of APA. Exercise for health appears most vulnerable to this type of ethical dilemma. Referring individuals to physical activity due to a physical or mental impairment is by itself ethically questionable. The term 'exercise prescription' is widely accepted in this regard, treating physical activity as another type of medicine, with specific dosage of pattern, intensity, repetitions and volume expected to induce certain biological benefits (Durstine and Moore 2003; Haskell et al. 2007). Since antiquity civilisation has gradually replaced physical labour with tools. Thus many individuals with and without disabilities disregard physical activity and prefer a sedentary lifestyle (Brown et al. 2005; Cavill et al. 2006). Most individuals, however, will be willing to participate even in intense physical activity if they find it motivating enough, i.e., provided it is under circumstances that generate competition, mastery and even social contact outcomes for the participant. Therefore providing choices for community-based physical activity instead of merely prescribing exercise to participants with disability after completing a rehabilitation programme not only avoids professional paternalism but appears to be much more effective. Thus satisfaction and enjoyment through the development of skills and relationships within health activity programmes are now encouraged as an alternative to exercise on prescription (Thurston and Green 2004).

Practitioners providing activity solutions for children with disability face an even trickier risk of being trapped within paternalistic decision-making. Children with disability tend to be less autonomous than adults and even age peers. Often, their parents or guardians decide about the nature of their practice and the type of activities in which the children are engaged. It is quite common to observe parents who, against the will of their children and the recommendations of the physical activity counsellor or instructor, compel their children to participate in a certain activity that is supposed to be beneficial for the child's health in the long run. From a service-provision perspective, although the practitioner may realise the need for a child-directed activity, the paying client and the legal guardian of the child is the parent, and he or she is to be satisfied. The APA practitioner's role in this case is extremely challenging, since he or she could be accused of professional paternalism in any position taken: supporting the child would be assumed to be paternalism towards the patents and vice versa. Mediating skills and collaborative decision-making could be a reasonable option.

The final principle appearing across task modifications is that of *self-determination*. Guttmann, one of the main initiators of the Paralympic movement, was eventually the first to witness the impact of self-selected sport activity for play and competition on motivation and participation in individuals with spinal cord injury who had developed by themselves the game of wheelchair hockey in Stoke Mandeville. (Guttmann 1976; Anderson 2003). Thus a shift of the practitioner's role towards a mediating rather than a dominating role is likely to increase self-tailored selection of activities, participation and long-lasting adherence. A systematic submission of choices to task accomplishment by participants was recommended by Davis and Burton (1991) who have developed ecological task analysis as an educational principle, now increasingly followed by APA practitioners (Davis and Broadhead 2007). Thus a shift from instructor-directed to participant-directed decision-making over activity alternatives across APA contexts should be preferred, in accordance with the empowerment and self-determination principle.

Environmental Modifications

The environmental conditions are critical for allowing patterns to emerge and tasks being successfully negotiated. The need for architectural modifications and accommodations in sport facilities such as swimming pools, gymnasium halls, and fitness centres are one of the main mandates of progressive legislation such as the Americans with Disability Act (Federal Register 1992) in the USA, or the Disability Discrimination Act in the UK, as well as in many other countries. Most structural accommodations include ramps and rails for wheelchair-users and facilities enabling visually impaired persons to orient and access the facility including its bathrooms and changing rooms. Changing environmental conditions for enabling and increasing performance is not unique for participants with disability. As early as the beginning of the nineteenth century, GutsMuths (1804; 1970) noted that environmental modifications should be used as a tool for increasing performance. For example, he had recommended the use of a descending incline to accelerate the run towards the long jump. Further contemporary examples are considered below.

Scaling down the playing area is another mode of environmental modification, practised for example in seven-a-side soccer for participants with cerebral palsy instead of full-size soccer. The rationale for this modification is that the reduced court size requires less energy for locomotion performed by individuals whose energy cost is considerably (50 to 100 per cent) higher than normal (Bar-Or and Rowland 2004). Such a modification is necessary in order to enable participation for the players with cerebral palsy in a meaningful soccer game. However, the ethical principle of self-determination may rule out such adaptations. Some participants may argue that they prefer being exhausted and ineffective rather than play on a field or surface different to that of their peers.

Using a treadmill to initiate infant walking. Based on the ecological perspective, gradually increasing velocity of a treadmill could facilitate a transition of infants with Down syndrome from standing to walking in participants who are late in acquiring this pattern (Ulrich et al. 1992). From an ethical point of view, it may be argued that such modifications are not aimed towards the benefit and pleasure of the participants, since they may resist and not comply. Nevertheless, the same rationale could be expressed towards almost any educational and therapeutic modality that during some point of time may be against the immediate pleasure of the participant in favour of improved function and extended activity repertoire and participation in later life.

Equipment modifications. The use of equipment is a unique human development, enabling movement performances beyond phylogenetic boundaries. Scuba diving, sky diving, hang gliding, surfing, sailing, cycling, climbing and skiing are only a few of the many alternative ways of confronting environmental challenge uniquely developed by humans. Using equipment as an assistive device may be considered an additional step on the evolutionary time scale. Thus, artificial prosthetic and orthotic devices enable movement solutions not within or compensatory to the original pattern. An artificial leg is a device intended to compensate for lost functions of the impaired body structure. The development of prosthetic legs has become so sophisticated that the J-shaped large-scale carbon-fibre 'blade' prosthesis (also called 'Cheetah leg') apparently provides athletes with lower limb amputations greater mechanical advantage than their peer athletes without disability.[2] This device is used by Oscar Pistorius for sprinting in regular competition and has been banned by the International Association of Athletics Federations as an assistive device due to the increased speed endurance it enables (Tucker and Dugas 2008a, 2008b). This decision was reversed by the Court of Arbitration for Sport on 16 May 2008. For a more complete ethical consideration of decision-making in this regard see other articles appearing in this volume.

Scaling down the ball size is a well established adaptation of equipment for children (Haywood and Getchell 2005). Females typically use decreased implement weights in field events and ball games, and novice participants often use modified equipment such as tennis rackets with increased circumference to assist hitting the ball. For participants with a disability the use of modified equipment may be critical to task accomplishment and participation. The degree of compensation for the loss in independent function and autonomy is a major decision, and one to be made with caution respecting the complexity of the unique physical and psycho-social circumstances. Personal choice and independence should sensitively be valued. For example, the use of manual versus electrical wheelchair often raises professional debates, since using the manual wheelchair might exercise the muscles and cardio-respiratory system, but provides a more limited mobility pace and distance, which could restrict participation in social events. In order to avoid paternalism and comply with the ethical principles of empowerment, the participant should be invited to take an active role in this decision-making process (e.g. Di Marco et al. 2003).

Rule Modifications

Particularly during game performance rules are important for structuring the activities performed. For example, the degree of body contact allowed according to the game rules determines the choices players take with respect to defensive and offensive actions in ball games. In the case of participants with disabilities, rules can compensate for limited function (e.g. strength, speed and endurance), allowing these players, who otherwise would drop out or remain unattended during the game, full or at least partial participation. One example for game modification, often practised (e.g. Kalyvas and Reid 2003) is a rule that all members of the group have to touch the ball before passing it over the net, throwing into the basket or kicking into the goal. This assures that participants with disabilities are included into the game. This rule change does not, however, control for the efficiency of their inclusion. Most groups would allow the child with disability a brief touch shortly after the ball is played and immediately take it over to the more effective players. Nevertheless, this constraint could result in peers' dissatisfaction. The ethical concern to be noted here, similar to that in task modification, is the likelihood of undue burden to the non-disabled participants. Therefore, practitioners should carefully consider different options for rule modifications, and preferably discuss these options with the participating students with and without a disability.

A final remark on rule modification concerns disability sports, where classification systems are widely used. The classification system is aimed at increasing participation of all individuals with disabilities (Strohkendl 1991; Vanlandewijck and Chappel 1996). Therefore ranges of functional limitations are identified, forming a competitive category enabling relatively equal but also broad enough competition. Since winning in disability sports competitions is associated with major social and sometimes economic benefits similar to able-bodied sports, ethical dispute is common. Due to technical and scientific inquiry, classification systems change from time to time, and many athletes who were previously winners abruptly become losers. This situation is sometimes psychologically unbearable and has already caused many dropouts from participation and apparent psychological distress (Wheeler et al. 1999). How can classification systems guarantee the *utilitarian* principle to all participants? Classification systems cope with the difficult task of avoiding exclusion of those with limited function on one hand, and facilitating competitive motivation challenging those with extraordinary function on the other hand. Spectators and competition organisers are further actors whose burden should be considered. Too many classes would bore the spectator and increase organisational complexity. Thus classification systems are compromises that should accept participants and scientific validity.

Instruction Modifications

Many ways exist to modify instructions in APA. A recent literature analysis suggests that more than 50 per cent of interventions reported in the principal scholarly APA journal, *Adapted Physical Activity Quarterly* (APAQ), across a ten-year period between 1995 and 2004 included instructional modifications (Hutzler 2006). While mostly applied within physical education, instructional modification has relevance in a variety of recreation and sport for all settings. One such area is skill acquisition, where gradual transition from verbal instruction through modelling to manual guidance is often implemented, particularly, in cases of participants with intellectual disability, coordina-tion disorders and autism (Sherrill 2004). The degree of cueing, prompting and providing feedback with increasing latency to enhance self-initiated decision-making is an instructional variable that requires attention. The ethical concern that should be considered in this regard is that of self-determination, that is the autonomous, intrinsic motivated and regulated behaviour, which may be a more distant outcome than behavioural outcomes and task accomplishment, often preferred by instructors, coaches and teachers.

Another instructional adaptation that requires attention is the use of human resources. The allocation of individual or across-the-class peer tutors is often recommended and has a supporting base of evidence (Houston-Wilson et al. 1997; Lieberman et al. 2000). Very limited, if any, research supports this instruction modification, however, from the perspective of the peer tutor. Do peer tutors socially or educationally distribute benefits equally? Do those peers with disability they help to instruct gain or lose benefits under given modifications? This utilitarian ethical concern warrants further study and debate.

Teacher assistants, resource APA professionals or volunteers represent other forms of support, which have increasingly been implemented in practice. This practice, however, often exacerbates ethical conflicts. Precisely who benefits from this additional support: the participant with disability or the instructor? It is likely that that the instructor would prefer assistance, while participants' benefit may indicate a preference for increasing independence. Also, from a utilitarian perspective, the question arises as to whether participants' benefits are more valuable than instructor's benefits?

Conclusion

Physical activity contexts are suitable for constructing the ability of individuals in spite of an existing disability. APA is the scientific field of study and professional expertise that enables individuals with a disability to participate in a variety of physical activity contexts. The examples of modifying activities to include participants with disabilities given in this article raises ethical concerns across participation and modification contexts. While many of the concerns related to the question of how to assure favourable consequences of participation for individuals with disabilities as well as their peers and practising personnel, other dilemmas concerned a range of service-provider and recipient relationships, from avoiding paternalism to assuring empowerment. These ethical concerns need further to be studied and appropriate criteria for decision-making rules outlined. Physical education teachers, sport coaches, administrators and referees should be aware of the ethical concerns regarding modifying tasks, environments, equipment, rules and instruction modalities. From an ethical and sociological perspective, the SEMA model appears suitable for structuring conduct criteria and warrants further study.[1]

ACKNOWLEDGEMENTS

The author wishes to thank the individuals who critically read primary drafts and provided valuable insights with respect to the ethical considerations and the praxis-related contents of the examples presented in this article. Gregory Reid, Michael McNamee and Ejgil Jespersen were particularly influential in structuring the final outcome.

NOTES

1. Dallas Mavericks Wheelchair Basketball: Mission Statement, available at http://wheel-mavs.org/philosophy.htm. See also A. Trabert, 'Professional Paralympic Athletes: Sport is still not Profession', Sport news, *The Paralympian* online 4 (2001), available at http://www.paralympic.org/paralympian/20014/2001425.htm, accessed 8 Feb. 2008.
2. 'Oscar Pistorius—independent scientific study concludes that Cheetah prosthetics offer clear mechanical advantages', press release, International Association of Athletics Federations (IAAF), 14 Jan. 2008. Available at http://www.iaaf.org/news/kind=101/newsid=42896.html, accessed 14 Feb. 2008.

REFERENCES

ALLABY, M. 1999. *A Dictionary of Zoology*. Oxford: Oxford University Press.

ANDERSON, J. 2003. 'Turned into taxpayers': Paraplegia rehabilitation and sport at Stoke Mandeville, 1944–56. *Journal of Contemporary History* 38: 461–75.

BAR-OR, O. and T.W. ROWLAND. 2004. *Pediatric Exercise Medicine*. Champaign, IL: Human Kinetics.

BOUFFARD, M. and W.B. STREAM. 2003. Critical thinking and professional preparation. In *Adapted Physical Activity*, edited by R.D. Steadward, G.D. Wheeler and E.J. Watkinson). Edmonton, AB: University of Alberta Press: 1–10.

BROWN, D.R., M.M. YORE, S.A. HAM and C.A. MACERA. 2005. Physical activity among adults ≥50 yr with and without disabilities, BRFSS 2001. *Medicine and Science in Sports and Exercise* 37: 620–9.

BURTON, A.W., N.L. GREER and D.M. WIESE-BJORNSTAL. 1993. Variations in grasping and throwing patterns as a function of ball size. *Pediatric Exercise Science* 5: 25–41.

CAVILL, N., S. KAHLMEIER and F. ROCIOPPI. 2006. *Physical Activity and Health in Europe: Evidence for Action*. Copenhagen: World Health Organization, Europe Regional Office.

DARWALL, S., ED. 2002. *Consequentialism*. Oxford: Blackwell.

DAVIS, W.E. and G.D. BROADHEAD. 2007. *Ecological Task Analysis and Movement*. Champaign, IL: Human Kinetics.

DAVIS, W.E. and A.W. BURTON. 1991. Ecological task analysis: Translating movement behavior theory into practice. *Adapted Physical Activity Quarterly* 8: 154–77.

DI MARCO, A., M. RUSSELL and M. MASTERS. 2003. Standards for wheelchair prescription. *Australian Occupational Therapy Journal* 50: 30–9.

DISABILITY DISCRIMINATION ACT. 1995. London: HMSO.

DURSTINE, L.J. and G.E. MOORE. 2003. *ACSM's Exercise Management for Persons With Chronic Diseases and Disabilitie,* 2nd edn. Philadelphia, PA: Lippincott, Williams & Wilkins.

FEDERAL REGISTER. The Americans with Disabilities Act. *Federal Register* 57, no. 189 (29 Sept. 1992). Washington, DC.

FREIRE, P. 1970. *The Pedagogy of the Oppressed*. New York: Continuum Publishing.

GIBSON, J.J. 1977. The theory of affordances. In *Perceiving, Acting, and Knowing: Toward an Ecological Psychology*, edited by R. Shaw and J. Bransford. Hillsdale, NJ: Erlbaum: 67–82.

GUTTMANN, L. 1976. *Textbook of Sport for the Disabled*. Aylesbury: HM&M.

GUTSMUTHS, J. 1803. *Gymnastics for Youth: Or A Practical Guide to Healthful and Amusing Exercises: For the Use of Schools. An Essay toward the Necessary Improvement of Education, Chiefly as it Relates to the Body*. Philadelphia: P. Byrne.

HAMILTON, L. 1997. The impact of an acquired disability on empowerment. *Journal of Leisurability* 24 (1), 12–16.

HASKELL, W.L., I.M. LEE, R.R. PATE, K.E. POWELL, S.N. BLAIR, B.A. FRANKLIN, C.A. MACERA, G.W. HEATH, P.D. THOMPSON and A. BAUMAN. 2007. Physical activity and public health: Updated recommendations from the American College of Sports Medicine and the American Heart Association. *Circulation* 116: 1081–1103.

HAYWOOD, K.M. and N. GETCHELL. 2005. *Life Span Motor Development*. Champaign, IL: Human Kinetics.

HOUSTON-WILSON, C., J.M. DUNN, H. VAN DEN MARS and J. MCCUBBIN. 1997. The effects of peer-tutors on motor performance in integrated physical education classes. *Adapted Physical Activity Quarterly* 14: 293–313.

HUTZLER, Y. 1990. The concept of empowerment in rehabilitative sports. In *Adapted Physical Activity: An Interdisciplinary Approach*, edited by G. Doll-Tepper, C. Dahms, B. Doll, and H. v Selzam. Heidelberg: Springer Verlag: 44–51.

———. 2006. Evidence based research in adapted physical activity: Theoretical and data-based considerations. *Revista da Sobama* 11: 13–24.

———. 2007a. A systematic ecological modification approach to skill acquisition in Adapted Physical Activity. In *Ecological Perspectives on Movement*, edited by W. Davis and J. Broadhead. Champaign, IL: Human Kinetics: 179–95.

———. 2007b. A systematic ecological model for adapting physical activities: Theoretical foundations and practical examples. *Adapted Physical Activity Quarterly* 24: 287–304.

HUTZLER, Y. and M. BAR-ELI. 1993. Psychological benefits of sports for disabled people: A review. *Scandinavian Journal of Medicine and Science in Sports* 3: 217–28.

HUTZLER, Y. and C. SHERRILL. 2007. Defining adapted physical activity: International perspectives. *Adapted Physical Activity Quarterly* 24: 1–20.

INTERNATIONAL PARALYMPIC COMMITTEE SPORT SCIENCE COMMITTEE. 1995. *The Paralympic Movement New Directions and Issues in Sport Science: Final Report of the Second Annual Meeting of the IPCSSC.* Berlin: German Olympic Institute.

KALYVAS, V. and G. REID. 2003. Sport adaptation, participation, and enjoyment of students with and without physical disabilities. *Adapted Physical Activity Quarterly* 20: 182–99.

KIPHARD, E.J. 1983. Adapted physical education education in Germany. In *Adapted Physical Activity: From Theory to Application: Proceedings of the 3rd ISAPA*, edited by R.L. Eason, T.L. Smith and F. Caron. Champaign, IL: Human Kinetics: 25–32.

KYDMAN, L. and W.E. DAVIS. 2007. Empowerment in coaching. In *Ecological Task Analysis and Movement*, edited by W.E. Davis and G.D. Broadhead. Champaign, IL: Human Kinetics: 121–40.

LIEBERMAN, L.J. and C. HOUSTON-WILSON. 2002. *Strategies for Inclusion: A Handbook for Physical Educators.* Champaign, IL: Human Kinetics.

LIEBERMAN, L.J., J.M. DUNN, H. VAN DEN MARS and J. MCCUBBIN. 2000. Peer tutors' effects on activity levels of deaf students in inclusive physical education. *Adapted Physical Activity Quarterly* 17: 20–39.

MCNAMEE, M., S. BOLIVIER and P. WAINWRIGHT. 2007. *Research Ethics in Exercise, Health and Sports Sciences.* London: Routledge.

NEAL, P. 1972. *Sport and Identity.* Philadelphia: M.A. Dorrance.

NEWELL, K.M. 1986. Constraints on the development of coordination. In *Motor Development in Children: Aspects of Coordination and Control*, edited by M.G. Wade and H.T.A. Whiting. Dordrecht: Martinus Nijhoff: 341–60.

NORMAN, T., J.T. SANDVIN and H. THOMMESEN. 2004. *A Holistic Approach to Rehabilitation.* Oslo: Kommuneforl.

RAPPAPORT, J. 1987. Terms of empowerment/Exemplars of prevention. *Toward a Theory of Community Psychology* 15: 121–45.

REED, E.S. 1988. Applying the theory of action systems to the study of motor skills. In *Complex Movement Behaviour: The Motor-action Controversy*, edited by O.G. Meijer and K. Roth. Amsterdam: Elsevier: 45–86.

REID, G. 2003. Defining adapted physical activity. In *Adapted Physical Activity*, edited by R.D. Steadward, G.D. Wheeler and E.J. Watkinson. Edmonton: University of Alberta Press: 11–25.

SCHMIDT, R.A. and T.D. LEE. 2005. *Motor Learning and Control: A Behavioral Emphasis,* 4th edn. Champaign, IL: Human Kinetics.

SCHMIDT, R.A. and C.A. WRISBERG. 2004. *Motor Learning and Performance,* 3rd edn. Champaign, IL: Human Kinetics.

SHAKESPEARE, T.W. 1996. Disability, identity and difference. In *Exploring the Divide*, edited by C. Barnes and G. Mercer. Leeds: The Disability Press: 94–113.

SHERRILL, C. 1998. *Adapted Physical Activity, Recreation and Sport: Crossdisciplinary and Lifespan,* 5th edn. Dubuque, IA: WCB/McGraw.

———. 2004. *Adapted Physical Activity, Recreation and Sport: Crossdisciplinary and Lifespan,* 6th edn. Boston, MA: McGraw-Hill Higher Education.

SILVERS, A. and D. WASSERMAN. 1998. Convention and competence: Disability rights in sports and education. In *Ethics in Sports*, edited by W.J. Morgan, K.V. Meier and A.J. Schneider. Champaign, IL: Human Kinetics: 409–19.

SINGER, R.N. 1980. *Motor Learning and Human Performance,* 3rd edn. New York: Macmillan.

SØRENSEN, M. 2003. Integration in sport and empowerment of athletes with a disability. *European Bulletin of Adapted Physical Activity* 2 (2), available at http://www.bulletin-apa.com/, accessed 18 Jan. 2004.

STAFFORD, G. 1939. *Sports for the Handicapped*. New York: Prentice-Hall.

STEADWARD, R.D., G.D. WHEELER and E.J. WATKINSON, eds. 2003. *Adapted Physical Activity*. Edmonton: University of Alberta Press.

STROHKENDL, H. 1991. The relevance of understanding sportspecific functional classification in wheelchair sports and its future development. In *Proceedings of the Kevin Betts Symposium on Functional Classification* (July 1991). Stoke Mandeville, England: International Stoke Mandeville Wheelchair Sports Federation.

THE AMERICAN HERITAGE. 2003. *Dictionary of the English Language*. Wilmington, MA: Houghton Mifflin Company.

THURSTON, M. and K. GREEN. 2004. Adherence to exercise in later life: How can 'Exercise on Prescription' programmes be made more effective? *Health Promotion International* 19 (3): 379–86.

TUCKER R. and DUGAS, J. 2008a. Oscar Pistorius banned by IAAF—carbon fibre blades offer 'Clear mechanical advantages'. *The Science Of Sport: Scientific Comment and Analysis of Sports and Sporting Performance*, available at http://scienceofsport.blogspot.com/2008/01/oscar-pistorius-announcement-banned_14.html, accessed 14 Feb. 2008.

———. 2008b. Pistorius to challenge ban—insight and overview of the debate so far. *The Science Of Sport: Scientific Comment and Analysis of Sports and Sporting Performance*, available at http://scienceofsport.blogspot.com/2008/01/oscar-pistorius-reaction-challenge-ban.html, accessed 14 Feb. 2008.

ULRICH, B.D., D.A. ULRICH and D.H. COLLIER. 1992. Alternating stepping patterns: Hidden abilities of 11-month-old infants with Down syndrome. *Developmental Medicine and Child Neurology* 34: 233–9.

ÚSTÚN, B.T. 2003. WHO's International Classification of Functioning, Disability and Health (ICF). In *Towards a Society for All Through Adapted Physical Activity. Proceedings of the 13th ISAPA, 2001*, edited by M. Dinold, G. Gerber and T. Reinelt. Vienna: Austrian Federation of Adapted Physical Activity: 71–7.

VANLANDEWIJCK, Y.C. and R. CHAPPEL. 1996. Integration and classification issues in competitive sport for athletes with disabilities. *Sport Science Review* 5: 65–88.

VAN LENT, M., ed. 2006. *Count Me In: A Guide to Inclusive Physical Activity, Sport and Leisure for Children with a Disability*. Leuven, Belgium: Acco.

WHEELER, G.D., R.D. STEADWARD, D. LEGG, Y. HUTZLER, E. CAMPBELL and A. JOHNSON. 1999. Personal investment in disability sport careers: An international study. *Adapted Physical Activity Quarterly* 16 (3): 238–50.

WHO (WORLD HEALTH ORGANISATION) 1980. *International Classification of the Impairments, Diseases and Handicaps*. Geneva: WHO.

———. 2001. *International Classification of Functioning, Disability and Health (ICF)*. Geneva: WHO. Available at http://www3.who.int/icf/icftemplate.cfm, accessed 11 Feb. 2008.

ZIMMERMAN, M.A. and J. RAPPAPORT. 1988. Citizen participation, perceived control and psychological empowerment. *American Journal of Community Psychology* 16: 725–50.

Yeshayahu Hutzler, Zinman College for Physical Education and Sport Science, Wingate Institute 42902, Israel. E-mail: shayke@wincol.ac.il

SELF-REGULATED DEPENDENCY: ETHICAL REFLECTIONS ON INTERDEPENDENCE AND HELP IN ADAPTED PHYSICAL ACTIVITY

Donna L. Goodwin

This article explores the ethical implications of the goal of functional independence for persons with disabilities. Central to independence is protection against the fear and uncertainty of future dependency and assurance of a level of social status. Moreover, independence reflects individualism, autonomy and control of decisions about one's life. Dependency, in contrast, implies the inability to do things for oneself and reliance on others to assist with tasks of everyday life. The ethics of independence are explored within the context of the medical and social constructionist models of disability and contrasted against the ethics of support that underscores self-regulated dependency. Self-regulated dependency gives emphasis to the need for support created through relationships, choices and the management of resources. Finally, the article concludes with a challenge to meaningfully translate the principles of ethics to the multiplicity of adapted physical activity contexts.

Resumen

El artículo explora las implicaciones éticas del objetivo de la independencia funcional de las personas con discapacidades. Clave para la independencia es la protección contra el temor y la incertidumbre de una futura depedencia y una garantía de cierto nivel de estatus social. Además, la independencia refleja individualismo, autonomía y control sobre las decisions en la vida de uno mismo. La depedencia, en cambio, implica la inabilidad para hacer las cosas por uno mismo y la dependencia en otros para ayudarnos con tareas cotidianas. La ética de la independencia es explorada dentro del contexto de los modelos de discapacidad construccionistas médicos y sociales, y es contrastada con la ética del sostenimiento que subraya la dependencia autoregulada. La dependencia autoregulada hace hincapié en la necesidad de un soporte creado a través de relaciones, elecciones, y la administración de recursos. Finalmente, el artículo concluye con el desafío a la hora de trasladar los principios de la ética, de un modo significativo, a la multiplicidad de contextos de la actividad física adaptada.

Zusammenfassung

Dieser Artikel untersucht die ethischen Implikationen, die sich aus dem Ziel ergeben, Personen mit Behinderung eine funktionale Unabhängigkeit zu ermöglichen. Zentraler Aspekt für Unabhängigkeit ist der Schutz vor Angst und Unsicherheit im Hinblick auf zukünftige Abhängigkeit und

Zusicherung eines bestimmten Levels an den Sozialstatus. Des Weiteren spiegelt Unabhängigkeit auch Individualismus, Autonomie und Kontrolle über eigene Lebensentscheidungen wieder. Im Gegensatz hierzu impliziert Abhängigkeit die Unfähigkeit, Dinge selbst erledigen zu können und die Abhängigkeit von anderen, die einen bei alltäglichen Aufgaben unterstützen. Die Ethik von Unabhängigkeit wird innerhalb des medizinischen und sozial konstruktivistischen Modells von Behinderung analysiert. Dies wird kontrastiert zu einer Ethik der Unterstützung, die eine selbstregulierte Abhängigkeit unterstreicht. Selbstregulierte Abhängigkeit betont die Notwendigkeit von Unterstützung, die durch Beziehungen, Entscheidungen und dem Management von Ressourcen entsteht. Abschließend wird versucht, die ethischen Prinzipien für den vielschichtigen Bereich Bewegung, Spiel und Sport in Prävention, Rehabilitation und Behinderung (APA = adapted physical activity) fruchtbar zu machen.

摘要

本文在探討殘障人士在機能獨立性目標上的倫理意義。獨立性(independency)的核心在於排除恐懼感及去除面對未來之不確定性，以確保個人的一種社會地位。除此之外，獨立性反映出個人主義、自律及對個人生命決定上之掌控。相對的，依賴性(dependency)所呈現的是一種無能力去為自己打點事務並需依賴他人來協助每日的生活。我們對於獨立性的倫理討論是放在醫學及社會建構下的殘障模式環境中來討論，這與自我調節式的依賴支持倫理學正好相反。自我調節式的依賴強調，所需要建立的支助在於透過關係、選擇、及資源上的管理。最後，本文的結語是在強調，將倫理學上的理論有意義的運用至適應身體活動環境中的各種多元層面中。

Most practitioners and researchers in the area of adapted physical activity would think of themselves as motivated by good intentions, honest and caring, and as such adhere to core ethical dispositions that guide their daily and professional activities. As a field of professional endeavour, however, we may be remiss in the lack of scholarly attention we have given to the ethical implications of our practice.[1] In this article, I first explore the medical and social models of disability and their importance in the definition of disability. I then explore the ethics of independence as a goal for persons with disabilities. In doing so, the concept of self-regulated dependency and the ethics of support will be contrasted against the backdrop of dependence, independence and interdependence. Finally, I describe the need to meaningfully translate the principles of ethics to the multiplicity of adapted physical activity contexts.

Medical and Social Models of Disability

The medical culture of decades ago reinforced a binary relationship between disability that disassociated the bodily manifestation of disability from the experience of disability. The early medical model, and the related field of rehabilitation, adopted a functional theory of disability whereby 'disabled individuals have inherently pathological conditions that can be objectively diagnosed, treated, and in some cases ameliorated' (Gabel and Peters 2004, 587). A decontextualised body lends itself to being treated, rehabilitated and normalised so that it can result in a return to a state of health and 'discharged' from the medical system (Armstrong 1995). As it became recognised that normalisation of the disabled body against the able-bodied norm was not always attainable, the construct of normalisation was remapped to mean functional independence and self-sufficiency became the underlying goal of rehabilitation sciences (Kerr and Meyerson 1987) and the standard of *normal* against which people with limiting conditions are measured (Koch 2001).

The medical model has been criticised for an approach to services for persons with disabilities that emphasises deficiencies of the person, disenfranchisement resulting from diagnosis and labelling, the loss of autonomy commensurate with the *sick role*, care or treatment by an expert and adjustment towards *normality* with little regard for the influence of environmental barriers on the person's functioning (Condeluci 1991; Asch 1998; Shakespeare 1998). In response, disability studies moved away from the embodied experience of disability for fear that the ideal body, based on statistical averages of 'normal', would be used as a standard that would stigmatise the body as weak, incapable and pitiful – would be used as a determinate of social worth (Goffman 1963; Shogan 1998; Goodwin et al. 2004; Taleporos and McCabe 2002).

Reindal (1999, 353) went so far as to state that 'disabled people argue that they are victims of an ideology of independence'. Negotiation can occur between the service provider and the consumer such that the person is 'sold on' certain goals such as independence and autonomy which may be more of a reflection of prevailing social and/or staff values than participant's full understanding of choices, risks and mutual accommodation resulting from deliberation between persons and service provider (Wegener 1996).

Rehabilitation care aims at independence for the patient or client. This is its chief value:

> Rehabilitation care tries to resort or to help the patient to achieve a level of functioning such that he or she can claim greater independence. Measures of impairment and performance in activities of daily living are key indicators of progress and are seen as essential to improving the patient's quality of life (Kuczewski and Fiedler 2005, 46)

The message that independence is important at all costs may not be the optimal way to view one's self over time given the demands on time, energy and motivation, in addition to the social and psychological isolation and separation that disability can bring (Kuczewski and Fiedler 2005). Moreover, following a trauma (e.g. spinal cord injury) many of the activities routinely performed may no longer be available to the person and it may be difficult, particularly soon after trauma to appreciate the possibilities the future may hold.[2]. 'From the vantage point of the life plan, goals, and values the person had developed over the years, his post-trauma prospects may seem nothing more than indignity, drudgery, and misery' (Kuczewski and Fiedler 2005, 33).

Measures of quality of life are most often those of contemporary mainstream culture and tend to place a premium on independence while devaluing dependency. To impose the standard or *ethic of independence* in rehabilitation may be reasonable and required for returning to the community. Although the goals of autonomy and functional independence are needed and required for returning to the community and may well be very appropriate short-term goals for post-traumatic injury care in acute care settings, the link to community engagement may not be linear. Reconstructions of self that may have occurred in rehabilitation may undergo further adjustments upon returning home. As the realities of returning to work, parenting, living in the community and relationship-building become realities, the autonomy that was the focus of rehabilitation may need to be recalibrated, refocused and augmented to include community and family supports. The needed assistance reinforces an *ethic of support* whereby people collaborate together to co-create understanding, interpretations, shared meanings and solutions to challenges (Cacinovic Vogrincic 2005).

This dualism of the mind and body had a powerful and deeply embedded influence on rehabilitation, education, employment and community services for people with disabilities (Condeluci 1991; Armstrong 1995). Health professionals who treat to maximum functional independence and community integration during rehabilitation can become frustrated when patients do not thrive in aftercare and cease to use many of the supports and aides upon returning to the complexities and environmental challenges of their homes (Albrecht and Devlieger, 1999; Kuczewski and Fiedler 2001). Accordingly, rehabilitation has sought to remove barriers to living independently by creating enabling processes that facilitate integration, albeit the extent to which rehabilitation has impacted physical and socio-cultural barriers can be debated (Kuczewski and Fiedler 2001).

A more recent emphasis in disability has been the prominence of a social definition of disability that insists that importance of physical differences lie in discriminatory social practice, social reactions or ignorance of the effect of that difference (Koch 2001). Disability studies have presented a social model of disability that focuses on the social implications for bodies that are deemed aberrant (subjectively), setting aside the constructs of health, illness, pathology and symptoms (objectively) while emphasising disability culture and social action (Bricher 2000; Snyder and Mitchell 2001). Having a clinically measurable functional limitation may not be grounds for labelling someone as having a disability, particularly if the environmental supports that may be exacerbating function are taken into consideration. What's more, the World Health Organisation (2001) grounds the determination of disability in an ecological framework that addresses the impact of structural change on activity restrictions and its impact in turn on participation in preferred activities.

The focus on discriminatory social practice has not been without criticism. Disability studies have been criticised for strategically neglecting the experience of disabled embodiment in order to be distanced from the objectification of the body resulting from the medical gaze (Snyder and Mitchell 2001). Rejecting the medical model and the reality of physical or structural difference in favour of purely social construction may be diminishing the multiplicity of disability and personal agency (Koch 2001).

Models of Disablement

Numerous models of disablement have been presented since the original work of Nagi (1965), which emerged in response to his belief that medicine was exerting a linear view of impairment whereby ameliorated changes in function and would result in similar incremental increases in community engagement (e.g. ICIDH 1980; ICF 2001; Verbrugge and Jette 1994; Peters 1996). This notion placed the burden of responsibility on the individual to change or improve given the supports of the medical community. Verbrugge's and Jette's (1994) model of disablement was based on Nagi's original model but reinforced the view that disablement was a dynamic process resulting from the interaction between the individual and physical and socio-cultural processes. Verbrugge and Jette (1994) further presented a distinction between intrinsic disablement and absolute disablement. They suggested that absolute disablement was the product of intrinsic disablement and the utilisation of personal assistance and specially designed equipment to reduce the impact of functional limitations on the person's actual ability (e.g. aids to daily living). Kuczeski and Fiedler (2001) criticised independence in rehabilitation being guided by assistive devices as it again reinforced a one-dimensional focus on the individual that emphasised labels, limitations and loss. Unfortunately, the submission that personal assistance may impact absolute disablement has received little research attention. Peters's (1996) model overtly addressed the subjective experience of disability as integral to the process of disablement given a two-directional expression of disablement, although did not go so far as to highlight the importance of personal support systems.

The World Health Organisation (WHO) International Classification of Functioning (ICF) is perhaps the best-known model of disability given its international reach in its development and dissemination, being translated and recognised by 191 countries (Masala and Petretto 2007). The purpose of the ICF was 'to establish a common language for describing health and health related states in order to improve communication between different users, such as health care workers, researchers, policymakers, and the public, including people with disabilities' (WHO 2001, 5), with the overall intent of emphasising the importance of functional health for people with disabilities and identifying facilitators of and barriers to the full participation of people with disabilities in society (Peterson and Threats 2005). The ICF presents the limitations of human functioning as the result of the dynamic interaction between contextual factors (personal factors and environmental factors) and health conditions as presented in the domains of the body functions (physiological and psychological), the body structures (anatomical parts), activities (execution of a task or action) and participation (involvement in a life situation or the actual context in which they live) (WHO 2001). Impairments are the manifestation of changes in body functions and structures. Disability refers to participation restrictions that can result from the interaction of health conditions with external factors within the context in which the person lives. In summary, 'ICF defines disablement as the result of the interaction among the domains of body, individual, and environment' (Marsala and Petretto 2007, 10).

The ICF is a valuable tool for the fields of rehabilitation and adapted physical activity as it focuses on health, disability and function and attempts to integrate the medical and social models of disability by addressing the biological, individual and societal perspectives of health (Peterson 2005). The ICF has not been without criticism and much debate. Ueda and Okawa (2003) suggest that the lived experience or subjective voice of the person is absent from the ICF, while others would say it may be implied in the 'personal factors' within the contextual component of the ICF (Marsala and Petretto 2007).

Dependence-Independence Dichotomy

It would appear that a position that brought together a more comprehensive view of the bodily, social and cultural contexts of disability is needed as individually the models are incomplete (Llewellyn and Hogan 2000). A recent trend in disability and other theorising explores a third dimension—the spaces between subjectivity and objectivity— thereby deconstructing subjective/objective and disability/impairment binaries to simultaneously examine material phenomena (e.g., the physical body) and symbolic meaning (e.g. interpretations of the body and/or oppression in dialectic with disablement) (Gabel and Peters 2004, 588).

For persons with acquired physical disabilities, striving to regain independence has a temporality that is closely associated with hospital-based rehabilitation and the period shortly following the return home and to family (Gustafson and Goodwin 2006). The need for acute help defines the first months of rehabilitation as the person's physical condition stabilises. Help through the rehabilitation regime becomes instrumental to the goal of independence in self-care and is the cornerstone to returning home (Braithwaite and Eckstein 2003). Once the person returns home, the message that further strides in independence are desirable remains. To do otherwise would be advocating dependency. The positioning of interdependence as a means by which to achieve physical and social inclusion in the community as people move beyond the medical or rehabilitative gaze has received much less attention or social value even when in reality we live in a state of mutual interdependence (Oliver 1989).

Dependence 'is depicted as being associated with practical helplessness, a state of need, incompetence, and functional incapacity' and independence 'typically emphasize[s] personal characteristics such as self-regulation, control, and the ability or opportunity to make choices about important aspects on one' life' (Gignac et al. 2000, 362). Nadler and Fisher (1986) characterised help-seeking as a threat to self-esteem because of its implied inferiority. Clearly, independence is a good thing, particularly when applied to those from whom it has been denied (Kerr and Meyerson 1987). It has inherent positive aspects including achievement of goals and can be psychologically and pragmatically self-supporting (Nadler and Fisher 1986).

Some conceptualise dependence and independence along a continuum. At the dependence end of the continuum people are on the receiving end of support, are under supervision or the expectations of others and are in genuine need of the support of others for part of their days. The other end of the continuum is independence, characterised by autonomy and ability, where support is not required or desired. As people require less support, they are expected to move along the continuum, accepting new independence challenges. This has been referred to as the 'continuum trap' in which the perception of others defines the 'goal' based on a perceived problem, judgement of the person's capability and assumptions about the resources required to complete tasks (e.g. energy expenditure, time to complete tasks) (Condeluci 1991). Independence is framed as the desirable end point and does not extend to self-direction through decision-making, control of resources or choosing to do complete tasks with assistance (Bricher 2000; Gignac and Cott 1998; Oliver 1989; Turnbull and Turnbull 1985).

It has been argued that dichotomising dependency and independence does not accurately reflect what we most desire; a human condition that reflects mutual interdependence based in partnership (Gignac and Cott 1998; Reindal 1999). The *ethics of independence* is properly the object of critical reflection when independence in basic living skills can claim the energy a person possesses, thereby limiting breadth of experiences (Bricher 2000). It can, moreover, lead to feelings of failure when a life-story that reflects achievement, cooperation, fulfilment and belonging is based on needing others (Goodwin and Thurmeier 2005), and loneliness as the bitter fruit of the hard-won autonomy of living alone and caring for oneself (Condeluci 1991; Mulderij 1997). The ethics of independence and reluctance to seek support must also be balanced against receiving support that is not needed or desired, thereby moving interdependence into forced dependency through lack of opportunity to demonstrate autonomy in actions (Gignac and Cott 1998).

Self-regulated Dependency

Interdependence is about relationships that lead to a mutual acceptance and respect as diverse people come together in a synergistic way to create environmental and attitudinal supports to foster full participation in preferred activities (Condeluci 1991). When contrasted against the medical and rehabilitation systems, interdependence focuses on capacities rather than deficits; stresses relationships rather than congregation; is driven by the person, not an expert; and promotes system change rather than change in the individual. Wegener (1996, 14) pondered the emphasis placed on independence and stated that 'While [separation, autonomy and personal independence] may be an integral and important goal for rehabilitation, it is possible we may overemphasise these goals at the expense of interdependence, deliberation, and empathetic understanding'.

As early as 1947, Ladieu, Hanfmann, and Dembo, in their work with returning Second World War veterans indicated that interdependence implied reliance on others for support (Ladieu et al. 1947). Seeking and accepting help when the situation seems to demand it becomes a social relationship that is based on understanding of contextual goals and control of the support provided. Koch (2001, 371) stated 'Social difference theorists insist that a physically dependent or interdependent life is no less full and viable than one that is autonomous and independent. Differences that may exist are inherently trivial except to the extent they reflect social prejudice or indifference.' Kerr and Meyerson (1987,173) went so far as to say:

> Rehabilitation is successful when the individual achieves the flexibility and skill to enter comfortably into a variety of dependence relationships. Particular emphasis is placed on the value of healthy dependency and the importance of facilitating changes in both the person and the culture to allow and encourage people with disabilities to develop interdependent and dependable roles with others.

The ethics of what some would refer to as self-imposed dependency is an interesting one. Dependence is viewed by some as intolerable and a situation to be rectified. Others view the development of interdependent relationships positively as it raises awareness of the physical and socio-cultural barriers people with disabilities encounter in those with whom they develop relationships. A qualitative study completed by Bedini (2000, 63) that investigated the perceptions of adults with disabilities as they engaged in community recreation described how the participants yielded to the challenges their disabilities posed in public settings, but did so without giving up control by 'relearning methods of daily living that were interdependent in nature'. Gignac and Cott (1998) also found that individuals may impose dependency upon themselves in certain contexts as a strategy for managing the energy and time needed to focus on other tasks. Seeking and receiving help is complex, as there is some evidence to suggest that seeking and receiving help may be domain-specific with help being more readily accepted for activities of daily living than discretionary activities such as leisure. In some instances recreational settings were avoided as they evoked and reinforced feelings of dependency (Bedini 2000; Gignac et al. 2000).

Baltes (1996) described self-imposed dependency as self-regulated dependency, thereby highlighting individual agency and control over situations where support is perceived to be an asset. Self-regulated dependence is also consistent with that which Condeluci (1991) believes are necessary for interdependence—the person with the disability defining the problem and being in charge to the extent that control of the situation is exercised. In this context, when help-seeking is recontextualised within a broader social context, it is viewed as adaptive behaviour.

Parameters of Support

Considerable literature exists on how and why people help one another. Nadler and Fisher (1986) summarised the reaction to help by suggesting that (a) situational conditions (characteristics of the helper and the helped) and personality variables of the recipient determine the extend to which help is self-threatening or self-supporting; (b) help that supports one's self-concept elicits positive, non-defensive reactions; (c) help that threatens one's self-concept can result in negative responses that can result in negative affect and harm the potential for future self-improvement or alternately lead to acquiescence and helplessness.

Help in itself can bring perceived dependency, loss of control, a threat to competence and admission of failure (Nadler 1987; Goodwin and Thurmeier 2005) but can be balanced against instrumental support that makes a task or acting on an opportunity possible (Braithwaite and Cunningham 2003; Goodwin 2001). Request for help can be well received when the recipient interprets the help to be 'the practical thing to do' or 'if I get help doing something, that's energy saved that I can use to more things for myself within the day' (Braithwaite and Cunningham 2003, 13).

Cutrona and Suhr (1992) categorised support into five social types: (a) informational support; (b) tangible support (or instrumental support); (c) esteem support; (d) emotional support; and (e) network support (connecting to others). Of these supports, instrumental support is perhaps the most salient to persons with disabilities on a daily basis given the challenges faced as they negotiate their physical surroundings. Barbee and Cunningham (1995, 389) defined instrumental support as 'something active or physical to help the seeker'. Well-received offers of assistance may have the following characteristics (Braithwaite and Cunningham 2003; Brooks 1978): (a) the request for assistance was initiated by the person in need of support; (b) offers of help are not patronising and permit the person to be active during the helping transaction; (c) the offer is natural or casual (the would-be helper does not make a big show of the help); (d) the would-be helper asks before assisting, then waits for the person's response; (e) the supervision of help is listened to and honoured; (f) the helper does not persist if the offer of help is ignored or declined as unnecessary; and (g) the help should only be offered if the person is willing to have it turned down. Furthermore, in a position when the help of strangers is needed, persons with disabilities may (a) carefully read nonverbal cues before asking or approaching someone; (b) approach those who assume a service role such as store clerks; and (c) select people who are physically non-threatening and are perceived to be less likely to take advantage of the situation (e.g. by stealing a purse or wallet).

Although there has been limited research on seeking and receiving help within the context of disability (Braithwaite and Cunningham 2003), even less attention has been given to its meaning on participation in disability sport, physical activity and recreation. An increased understanding of the meaning of help-seeking and receiving (i.e. self-regulated dependency) and the manner in which to best provide help so as to promote collaboration and empathetic relationships is an integral part of ethical practice.

Ethics of Support

Ethics can be defined as the science of balancing values towards the development of guidelines or rules that are concerned with that which is deemed right, proper, desirable or worthwhile (Haas and Mackenzie 1993; Corey et al. 1998). Ethics is described by Haas and Mackenzie (1993, 48) as the 'science of duty' that balances the values on either side of a moral dilemma, which can be recognised by the sense that your are sure that an error will be made regardless of the path chosen.

Ethically, five problems arise when the question of independence and self-regulated dependency is discussed: (a) it is difficult for a person to evaluate how beneficial a care plan will be until partaking in it (e.g. walking for someone who is a double above-knee amputee over using a wheelchair); (b) applying able-bodied values (e.g. independence) such that non-compliance or the inability to reach the imposed goal results in stigmatisation or feelings of failure; (c) the short-term aim of autonomy and functional independence as experienced in a rehabilitation context may not transfer well to the environmental and socio-cultural barriers that exist in the larger social context; (d) contra-indicating some activities because they may interfere with independence places an objective value on happiness rather than something that is individually meaningful (e.g. avoiding wheelchair sport due to potential shoulder overuse injuries) (Kuczewski and Fiedler 2005); and (e) providing assistance that is not needed results in imposed role-dependency and conversely not providing assistance when the person needs it results limits independence. Fundamental ethical questions arise when professionals advocate what is good/bad or right/wrong when the consequences of one stance (e.g. independence over self-regulated dependency) can impact upon the health (pain) or social networks (social isolation resulting from autonomy) of the other and restrict the breadth of daily activities due to energy expenditure (fatigue prevents engagement in leisure activities) (Albrecht and Devieger 1999; Reid 2000). Answers to ethical questions are not easily attained and because they often involve conflicts of values it is difficult to resolve them to the satisfaction of all. For these reasons, we often look to guidelines or principles to guide our decision-making processes.

The dominant model of ethics is that of principlism or the practice of using principles to deal with moral problems (Hanford 1993). The principles of non-maleficence, beneficence, autonomy, justice and fidelity have been identified as universally accepted constructs of ethical theory and hence appropriate to healthcare, rehabilitation medicine and psychology (Haas and Mackenzie 1993; Kitchener 2000; Rumrill and Bellini 2000; Beauchamp and Childress 2001) and were used to inform the ethical use of the ICF (WHO 2001). Non-maleficence refers to the 'do no harm' maxim. In addition to ensuring that our actions do not subject persons to negative consequences, we are also bound to vigilance in assessing and eliminating potential risks and informing participants of the unintended risks that cannot be controlled. Beneficence, or acting in a manner that promotes the well-being of others, is the corollary principle to non-maleficence. In terms of Beauchamp and Childress (2001) collectively it means preventing harm, removing harm and promoting good. It refers to the positive purpose of adapted physical activity programming and policies in promoting the physical and social well being of others.

Creating learning environments based on adaptation principles to promote success demonstrates the principle of beneficence. Implicit in the principle of beneficence is that ethical obligation that the professional possesses the appropriate preparation and skills to support the person on whose behalf they are advocating or instructing.

Autonomy refers to the freedom of the individual to act independently, in accordance with one's interests, ambitions and values and the respect of others in their exercise of choice (Haas and Mackenzie 1993; Rumrill and Bellini 2000). This principle translates into the person's right to participate or not participate of his/her own volition and without negative consequence in programmes or activities. The person retains an absolute prerogative as to whether, with whom, when and to what extent he/she engages in an activity. Justice implies that services and resources and fairly dispersed according to need and not just those who are perceived to be most likely to benefit. In other words, no one is disadvantaged in the procurement of programmes and services. Fidelity is core to helping relationships as it means faithfulness. Faithfulness is manifest by honouring agreements, keeping promises, being honest, being devoid of deception and maintaining confidentiality—common ways of ensuring fidelity.

Challenges to the Field

The paper has focused on the ethics of independence and the ethics of support that are embedded in the professionally driven ideal of functional independence for persons with disabilities. It is difficult to discuss this topic area without asking questions about what constitutes ethical practice. There are many other ethical issues in the field of adapted physical activity that require consideration and discussion (e.g. waiting lists for adapted programming, availability of choice in programme offerings, evidence-based program-ming, confidentiality etc). The published literature addressing ethics practice in adapted physical activity and the preparation of our future professionals is woefully lacking.

In looking to principles or guidelines as a starting point for the discussion of ethics in our field, we must be cognisant of the medical model from which principlism is based (mind and body dualism and correction and normalising) and the extent to which the sociology of disablement is present in our discussions (disablement imposed by barriers of an excluding society) (Hughes and Peterson 1997). To not carefully negotiate both sides of the discussion, or include those with disabilities and those who reinforce or sustain disability through exclusion practices or omissions may result in the ethical deliberations being reduced to the status of that which must be controlled rather than the recognition that subjectivity focuses on the whole self and personal agency that is embedded in time and contexts (Clapton 2003; Clegg 2004).

Principlism can create an otherness that reinforces a sense of professional superiority over those on whose behalf we advocate (Hanford 1993). Further, principlism can promote a cookbook approach to ethics in which security can be taken in achieving the *right*, which can lead to complacency in the evaluation of the systems and institutions we create.

Considerable discussion is needed to meaningfully translate principles of ethics for the multiplicity of contexts of adapted physical activity (e.g. disability sport, educational settings, recreational contexts, instructional settings) and the various roles held by professionals (e.g. coach, mentor, instructor, assessor, classifier). I humbly suggest that leadership in the field of adapted physical activity is needed and further that there is a need to assemble a task force to examine ethical landscapes in adapted physical activity and how we are addressing professional practice; to publish the results of the task force discussions;

to develop ethical guidelines for professional practice in adapted physical activity; and to formulate education plans to promote ongoing awareness and debate exploring the efficacy of different formats (e.g. in-service, curriculum infusion, group discussion with team leaders, ethical consultants, video with group leader or self-instruction).

NOTES

1. The exception may be those who are employed as adapted physical educators with schools systems and are bound by the codes of conduct of their teaching associations or required professional certifications (Kelly 2006).
2. The focus of this paper will be persons with physical disabilities. The issues facing persons with developmental disabilities, their families and service providers have considerable overlap with those of persons with disabilities, but out of respect for the distinct challenges faced by both communities, for the purposes of this paper the discussion will focus on physical disability.

REFERENCES

ALBRECHT, G.L. and P.J. DEVLIEGER. 1999. The disability paradox: High quality of life against all odds. *Social Science and Medicine* 48: 977–88.

ARMSTRONG, D. 1995. The rise of surveillance medicine. *Sociology of Health & Illness* 17: 393–404.

ASCH, A. 1998. Distracted by disability. *Cambridge Quarterly of Healthcare Ethics* 7: 77–88.

BALTES, M.M. 1996. *The Many Faces of Dependency.* Cambridge: Cambridge University Press.

BARBEE, A.P. and M.R. CUNNINGHAM. 1995. An experimental approach to social support communications: Interactive coping in close relationships. *Communication Yearbook* 18: 381–413.

BEAUCHAMP, T. and J. CHILDRESS. 2001. *Principles of Biomedical Ethics,* 5th edn. Oxford: Oxford University Press.

BEDINI, L.A. 2000. 'Just sit down so we can talk': Perceived stigma and community recreation pursuits of people with disabilities. *Therapeutic Recreation Journal* 34: 55–68.

BRAITHWAITE, D. and N.J. ECKSTEIN. 2003. How people with disabilities communicatively manage assistance: Helping an instrumental social support. *Journal of Communication Research* 31: 1–26.

BRAITHWAITE, D.O. and N.J. ECKSTEIN. 2003. How people with disabilities communicatively manage assistance: Helping as instrumental social support. *Journal of Applied Communication Research* 31: 1–26.

BRICHER, G. 2000. Disabled people, health professionals and the social model of disability: Can there be a research relationship? *Disability and Society* 15: 781–93.

BROOKS, N.A. 1978. Receiving help: Management strategies of the handicapped. *Journal of Sociology and Social Welfare* 5: 91–9.

CACINOVIC VOGRINCIC, G. 2005. Teaching concepts of help in social work: The working relationship. *European Journal of Social Work* 8: 335–41.

CLAPTON, J. 2003. Tragedy and catastrophe: Contentious discourses of ethics and disability. *Journal of Intellectual Disability Research* 47: 540–7.

CLEGG, J. 2004. Practice in focus: A hermeneutic approach to research ethics. *British Journal of Learning Disability* 32: 186–90.

CONDELUCI, A. 1991. *Interdependence: The route to Community.* Winter Park, FL: GR Press.

COREY, G., M. COREY and P. CALLANAN. 1998. *Issues and Ethics in the Helping Professions,* 5th edn. Pacific Grove, CA: Brooks/Cole.

CUTRONA, C.E. and J.A. SUHR. 1992. Controllability of stressful events and satisfaction with spouse support behaviors. *Communication Research* 19: 154–74.

GABEL, S. and S. PETERS. 2004. Presage of a paradigm shift? Beyond the social model of disability toward resistance theories of disability. *Disability and Society* 19: 585–600.

GIGNAC, M.A.M. and C. COTT. 1998. A conceptual model of independence and dependence for adults with chronic physical illness and disability. *Social Science and Medicine* 47: 739–53.

GIGNAC, M.A.M., C. COTT and E.M. BADLEY. 2000. Adaptation to chronic illness and disability and its relationship to perceptions of independence and dependence. *Journal of Gerontology* 55B: 362–72.

GOFFMAN, E. 1963. *Behavior in Public Places.* New York: Free Press.

GOODWIN, D.L. 2001. The meaning of help in PE: Perceptions of students with physical disabilities. *Adapted Physical Activity Quarterly* 18: 289–303.

GOODWIN, D.L. and R. THURMEIER. 2005. Negotiating independence against the landscape of Physical activity. Presentation at the International Federation of Adapted Physical Activity Symposium, Vienna, Austria.

GOODWIN, D.L., R. THURMEIER and P. GUSTAFSON. 2004. Reactions to the metaphors of disability: The mediating effects of physical activity. *Adapted Physical Activity Quarterly* 21: 379–98.

GUSTAFSON, P. and D.L. GOODWIN. Transition from rehabilitation to community wellness: What does it take? Paper presented at the Leaders in Rehabilitation Conference, Calgary, AB, Sept. 2006.

HAAS, J.F. and C.A. MACKENZIE. 1993. The role of ethics in rehabilitation medicine. *American Journal of Physical Medicine and Rehabilitation* 72: 48–51.

HANFORD, L. 1993. Ethics and disability. *British Journal of Nursing* 2: 979–82.

HUGHES, W. and K. PETERSON. 1997. The social model of disability and the disappearing body: Towards sociology of impairment. *Disability and Society* 12: 325–40.

KELLY, J.E. 2006. *Adapted Physical Education National Standards.* Champaign, IL: Human Kinetics.

KERR, N. and L. MEYERSON. 1987. Independence as a goal and a value of people with physical disabilities: Some caveats. *Rehabilitation Psychology* 3: 173–80.

KITCHENER, K.S. 2000. *Foundation of Ethical Practice, Research, and Teaching in Psychology.* Mahwah, NJ: Erlbaum.

KOCH, T. 2001. Disability and difference: Balancing social and physical constructions. *Journal of Medical Ethics* 27: 370–7.

KUCZEWSKI, M.G. and I. FIEDLER. 2001. Ethical issues in rehabilitation: Conceptualizing the next generation of challenges. *American Journal of Physical Medicine and Rehabilitation* 80: 848–51.

———. 2005. Ethical issues in physical medicine and rehabilitation: Treatment decisions making with adult patients. *Critical Review in Physical and Rehabilitation Medicine* 17: 31–52.

LADIEU, G., E. HANFMANN and T. DEMBO. 1947. Studies in adjustment to visible injuries: Evaluation of help by the injured. *Journal of Abnormal and Social Psychology* 42: 169–92.

LLEWELLYN, A. and K. HOGAN. 2000. The use and abuse of models of disability. *Disability and Society* 15: 157–65.

MASALA, C. and D.R. PETRETTO. 2007. From disablement to enablement: Conceptual models of disability in the 20th century. *Disability and Rehabilitation* 29: 1–12.

MULDERIJ, K.J. 1997. Peer relations and friendship in physically disabled children. *Child: Care, Health and Development* 23: 379–89.

NADLER, A. and J.D. FISHER. 1986. The role of threat to self-esteem and perceived control in recipient reaction to help: Theory development and empirical validation. In *Advances in experimental social psychology*, edited by L. Berkowitz. New York: Academic Press.

NADLER, A. 1987. Determinants of help seeking behaviour: The effects of helper's similarity, task centrality and recipient's self-esteem. *European Journal of Social Psychology* 17: 57–67.

NAGI, S.Z. 1965. Some conceptual issues in disability and rehabilitation. In *Sociology and Rehabilitation*, edited by M.B. Sussman. Washington, DC: American Sociological Association.

OLIVER, M. 1989. Disability and dependency: A creation of industrial societies? In *Disability and Dependency*, edited by L. Barton. Bristol, PA: The Falmer Press.

PETERS, D.J. 1996. Disablement observed, addressed, and experienced: Integrating subjective experience into disablement models. *Disability and Rehabilitation* 18: 593–603.

PETERSON, D.B. 2005. International classification of functioning, disability and health: An introduction for rehabilitation psychologists. *Rehabilitation Psychology* 50: 105–112.

PETERSON, D.B. and T.T. THREATS. 2005. Ethical and clinical implications of the International Classification of Functioning, Disability and Health (ICF) in rehabilitation education. *Rehabilitation Education* 19: 129–37.

REID, G. 2000. Future directions of inquiry in adapted physical activity. *Quest* 52: 369–81.

REINDAL, S.M. 1999. Independence, dependence, interdependence: Some reflections on the subject and personal autonomy. *Disability and Society* 14: 353–67.

RUMRILL, D. and J.L. BELLINI. 2000. Perspectives on scientific inquiry: Ethics in the conduct of rehabilitation research. *Work* 14: 67–74.

SHAKESPEARE, T. 1998. Choices and rights: Eugenics, genetics and disability equality. *Disability and Society* 13: 665–81.

SHOGAN, D. (1998). The social construction of disability: The impact of statistics and technology. *Adapted Physical Activity Quarterly* 15: 269–72.

SNYDER, S.L. and D.T. MITCHELL. 2001. Re-engaging the body: Disability studies and the resistance to embodiment. *Public Culture* 13: 367–89.

TALEPOROS, G. and M.P. MCCABE. 2002. Body metaphor and physical disability: Personal perspectives. *Social Science and Medicine* 54: 971–80.

TURNBULL, A.P. and R. TURNBULL. 1985. Developing independence. *Journal of Adolescent Health Care* 6: 108–19.

UEDA, S. and Y. OKAWA. 2003. The subjective dimension of functioning and disability: What is it and what is it for? *Disability and Rehabilitation* 25: 596–601.

VERBRUGGE, L.M. and A.M. JETTE. 1994. The disablement process. *Social Science and Medicine* 38: 1–14.

WEGENER, S.T. 1996. The rehabilitation ethic and ethics. *Rehabilitation Psychology* 41: 5–17.

WHO (WORLD HEALTH ORGANISATION). 1890. *ICIDH: International Classification of Impairment, Disability and Handicaps*. Geneva, Switzerland: WHO.

———. 1997. *The International Classification of Impairments, Activities, and Participation: A Manual of Dimensions of Disablement and Functioning*. Geneva: WHO.

———. 2001. *ICF: International Classification of Functioning, Disability and Health*. Geneva: WHO.

Donna L. Goodwin, W1-67 Van Vliet Centre, Faculty of Physical Education and Recreation, University of Alberta, Edmonton, Canada T6G 2H9.
E-mail: donna.goodwin@ualberta.ca

CONVERSION GAIT DISORDER—MEETING PATIENTS IN BEHAVIOUR, REUNITING BODY AND MIND

Anika A. Jordbru, Ejgil Jespersen and Egil Martinsen

The Hospital for Rehabilitation, Stavern, in Norway has treated patients with physical symptoms with no organic cause, so called conversion disorder patients, for over a decade. For four years research on the treatment has been carried out. Patients with conversion disorder seem not to fit in traditional somatic hospitals because their patienthood depends upon psychiatric diagnosis. Ironically, they appear not to belong in psychiatric hospitals because of their physical symptoms. The treatment offered these patients at hospitals for rehabilitation is adapted physical activity consisting of behaviour elements such as positive reinforcement of normal function and lack of positive reinforcement at dysfunction. The pedagogical approach is seen as crucial in the successful rehabilitation of the patients. The disorder and treatment can be understood by using theories about the ecstatic body, radical behaviourism and phenomenology. When patients have problems in behaviour concerning both body and mind, it would be natural to employ both in the road to recovery. This article describes the various treatments and discusses them from phenomenological, ethical and philosophical perspectives.

Resumen

El hospital para la rehabilitación Stavern, en Noruega, ha tratado a pacientes con síntomas físicos sin causa orgánica, los llamados pacientes con desorden de conversión, durante más de una década. La investigación sobre el tratamiento ha sido llevada a cabo durante cuatro años. Los pacientes con desorden de conversión parece que no cuadran en los hospitales somáticos tradicionales porque su estado como pacientes depende de un diagnóstico psiquiátrico. Irónicamente, parece que no pertenecen en hospitales psiquiátricos a causa de sus síntomas físicos. El tratamiento que se ofrece a estos pacientes en los hospitales de rehabilitación consiste en una actividad física adaptada de elementos de comportamiento tales como el refuerzo positivo de la función normal y la omisión de refuerzo positivo de la disfunción. El enfoque pedagógico se entiende como crucial a la hora de la rehabilitación con éxito de los pacientes. La enfermedad y su tratamiento pueden ser entendidos por medio de teorías acerca del cuerpo extático, la teoría del comportamiento radical [radical behaviourism], y la fenomenología. Cuando los pacientes tienen problemas de comportamiento en cuanto a su cuerpo y mente, sería natural el implicar ambos en el camino hacia la recuperación. Este artículo describe varios tratamientos y los discute desde perspectivas fenomenológicas, éticas y filosóficas.

Zusammenfassung

Die Reha-Klinik Stavern in Norwegen behandelt seit mehr als einem Jahrzehnt Patienten, die körperliche Symptome ohne organische Grundlage aufweisen, sogenannte Konversionsstörungen. Es wurden über vier Jahre Behandlungsmöglichkeiten erforscht. Patienten mit Konversionsstörungen passen scheinbar nicht in traditionelle somatische Kliniken, da ihre Krankheit psychischer Natur ist. Ironischerweise gehören sie nicht in eine psychiatrische Klinik, da sie körperliche Symptome aufweisen. Die Behandlung, die diesen Patienten in Reha-Kliniken zuteil wird, besteht aus APA (adapted physical activity = Bewegung, Spiel und Sport in Prävention, Rehabilitation und Behinderung), insbesondere aus Elementen zum Verhalten, wie zum Beispiel positive Verstärkung normaler Funktionen und das Weglassen dieser Verstärkung bei Dysfunktionen. Die pädagogische Herangehensweise ist besonders wichtig für eine erfolgreiche Rehabilitation der Patienten. Zum Verständnis und zur Behandlung der Störung werden Theorien über ekstatische Körper, radikalen Behaviorismus und Phänomenologie herangezogen. Wenn bei Patienten Verhaltensprobleme auftauchen, die Körper und Geist betreffen, so erscheint es nur natürlich, beide in den Heilungsprozess einzubeziehen. Dieser Artikel beschreibt die verschiedenen Behandlungsmöglichkeiten und bespricht diese aus phänomenologischer, ethischer und philosophischer Perspektive.

摘要

在挪威有一家復健醫院叫 Stavern，是用無機的方式在治療病人的身體症狀，這種叫做轉換失調患者，這種治療方式已有十年之久。對於這種治療法的研究已經執行了四年。這類轉換失調患者似乎無法適應傳統的醫院，因為他們的病患需依賴一些精神病學上的診斷。諷刺的是，由於他們的身體症狀，他們並不隸屬於精神醫院中。 復健醫院提供給這些病患的治療處理方式是一種適應身體活動，這個活動內容包括對於正常行為機能的正向增強，並對於機能障礙部分減少正面的增強。教育學上的方法被視為對病患復健上的主要關鍵。這種失調及治療方法，可以藉由一種有關欣喜若狂的身體理論、徹底行為主義理論及現象學理論來理解。當病患在身與心的行為上有問題時，就很自然地去指引兩者到恢復的道路上。本文描述各種治療理論，並從現象學上、倫理學上及哲學的層次上來加以討論。

Introduction

What would you do if your legs suddenly where paralysed? You would probably become genuinely scared and seek a doctor to find out the reason(s) why. This article is about those who have undergone thorough medical examinations and yet are left with the conclusion that there is nothing wrong with them. Yet they are still not able to walk and there is no specific treatment for them.

Loss of walking ability without any organic cause is termed conversion disorder (Malt et al. 2003; Hurwitz 2004, 49; Krem 2004, 65), and this is classified among the 'somatoform' disorders. Freud used the term 'hysteria', which still is a term used for these kinds of paralyses (hysterical paralyses) (Torgersen 2002, 122). In Freud's days this was a well-known and more frequent condition. It is more rare in our time, and in many cases neither the patient nor the treating staff are familiar with it (Heruti et al. 2002). Today another form of illness in the intersection of body and mind, such as chronic fatigue syndrome, is more common. This is also a disorder with somatic symptoms, where no organic aetiology has been identified. The same principles of treatment seem to be effective for this disorder as well: adapted physical activity and cognitive behavioural therapy (Powell et al. 2004).

Persons presenting bodily symptoms without any organic illness seem to fit neither in the somatic hospital, as they have no organic illness, nor in psychiatric hospitals, because their main symptoms come bodily registered. In this paper we present challenges related to meeting patients with one of these illnesses, conversion disorder, who receive treatment in a somatic hospital with a specialist in adapted physical activity who is the main actor on the road to recovery.

This article aims to present the use of adapted physical activity in rehabilitation for conversion gait disorder and emphasises how adapted physical activities help persons to forget the body by using the body (Duesund and Skårderud 2003). Adapted physical activity is a tool to re-direct attention from the 'sick' body into activity and mastery, and may be viewed as an existential approach. This will be discussed in this paper, together with ethical and philosophical considerations concerning this treatment approach. But we start with some background information about conversion disorder and its treatment.

Classification and Understanding

The term 'conversion' was first used by Sigmund Freud (Torgersen 2002), who believed that the condition was caused by repression of forbidden impulses or conflicts which converted into physical symptoms. According to the ICD-10 classification system of the World Health Organisation (WHO) conversion disorder is a psychiatric diagnosis among the dissociative disorders. In the Diagnostic and Statistical Manual of Mental Disorders (DSM-IV), which is used in the USA (American Psychiatric Association 1994), conversion disorder is classified among the somatoform disorders. In both systems the disorder is defined as a condition with neurological symptoms where no organic cause of the disease is detected.

Patients with conversion disorder are heterogeneous, and various labels have been used to classify them. Commonly used terms to cover these patients and their maladies are 'medically unexplained condition', 'psychogenic disorder', 'functional disorder', 'somatoform disorder' or 'hysteria'. The inconsistency of nomenclature can affect what kind of patients are recruited in the various programmes/studies and this will affect the outcomes of these programmes/studies.

Somatoform disorders represent 25 per cent of patients consulting medical practitioners (Fink et al. 1999). The prevalence of conversion disorder varies between 0.01 and 0.03 per cent of the normal population (Malt et al. 2003). The disorder tends to be more common among females, but is longer-lasting among males (Sandanger et al. 1999). The typical time of onset of conversion symptoms is between the second and fourth decades (Sandanger et al. 1999; Reuber et al. 2005). The disorder seems to be more common in less developed countries (Malt et al. 2003).

Treatment

Patients with conversion disorder may experience severe and long-lasting dysfunction. In a study by Stone and co-workers including 60 persons with conversion disorder, 83 per cent still had serious dysfunction after 12 years (Stone et al. 2003). There are few good treatment studies (Moene et al. 2002; Brown et al. 2005). A controlled study by Moene and co-workers did not find any significant effect of adding hypnosis behavioural therapy (Moene et al. 2002). A retrospective study on the effects of behavioural therapy found good results in the short run, but the long term results were more uncertain (Stone et al. 2003).

A recent meta analysis concluded that it is possible to perform randomised, controlled treatment studies, but due to methodological limitations no firm conclusion about treatment effects could be drawn from the 260 studies that were scrutinised (Ruddy and House 2005). Adequate descriptions of patients included and treatment given were rare. Previous treatment studies have included various forms of psychotherapy such as short-term group therapy, cognitive behavioural therapy and psychodynamic psychother-apy (Brown et al. 2005; Reuber et al. 2005; Schwartz et al. 2001), and hypnosis (Moene et al. 2003, 51). Research suggest that each of these treatments can be used successfully to some extent, but the documentation is limited (Brown 2004, 130). Several studies report using physical training, defocusing on symptoms and focusing on achievement (Brazier and Venning 1997; Malhi and Singhi 2002; Calvert and Jureidini 2003; Shapiro and Teasell 2004). These studies report general improvement by using physical activity, but in none of the studies had patients been randomly assigned to various treatment conditions. In treatment projects, physical activity and psychiatric treatment are often combined, and this makes it difficult to evaluate what precisely it is that is seen to be working. Shapiro and co-workers found good results with interdisciplinary in-patient treatment (Shapiro and Teasell 2004). There is a need for well designed randomised controlled studies (Stone et al. 2003). Establishing and evaluating effective treatment for these patients is a major challenge.

Clinical Experience and Research from the Hospital for Rehabilitation

The Hospital for Rehabilitation in Stavern, Norway, has treated persons with conversion gait disorder during the last decade, using an interdisciplinary team consisting of a specialist in adapted physical activity (APA specialist), medical doctor, nurse, nurse assistant and usually a physiotherapist. A specialist in adapted physical activity is a pedagogue and uses pedagogical interventions as the main tool in his/her work. Adapted physical activity is an important part of the treatment. This implies using sport activities in spite of the dysfunction to increase function and mobility. This approach is built on the patients' own resources in order to make a change; the patient has to make an effort. This message is used to motivate patients to contribute to successful treatment. The education for a specialist in adapted physical activity is based on sport, activities, medicine and last but not least pedagogy. Pedagogy is a new profession in most hospitals. In the Hospital for Rehabilitation, Stavern, there are now ten pedagogues who are specialists in adapted physical activity, and pedagogy seems to be of increasing importance. The main focus of the APA specialist is to adjust activities to the dysfunction or illness. Pedagogy is a very important part of the work of the APA specialist in motivating, focusing on the positive aspects of the treatment, and in coaching people to bring out the best in themselves in order to achieve their goals. Training and exercise is a joint approach for the interdisciplinary team, but where the physiotherapist[1] conducts treatment on the affected/sick part of the body, the pedagogue uses sport activities such as bicycling, paddling, indoor climbing, archery and different ball games. A pedagogical approach is an important part of adapted physical activity, giving the persons opportunity for achievement, reaching their own goals and gaining self esteem.

Adapted physical activities are best performed in the natural environment, where the activities themselves give feedback. Here there are ample and important opportunities for positive reinforcement. Adapted physical activity gives natural motivation in multi-task activities, focusing on accomplishing the activities.

The model for treatment on conversion disorder comes from practical clinical experiences and it has been tested in a clinical trial (Jordbru 2006). Patients were recruited from neurological departments, and were randomised to immediate treatment or treatment after waiting three weeks (such were the 'controls' of the experiment). The level of function before and after treatment was assessed by standardised instruments and self-report questionnaires, and 11 patients with conversion gait disorder were included.

Patients significantly improved their general function and walking ability following a three-week rehabilitation programme, compared to controls on the waiting list. Patients kept their improvements at follow-up.

The Treatment Model at the Hospital for Rehabilitation

The treatment programme consists of physical training with a pedagogical approach. Cognitive behavioural elements are included, aimed at positive reinforcement of normal gait. If no improvement occurs, positive attention is held back.

The patients are treated by an interdisciplinary team comprising medical doctor, nurse, assistant nurse, physiotherapist and APA specialist. The team spends sufficient time discussing each client to reach a common understanding of the patients and their treatment. This enables all team members to meet individual patients with a consistent and common attitude. When patients receive the same response from all members of the staff, this facilitates change.

The programme includes four elements: (1) symptom explanation; (2) positive reinforcement of normal function; (3) lack of positive reinforcement on dysfunction; and (4) discharge if no improvement occurs.

1. Symptom Explanation

At admission the patient is examined by a medical doctor/specialist in rehabilitation medicine together with an APA specialist. The examination includes an adapted medical explanation of the patient's functional disturbances. Besides ordinary medical evaluation, the thorough explanation of the symptoms is seen as a therapeutic intervention and an important start of the treatment. Though medicine likes to think it has all the answers and is even able to transplant hearts, there is still no cure for the common cold. This we tell the patients too as well as saying that we do not really know the course for their symptoms, which is true. Furthermore, the patients are told that there is no exact explanation of the symptoms, only that it commonly arises from stressful life situations. Typically, explanations would entail telling the patient that thorough examinations show no critical illness or disease. In fact, these tests show that the central nervous system is in order and the muscles are intact. The doctor and the APA specialist reassure the patient that it is common to see a disconnection between the nervous system and muscles. And that there are good chances for reconnection by attending multi-activities focusing on achieving goals. By attending the programme the patient will be given guidance in what to do to get better. Further that it is possible to get well with training and quick recovery can be expected.

This is typically what we say:

> Neurological examinations have revealed that there is no organic cause. Both muscles and the central nervous system are intact. Still, sometimes the central nervous system looses track of the muscles. There are good chances for reconnection by attending to multi task activities focusing on achieving goals. We can help you get better. Medicine likes to think it has all the answers, being able to transplant hearts; yet we still have no cure for a common cold. We can't say why you lost control over your muscles, but it often happens in stressful life situations. We often see that this can happen, and we often see quick recovery, given the right treatment.

2. Positive Reinforcement of Normal Function

The patients work together with an interdisciplinary team, aiming at positive reinforcement of normal gait. The positive response is mainly oral, both during physical training as well as other daily activities. Patient goals are set in collaboration with the patient and the interdisciplinary team. An example might be: walk with two crutches the first week; then one crutch the second week; and finally without crutches the last week. When the patient does improve in gait or posture, the team reacts with positive reinforcement. Video feedback is used to illustrate progress, but mainly oral feedback is used in the training situations. Inpatients have contact with hospital staff on a 24-hour basis also outside training sessions, especially with nurses and nurse assistants during evenings and nights. Encouraging and reinforcing normal function is a joint treatment strategy, which also occurs when patients are not in training situations. This makes the institution a round-the-clock arena for treatment, aiming at encouraging independent function and normal gait.

3. Lack of Positive Reinforcement of Dysfunction

When improvement is lacking, the positive reinforcement from the interdisciplinary team is held back. The team aims to minimise the attention on sick or ill behaviour. This attitude is much more difficult to standardise, because care and consideration are a strong element in hospital treatment. But by emphasising the importance of this element in treatment, and drilling the personnel in this intervention, we believe that it can be accomplished. It is much more difficult to standardise the concern and attention from other patients, but the in-patient situation gives the staff some control over environmental contingencies.

4. Discharge If No Progress Is Achieved

The standard length for the rehabilitation is three weeks, but this will be reduced if no progress has taken place within the first week. Quick recovery is seen in most cases. For example, most wheelchair users start to walk with no assistant within two to three weeks. So it is safe to say that if this is the right rehabilitation for the person, some recovery should occur after a one week of intensive training.

An example of a typical day for a patient with conversion gait disorder at the Hospital for Rehabilitation, Stavern, could be as shown below, though not all days are equal and there are not always so many activities in one day.

08.30: Breakfast
09.30: Group training with a specialist in adapted physical activity
10.30: Individual training with a specialist in adapted physical activity (bicycling, outdoor walking, climbing etc.)
11.30: Lunch
12.30: Individual training with a physiotherapist
13.00: Pool activities in group
16.00: Dinner

In all of these activities the positive reinforcement of normal function and lack of positive reinforcement for dysfunction is carried out by the personnel at the hospital. Moreover, this process is carried over into daily living activities, such as getting up and into the bathroom in the morning, getting ready for the day.

Role of the Specialist in Adapted Physical Activity

In a hospital with an interdisciplinary team, the staff person with the main role in treatment will vary from patient to patient, and also for the same patient at different times in the rehabilitation process. In rehabilitation of conversion disorder, however, the APA specialist always plays the main role. This is logical as the main principles of treatment are pedagogical. We think there is an advantage in not being a healthcare professional, with its socialisation based on a trained focus upon diagnoses, attention to medical history and care-giving, tending or nursing. The APA specialist focuses on the healthy part of the person and on the resources, and is less focused on the symptom and lack of function. This may help convey a clear message that the person can get better simply by training and focuses on activities that persons with gait disturbance can do in spite of their dysfunction. The main goal is to shift the attention from 'cannot do' to 'can do'.

Treatment and Ethics

One of the aims in this article is to explore some ethical consideration about the treatment. Though the treatment previous described is recommended by a regional committee of ethics, an ongoing repercussion is still important.

The diagnosis of conversion disorder is set by excluding neurological injury or illness. The neurologists have a challenge offering an explanation of symptoms and treatment to a person with no organic illness, but who still has symptoms resembling those of neurological disorder. Some patients are left feeling mistrusted and stigmatised when they interpret their doctor's message as being like 'it is all in your head, the symptoms are something you're making up, get a hold of yourself and you will be all right'. In this section we will discuss the four elements of our treatment programme from an ethical perspective.

Explanation of the Symptoms

Persons with conversion symptoms have often received a variety of explanations or a lack of them from several doctors. There is great discomfort in thinking one has a serious neurological illness that is so severe that most doctors don't know what it is. Getting the feeling of not being taken seriously and therefore not examined thoroughly is even worse. An explanation of the symptoms is therefore an important part of the treatment. To accommodate a joint understanding of symptoms in the interdisciplinary team and with the patient, emphasis is put on presenting a good explanation.

This pedagogical approach with joint terminology and understanding of the treatment is achieved by extensive interdisciplinary cooperation between doctor, physiotherapist, APA specialist, nurse and nurse assistant. When in need of other professionals, such as for example a social worker or occupational therapist, a shared ideology gives further good internal communication. Many of those with conversion symptoms have previously been given a broad variety of explanations for their illness, by friends and relatives and other professionals in the healthcare system. The patients are given the same explanation consistently over time from different staff members working with them. This will validate the message and the credibility of the given explanation.

The aim of this pedagogical approach is to present for the patient an alternative understanding of his/her symptoms. One's imagination of one's body dictates the way one uses it (Indahl 2003). This means that if the patient's legs feel paralysed and the patient is afraid there is something dangerous wrong with them, the behaviour and the use of the body naturally will change. Careful symptom explanation, hopefully, helps the imagining of the body as something broken that can be fixed. In addition, the aim of the team is to obtain a standardised explanation model and common terminology within the interdisciplinary team, in order to minimise inconsistency between various team members.

There is no mention of psychiatric or mental disorders, or that it is all in their mind. One might argue that it is unethical not to mention that conversion disorder is a mental disorder. This could be seen as lying or deception, and that is not thought to be a good basis for a patient-therapist relationship. The aim is to communicate in such a manner that the patient receives messages that are useful. By indicating that symptoms are due to psychological factors, a patient's response might be an attempt to convince the staff that it is biological. This again might lead to increase in symptoms, and eventually new symptoms, which again would generate new rounds of medical investigations (Brazier and Venning 1997). The more seriously the patient is affected by these new symptoms, the more difficult it would be for others to question them. When further medical investigation has ruled out organic conditions, the possibility of a psychiatric aetiology often is raised. A vicious circle then ensues, with the consequence of an escalation of the problem. The availability of a face-saving medical intervention may allow the patient to get better. If no such intervention is offered, and/or the precipitating stressor is still present, then a safer response would be to maintain the symptoms (Fink et al. 2005).

Not labelling the symptoms as psychiatric also makes it easier to reach out with the message that this is not a dangerous disease but a condition where you can get better by your own efforts, in this case adapted physical activity. This is the major message to the patients. We argue that it is ethically acceptable to give adjusted information in the best of interest for the patient. This approach is important to strengthen the person's beliefs about his or her ability to solve their problems. It is important for people to contribute to their own personal health. Interdisciplinary cooperation is essential and an important contribution to success. Joint approaches make the patient feel safe and able to concentrate on the training and to get better. Although conversion disorder is labelled a mental disorder, we do not know its aetiology for sure and there is no available psychiatric treatment, neither psychotherapy nor medication. What we have is hypotheses and speculations about aetiology. Therefore, we do not lie when we say we do not know its aetiology.

Positive Reinforcement of Normal Function

An interdisciplinary team contributes with a joint treatment culture positively reinforcing normal gait. The underlying thought is simple yet useful. Behaviour will increase when it is rewarded. During admission the patients formulate specific and concrete goals for bodily improvement in cooperation with the interdisciplinary team. When patients during training improve gait ability according to their goals, a massive positive reinforcement is afforded. Video recording is used to encourage for more improvement and also allowing the persons to see how their walking patterns appears. When patients look at the recorded walk, many are surprised to see how they walk and comment how odd it is. Sometimes we take pictures or videos of the patients in activity using their own mobile phones. They can then send them to families and friends. Other patients show remarkable little satisfaction from improvement in function. Getting better can be scary: one implication for patients is that soon they will have to go back to their normal life. This entails being 'grown up' and requires the taking up of everyday responsibility which can be a bitter pill to swallow. Hearing about some of the patients' everyday challenges makes it understandable that some of them are in need of a break, to have time to recover and rethink their lives. But still, being paralysed is not the best way to solve a troublesome life situation. Being an in-patient, being taken seriously, given positive attention and mastering activities may give patients motivation and help to get their life and function back on track and enable them to make their lives better. Two statements from patients illustrate this:

> I was overwhelmed by being able to take some small steps today. It was a scary feeling. Maybe tomorrow I am a walking person. (Tina, 30 years old)
> I can't really go. I just walked, no, because you stood beside me. It doesn't count. (Sara, 32 years old

The approach with positive reinforcement can be described as operant behavioural treatment. This is often criticised for being manipulative. Yet the patient always has a choice. To take care of one's self-esteem and offer the patient face-saving opportunities is useful, whether improvement ensues or not. Accomplishing new skills and experiencing achievements are important elements of positive reinforcement. Patients who are not able to walk are given the opportunity to master activities such as bicycling, indoor climbing, kayak paddling, indoor activity, archery and golf. Those are high-status activities that contribute to self-esteem. The contradiction and variety in function, like for instance not being able to walk while being able to master cycling, is typical for persons with conversion disorder and is very untypical for all other kind of illness or injury. This, along with the often quick recovery, is fascinating.

The aim is to create a process where individuals regain improvement in gait, and hopefully this contributes to better self-esteem and an ability to improve life situations in general.

Lack of Positive Reinforcement by Dysfunction

It is an everyday ethical expectation in our culture that we give attention and care to those who are sick, both generally and specifically in the world of medicine. Being sick is a ticket to treatment, but also, for many, to a means of getting care and consideration from friends and family. This can cause secondary sickness advantages for patients. During three weeks of interdisciplinary treatment at the Hospital for Rehabilitation, Stavern, all this is turned upside down. When patients do not show any improvement, positive reinforcement is withheld. To gain positive feedback patients have to make an effort that leads to an improvement in function. The team gives massive positive feedback on achieving goals. The positive feedback has to be due to real improvement and be meaningful to the patient. Giving attention and support to negative behaviour may lead to increase in helplessness and therefore reduced function.

The patient's focus on symptoms and demonstrations of dysfunction is given minimal attention, but not totally ignored. It is important to reassure the patient that members of the staff see them and care about them. This kind of 'ignoring' of symptoms and maladaptive behaviour often seems unnatural for healthcare workers but is in fact a crucial ingredient in the treatment of conversion symptoms. The APA specialist plays an important role here by overlooking limitations and focusing on achievements in spite of dysfunction. An APA specialist aims at achieving during activities, by defocusing on symptoms. This corresponds with the treatment strategy for conversion disorder. When patients receive attention or material benefits when expressing subjective health complaints and loss of function, this response will positively reinforce the symptoms and contribute to their maintenance.

Discharge If No Progress is Achieved

Having discussed the lack of attention given to dysfunction or to the lack of improvement, as in the third element above, a consequence of no progress for patients is to be discharged. If no progress has taken place, there is no use staying in hospital because this may reinforce the experience of being ill. One might argue that one week is a very short time for a paralysed person to achieve improvement. Based, however, on the fact that there are no neurological malfunctions and no muscular atrophy, a quick recovery is indeed to be expected. Persons who are dependent on a wheelchair and need help with daily living activities become independent and are able to walk after three weeks. After one week the interdisciplinary team can therefore give a qualified judgement of whether or not the patient will benefit from further treatment. Keeping a person in an institution for three weeks while they know that they are most likely to experience failure will decrease the person's self-esteem and well-being, and is therefore considered unethical.

Phenomenological Perspectives

A phenomenology of the body provides perspectives on the relation between the body as an object and the body as a subject. This calls for an existential dimension in the treatment of conversion gait disorder. An example from the clinical practice at the Hospital for Rehabilitation in Stavern serves to illustrate this.

The patient is a 50-year-old woman, sitting in a wheelchair, unable to walk. Outside the hospital there is a building with regular bicycles. I tell the patient that that since her central nervous system and muscles are intact, they may get connected when she tries to perform a familiar activity such as bicycling. She is sceptical at first, but I manage to convince her that I really believe she can do this. We both find nice bikes and put on our helmets. After helping her on the bicycle I hold her for a couple of metres. Then I let her go on by herself while I am getting on my bike. The crucial point is that I believe she can do it, and my actions confirm what I believe. After one kilometre we are back where we started and the woman is reinstalled in her wheelchair. This illustrates how the APA specialist uses adapted physical activity to put attention away from the gait-disturbed body. Mastering the activity hopefully gives a feeling of flow and makes the person to forget the body. This feeling can also be described as existential. Leder (1990) has described three bodily dimensions to illustrate the process of being present in the world. These three dimensions are: the recessive body, the dys-appearing body and the ecstatic body.

The recessive body is the physical body, such as heart, lungs, liver and so on. When one examines the body with an X-ray or CT scan one can find out whether the recessive body is sick or healthy. Patients go through such examinations before the diagnosis of conversion disorder is established. One can say that in this case the recessive body has no signs of disease, and this is what the neurologists conclude when they tell patients who are paralysed—that there is nothing wrong with them. It is a paradox that specialists in medicine conclude there is nothing wrong with a person, when everyone else without any medical education can see that something must be wrong.

The dys-appearing body presents itself when something is broken or troublesome in the body. Most of us usually can walk up and down stairs without thinking about it. It is just something we do to get somewhere, probably thinking about something else that we are occupied with. But if your leg is broken, for instance, and you need crutches, then walking on stairs would be troublesome and you would notice the body as it struggled to get up or down a stair. The body would be dys-appearing.

Merleau-Ponty highlighted the meaning of setting aside the mechanistic construction of the body as a machine in order to explore the body as ecstatic in the world (Leder 1990). We are our bodies, meaning that when the body is functional we are not aware of it; the body is not in our consciousness. Being ecstatic means being engrossed and unconscious of our body. The ecstatic body forgets it own body because it is preoccupied with something else. The body is present in an absent way. An example would be an activity such as walking without thinking about the activity or the body. The body is unconscious for us. But if one has trouble walking, the essential feeling will be ripped apart, and the focus will be upon the body. The troubled body takes all the attention. According to this you could say that conversion disorders will disturb the ecstatic body.

Our intervention is a form of behaviour therapy. As in behaviour theory, the treatments at hospital for Rehabilitation in Stavern reward a wanted behaviour—here normal gait. This form of therapy has often been criticised. However, a radical phenomenology of behaviour may shed some new light on this relationship.

Skinner (1904–1990) established his own philosophy of science: radical behaviourism. He examined behaviour in a psychological perspective in a manner close to a traditional scientific approach. Perhaps his main lesson was this: reinforcement means learning. Despite their paradigmatic differences, one of the primary aims of an explicitly phenomenological approach is to let what is given appear as pure phenomenon (the thing as meant) and then work to describe the invariant features of such phenomena (Toombs 2001).

The theory of phenomenology gives insight in humans' perspective of their body as something different from that of naturalism and objectivism. Phenomenology brings in a holistic way of thinking that many of us take for granted and that is implemented in our daily life. Merleau-Ponty maintains that the body does not contain an either/or but a both/and (Leder 1990). The body is both subject and object, with a simultaneous and mutual relationship between these levels. People with physical disability often criticise other people for just seeing them as disabled (object) instead of their real them as a person (subject) (Duesund 1995). In contrast, it might seem like people with conversion disorder prefer (unconsciously or otherwise) to be seen as an object with a dysfunctional body, instead of the real them. Phenomenology provides an explication of the fundamental and important distinction between the immediate pre-theoretical experiencing of the world of everyday life and the theoretical, scientific account for such experience.

Radical behaviourism and phenomenology are usually seen as two very different perspectives, but show some remarkable similarities, especially in their rejection of the dualistic philosophy (Kvale and Grenness 1967). In that way it is relevant for meeting patient in between body and mind.

In the following some similarities between the radical development of behaviourism by Skinner and the phenomenology of Merleau-Ponty will be presented. They both strongly objected to what may be called 'the illusion of the double world'. The double world involves the assumption of an external, objective, physical world and its internal, subjective psychological copy (Kvale and Grenness 1967). Skinner and Merleau-Ponty argue that perception is no duplicating of the external world into an internal one. And just as action reaches to the world directly, so does perception. The phenomenologist further claims that by discarding what Merleau-Ponty has termed 'the prejudice of the objective world', no inner reduplication is necessary to account for our perception of the world. By arguing that the individual simply reacts to his/her environment, rather than to some inner experience of that environment, the bifurcation of nature into physical and psychic can be avoided (Kvale and Grenness 1967) It is most convenient, for both patients and therapists, if the external world is never copied—if the world we know is simply the world around us. A parallel to the illusion of the double world is what Skinner has termed 'the flight to the internal man'. Just as psychology had to create an internal world to account for perception, it had to construct an internal man to account for action. This 'internal man' is rudiment of the now unacceptable 'soul' but in a disguised form. The 'inner man' is especially distinct within psychoanalytic therapy with its id-ego-superego. Merleau-Ponty elaborates a conception of the relationship between the body and the soul that both retains and transforms the conception of consciousness and nature. This way of thinking and taking the whole body into account seems to be a useful thing to consider when treating a person with conversion disorder.

Conclusion

Our guiding aspiration is to meet patients in behaviour while reuniting body and mind. Perhaps it is more correct to say that we aim at a meeting of patients concerning both body and mind. It would be helpful to erode the black-and-white distinction between the body and the mind. Conversion disorder is a mix of embodiment and mind. The symptoms reveal themselves in the body, but we believe they have a mental source and nature. That is why we need to take the whole body into consideration when treating this disorder. The Hospital for Rehabilitation in Stavern is a somatic hospital and the treatment is based on adapted physical activities. If a patient cannot walk, then that is what we will focus on. But the adaptations and adjustment of the activities function better when they are integrated in a pedagogical/psychological frame. Conversion disorder was conceived of as a medical illness among the ancient Egyptians (Krem 2004) and a mental disorder in Freud's time. Now maybe it is time to give them both their due, meeting the patients in behaviour reuniting the body and the mind.

NOTE

1. Here the role of therapist and pedagogue are described in a stereotypical way for ease of explanation whereas in reality matters are less clear cut.

REFERENCES

AMERICAN PSYCHOLOGICAL ASSOCIATION. 1994. *Diagnostic and Statistical Manual of Mental Disorders (DSM-IV)*. Washington DC: Pilgrim Press.

BRAZIER, D.K. and H.E. VENNING. 1997. Conversion disorders in adolescents: a practical approach to rehabilitation. *British Journal of Rheumatology* 36 (5): 594–8.

BROWN, R.J. 2004. Psychological Mechanisms of medically unexplained symptoms: An integrative conceptual model. *Psychological Bulletin* 130 (5): 793–812.

BROWN, R.J., A. SCHRAG and M.R. TRIMBLE. 2005. Dissociation, childhood interpersonal trauma, and family functioning in patients with somatization disorder. *American Journal of Psychiatry* 162 (5): 899–905.

CALVERT, P. and J. JUREIDINI. 2003. Restrained rehabilitation: An approach to children and adolescents with unexplained signs and symptoms. *Arch. Dis. Child* 88 (5): 399–402.

DUESUND, L. 1995. *Kropp, kunnskap og selvoppfatning* [The Body in the World]. Oslo: Universitetsforlaget.

———. 2003. *Kroppen i verden*. Oslo: Universitetsforlaget.

DUESUND, L. and F. SKÅRDERUD. 2003. Use the body and forget the body. Treating anorexia nevrosa with adapted physical activity. *Clinical Child Psychology and Psychiatry* 8 (1).

FINK, P., M. ROSENDAL and F. OLESEN. 2005. Classification of somatization and functional symptoms in primary care. *Aust N Z J Psychiatry* 39 (9): 772–81.

FINK, P., L. SORENSEN, M. ENGBERG, M. HOLM, and P. MUNK-JORGENSEN. 1999. Somatization in primary care: Prevalence, health care utilization, and general practitioner recognition. *Psychosomatics* 40 (4): 330–8.

HERMANSEN, M. 1996. *Læringens Univers* [The Educational Universe]. Århus: Klim forlag.

HERUTI, R.J., A. LEVY, A. ADUNSKI and A. OHRY. 2002. Conversion motor paralysis disorder: overview and rehabilitation model. *Spinal Cord* 40 (7): 327–34.

HURWITZ, T.A. 2004. Somatization and conversion disorder. *Can J Psychiatry* 49 (3): 172–8.

INDAHL, A. 2003. *Når ryggen krangler* [When the Back Acts up]. Norway: Valdisholm forlag.

JORDBRU, A.A. 2006. *Når å gå går i stå. Multidisiplinær rehabilitering av konversive gangforstyrrelser* [Multidisciplinary Rehabilitation on Conversion Gait Disturbance, a Randomised, Controlled Study]. Oslo: Norges Idrettshøgskole.

KREM, M.M. 2004. Motor conversion disorders reviewed from a neuropsychiatric perspective. *J Clin. Psychiatry* 65 (6): 783–90.

KVALE, S. and C.E GRENNESS. 1967. Skinner and Sartre: Towards a radical phenomenology of behavior? *Review of Existential Psychology and Psyciatry* 7: 128–50.

LEDER, D. 1990. *The Absent Body*. Chicago: University of Chicago Press.

MALHI, P. and P. SINGHI. 2002. Clinical characteristics and outcome of children and adolescents with conversion disorder. *Indian Pediatr* 39 (8): 747–52.

MALT, U.F., N. RETTERSTØL and A.A DAHL. 2003. Psykosomatiske lidelser [Somatisation disorder]. *Lærebok i psykiatri*, 403–50. Oslo: Gyldendal Akademisk.

MOENE, F.C. 2003. A randomized controlled trial of hypnosis-based treatment for patients with conversion disorder, motor type. *Clin Exp Hypn* 51: 29–50.

MOENE, F.C., P. SPINHOVEN, K.A. HOOGDUIN and R. VAN DYCK. 2002. A randomized controlled trial on additional effects of hypnosis in comprehensive treatment programme for inpatients with conversion disorder of the motor type. *Psychoter Psychosom* 71 (71): 66–76.

POWELL, PAULINE, RICHARD P. BENTALL, FRED J. NYE and RICHARD H.T. EDWARDS. 2004. Patient education to encourage graded exercise in chronic fatigue syndrome: 2-year follow-up of randomised controlled trial. *The British Journal of Psychiatry* 184 (2): 142–6.

REUBER, M., A.J. MITCHELL, S.J. HOWLETT, H.L. CRIMLISK and R.A. GRUNEWALD. 2005. Functional symptoms in neurology: questions and answers. *Journal of Neurology, Neurosurgery and Psychiatry* 76 (3): 307–314.

RUDDY, R. and A. HOUSE. 2005. Meta-review of high-quality systematic reviews of interventions in key areas of liaison psychiatry. *British Journal of Psychiatry* 187: 109–20.

SANDANGER, I., J.F. NYGARD, G. INGEBRIGTSEN, T. SORENSEN and O.S. DALGARD. 1999. Prevalence, incidence and age at onset of psychiatric disorders in Norway. *Soc. Psychiatry Psychiatr. Epidemiol* 34 (11): 570–9.

SCHWARTZ, A.C., A.W. CALHOUN, C.L. ESCHBACH and B.J. SEELIG. 2001. Treatment of conversion disorder in an African American Christian woman: cultural and social considerations. *American Journal of Psychiatry* 158 (9): 1385–91.

SHAPIRO, A.P. and R.W. TEASELL. 2004. Behavioural interventions in the rehabilitation of acute v. chronic non-organic (conversion/factitious) motor disorders. *The British Journal of Psychiatry* 185 (2): 140–6.

STONE, J., M. SHARPE, P.M. ROTHWELL and C.P. WARLOW. 2003. The 12 year prognosis of unilateral functional weakness and sensory disturbance. *Journal of Neurology, Neurosurgery and Psychiatry* 74 (5): 591–6.

STONE, J., R. SMYTH, A. CARSON, S. LEWIS, R. PRESCOTT, C. WARLOW and M. SHARPE. 2005. Systematic review of misdiagnosis of conversion symptoms and 'hysteria'. *BMJ* 331 (7523): 989.

TOOMBS, S.K. 2001. *Handbook of phenomenology and medicine.* London: Kluwer Academic Publishers.

TORGERSEN, S. 2002. Genetikk og somatoforme forstyrrelser [Genetics and somatisation disorder]. *Tidsskrift for Den norske lægeforening* 122 (14): 1385–8.

WHO (WORLD HEALTH ORGANISATION). 2000. ICD-10 *Internasjonale statistiske klassifikasjon av sykdommer og beslektede helseproblemer.* Oslo: Eladerst Publishing AS.

Anika A. Jordbru (corresponding author), Rikshospitalet University Hospital HF, Hospital for Rehabilitation, PO Box 160, 3291 Stavern, Norway, and Norwegian School of Sport Sciences, Department of Physical Education.

E-mail: Anika.Jordbru@rehabilitering.net

Ejgil Jespersen, Norwegian School of Sport Sciences, Department of Physical Education

Egil Martinsen, Aker University Hospital, Clinic for Mental Health

CELEBRATING THE INSECURE PRACTITIONER. A CRITIQUE OF EVIDENCE-BASED PRACTICE IN ADAPTED PHYSICAL ACTIVITY

Øyvind F. Standal

Over the past decade there has been a trend within adapted physical activity (APA) to question the hegemony of the medical understanding of disability. This debate has consequences for professional practice, which some argue should be regarded as a learning situation with a pedagogical orientation. The concept of evidence-based practice and research has spread from its origin in medicine to other allied health fields and education. In this article I discuss the limitations of applying evidence-based practice to a pedagogical approach to APA. More specifically, I use the Aristotelian notion phronesis to show that professional practice of APA is essentially characterized by an indeterminacy that cannot be eradicated through the technological thinking inherent in evidence-based practice.

Resumen

Durante la última década ha habido una tendencia dentro de la actividad física adaptada (AFA) [adaped physical activity (APA)] a cuestionar la hegemonía de la concepción médica de la discapacidad. Este debate repercute en la práctica profesional, que algunos arguyen, debería ser considerada como una situación de aprendizaje con una orientación pedagógica. El concepto de práctica basada en la evidencia se ha extendido desde su orígen en medicina a otros campos de la salud aliados y la educación. La posibilidad de práctica basada en la evidencia ha sido debatida en el campo de la AFA hasta cierto punto. Dado que el campo de la AFA misma se encuentra en un proceso de redefinición como una profesión que depende de más perspectivas que las meramente médicas, este artículo indaga algunos problemas potenciales al aplicar una conceptualización de práctica professional que ha surgido desde el campo de la medicina.

Zusammenfassung

Über die letzten zehn Jahre zeichnete sich innerhalb der APA (adapted physical activity = Bewegung, Spiel und Sport in Prävention, Rehabilitation und Behinderung) ein Trend ab, der die Vormachtstellung des medizinischen Verständnisses von Behinderung infrage stellt. Diese Debatte hat Konsequenzen für die professionelle Praxis, von der einige behaupten, sie sei als pädagogische Lernsituation zu betrachten. Das Konzept der evidenzbasierten Praxis und Forschung hat sich von seinen Ursprüngen in der Medizin in andere gesundheitsbezogene Felder weiter verbreitet. Die Möglichkeiten der evidenzbasierten Praxis wurden bisher nur in begrenztem Maße in der APA diskutiert. Dieser Artikel untersucht potenzielle Probleme der Anwendung von Konzepten professioneller Praxis, wie sie sich seitens der Medizin verbreitet haben Dies geschieht unter der Annahme, dass dieses gesundheitsbezogene Feld von APA in seinem fachlichen Erneuerungsprozess von mehr als nur medizinischen Perspektiven abhängig ist.

摘要

在過去十年中，有一股針對適應身體活動 (APA) 的研究潮流，主要在於質問醫學上對於殘障理解上的權威性。這個討論的結果，對專業治療活動來說，在於有一些人主張，這種活動應被視為一種帶有教育學導向之學習情況。有關這種以證據為基礎的治療活動與研究已從醫學的源頭擴散到其它與健康及教育結合的領域上。這種以證據為基礎的醫療行為活動在適應身體活動中的探究目前只限於一小部分的研究群。由於 APA 這個領域現在目前正朝向重新定義其本身做為一種專業，其論點已超出僅是從醫學的觀點來看。本文在於探究出一些潛在性問題，是從醫學領域中所擴散出來而可應用在專業治療活動上的問題。

Adapted physical activity (APA) is a cross-disciplinary field of study that takes its theories and methodologies from the mother-disciplines physical education, medicine and special education (Reid and Stanish 2003). The focus of APA has primarily been directed towards professional practice in the sense that research and theory in APA aim at enabling 'professionals to interact with people experiencing difficulties with movement' (Reid 2003, 20). Thus, there is a strong emphasis on providing services that help people with disabilities (and others) who experiences difficulties with movement to take part in physical activities.

The historical roots of adapted physical activity can be traced to the system of medical gymnastics developed by the Swede P.H. Ling (Sherrill and DePauw 1997). In the early years of the discipline, people with disabilities were for the most part exempted from participation in physical education and sports, and if they did participate, expectations and challenges were low (Reid 2003). Physical activities were used almost exclusively as corrective therapy, in efforts to alleviate problems connected to people's impairments. As Reid (2003, 13) points out, 'The medical perspective of correctives was consistent with the historical fact that early physical education was dominated by physicians who realized that exercise were beneficial in the treatment of some physical disabilities.'

Over the past decade, there has been a trend in APA to question the hegemony of the medical understanding of disability (cf. DePauw 2000; Grenier 2007). More specifically, the critique is directed towards the idea of disability as a problem mainly connected to the individual's body, rather than seeing disablement as a socio-contextual process. The medical understanding of disability has, as DePauw (2000) pointed out, consequences both for research and practice. Research in APA has been characterised as an atomistic study directed at specific structures or functions of the body, seen unrelated to each other (DePauw 1997). Also the practice of APA has been characterised by a categorical approach to movement activities. A categorical approach is such that 'physical activity options and adaptations for an individual can be generalized based on the disability and the associated implications' (Emes et al. 2002, 404).

The notion of viewing APA as distinct from medical endeavours is not all together new. Hutzler (2007) refers to Lorenzen's German textbook on disability sports (*Versehrtensport*) from 1961, where Lorenzen made the distinction between disability sports and physical therapy. Whereas the former, according to Lorenzen, is based in a pedagogical perspective on participation in movement activities, the latter is based in a medical perspective. Physical therapy is founded on prescribed treatment of impairments; whereas disability sport is concerned with self-determined participation in physical activities, focusing on the whole person rather than her impairments (Lorenzen 1961, cited in Hutzler 2007, 48).

Emes and co-workers (2002) maintain that the trend of criticising the medical model in APA is not necessarily reflected in professionals' actual practice. In their critique of the medical dominance of professional practice in APA, these authors reached much the same conclusions that Lorenzen did: they advocated an abilities-based approach to professional practice where the focus is on 'the person in a learning situation' (Emes et al. 2002, 403) rather than in a treatment situation.

Thus, if we want to conceptualise professional practice in APA in a manner distinct from medical practice, it might be useful to see it as a learning process that aims at self-determined participation in activities that are experienced as inherently meaningful in the perspective of the participant. We can say that this is an educational[1] rather than a medical approach to professional practice.

To a very limited degree, evidence-based practice (EBP) has been debated in APA. An exception is Hutzler (2006, 13), who defines it as 'the conscientious, explicit and judicious use of current best evidence in making decisions about the professional service provided to participants in APA programs'. Hutzler argues that there is a need for more evidence-based research (EBR) in APA where there is a clear theoretical link between the intervention and the expected outcome effects.

EBP originated from medicine but has spread to other areas, e.g. education, nursing and social work. In educational research there has been a large debate about whether the principles of EBP can be imported from medicine (cf. Slavin 2002; Olson 2004; Biesta 2007). In this article I want to critically examine the idea of EBP as applied to APA. More specifically, I want to discuss the possible problems of applying a conceptualisation of professional practice that has emanated from medicine when the field of APA is on its way to re-defining itself as a profession relying on socio-pedagogical perspectives more than medical ones.

The Controversies of Evidence-based Practice in Education

Slavin (2002) states that education has not embraced the idea of developing scientifically based evidence-effectiveness. He notes that in other fields, such as medicine, transportation and technology, the adoption of EBP has lead to progressive, systematic improvement over time, something that has been lacking in education. Slavin maintains that change in educational practice is characterised as a process that 'more resembles the pendulum swings of taste characteristic of art or fashion' (Slavin 2002, 16). One of the reasons that educational practice has been condemned for being largely a matter of personal taste is that educational research has failed to deliver proper cumulative evidence that could guide practice as well as policy (Clegg 2005). The strategy behind advocating EBP in education is that it is thought to provide practitioners with a secure foundation on which to make their choices between different teaching methods and instructional strategies. In addition, policy-makers will be able to base their decisions on the best scientific evidence available. Thus, when properly conducted it is said that the adoption of EBR will improve the professional practice of education and will effectively inform decision-making regarding educational policies.

The idea that teachers and policy-makers should base their decisions on scientific evidence of what works, rather than according to the personal taste of the professional, seems reasonable. Why then has this issue sparked controversies? One answer lies in the forms of knowledge that are privileged in EBP. In relation to EBP, researchers will investigate whether an intervention gives an intended effect on those people receiving the intervention. The researcher wants to detect whether the intervention, and the intervention alone, causes the desired outcome. This means that researchers must use some form of experimental method, preferably the randomised controlled trial (RCT) (Slavin 2002). The RCT is reckoned as a 'gold standard' for EBR because it is the best 'methodological route to ferreting out systematic relations between actions and outcome' (Feuer et al. 2002, 8). The reason for this is that it tests the effects of a specific intervention in an experimental group, as compared to a control group, in a manner so that spurious causality and bias is removed. When properly conducted the difference in pre- and post-test results between the two groups can be ascribed to the intervention and the intervention alone. Other experimental studies deviate from the RCT in some ways, where the deviations result in confounding factors and increased risks of researcher's bias (hence, the notion of a gold standard). This produces a hierarchical system of evidence and knowledge, ranging from metasynthesis of RCTs to the lowest acceptable level, which is reports from expert committees (Odom et al. 2005).

An example of this hierarchy of knowledge and how it is implemented is found in the recommendations about physical activity for people with disabilities from the Norwegian directorate of health and social affairs (SHDIR) (SHDIR 2004). In the report, knowledge is graded in four levels, where levels one and two (highest) range from evidence generated from a metasynthesis of randomised controlled trials to other experimental studies; level three is evidence from well designed non-experimental studies; and level four is opinions from expert committees or clinical expertise.[2] Ideally, advice should be grounded in the theoretical knowledge from levels one to three (SHDIR 2004). Thus, the report from SHDIR follows the standard of prioritising scientific and theoretical knowledge.[3] The example from SHDIR, and EBP in general, indicate that:

> a common element across professions is the extent to which the legitimacy of professional decision-making is no longer based on what might be accounted as professional wisdom.... Instead [the legitimacy] is thought to reside in the weight of evidence, produced by other members of the community or by the researcher community, independently sifted through external review (Clegg 2005, 417).

The methodological hierarchy of EBP suggests that there is one best way of finding out what works. Berliner (2002, 18) argues, however, that seeing randomised controlled trials as *the* method for gaining evidence in education 'reveals a myopic view of science in general and a misunderstanding of educational research in particular'. More specifically, he points out that educational researchers must deal with problems like the power of context and the ubiquity of interactions, which limits the possibility of generalisations from experimental studies. The complex networks of social interactions that take place in an educational setting cannot be totally controlled and are thus confounding factors that makes it inappropriate to generalise findings.

A related issue is that in complex contexts, factors such as student characteristics, motivation, socio-economic status and curriculum material interact with each other in a myriad of reciprocal ways. Again, according to Berliner, the ubiquity of interactions limits the possibility of finding out what actually works. In education, both the inputs and outputs, and the relations between them, are highly complex (Berliner 2002; Clegg 2005). This means that one needs to question whether the practice of experimentation valued in EBR is in any way analogous to the practice of professional education where the experimental results are going to be applied.

In a critique of EBP in education, Biesta (2007) raises the question of whether there actually is a homology between medicine and education which could justify the application of EBP in education. According to Biesta, EBP conceives of professional action as a form of intervention. A consequence of this conception of professional practice is that it relies on a causal model: a treatment or intervention is administered in order to produce certain measurable effects. Hammersley refers to this as the linear model of professional practice, where 'it is assumed that [professional practice] should take the form of specifying goals explicitly, selecting strategies for achieving them on the basis of objective evidence about their effectiveness, and then measuring outcomes in order to assess their degree of success (thereby providing the knowledge required for improving future performance)' (Hammersley 2001, 3).

Both Biesta and Hammersley argue that this model of professional practice is defective, though not totally inaccurate, when applied to the educational domain. Professional practice in education usually involves multiple goals that are not readily operationalised in explicit terms (Hammersley 2001). The linear model also portrays the relation between means and ends as an external, causal one. Biesta objects to this by claiming that the means and ends of education are linked in an internal way. This is to say that the means 'contribute qualitatively to the very character...of the goals which they produce' (Carr 1992, 249, as quoted in Biesta 2007, 10). The means are not neutral but value-laden, and this is why most of us would not endorse corporeal punishment, even if it should be shown that this type of intervention is effective in producing better school results (Carr 2001). Interaction in education is thus not a neutral process of applying means to ends, but rather a value-laden practice.

Biesta further claims that through the rhetoric of EBP the only research questions regarded as relevant are those that deal with the effectiveness of interventions, i.e. questions of 'what works'. The question of what works is therefore prioritised to the exclusion of questions like 'effective for what?' Thus, according to Biesta, EBP leaves out questions of what is educationally desirable. Consequently, EBP severely limits 'the opportunities for educational practitioners to make such judgments in a way that is sensitive to and relevant to their own contextualised settings' (Biesta 2007, 5).

In summary, proponents of EBP claim that in order to give practitioners and policy-makers a proper foundation for decision-making, there is a need to investigate what works, primarily through some form of experimentation. Basing professional judgment on secure scientific evidence is the best way to ensure that the best possible services are delivered. The lack of EBP makes professional practice a matter of subjectivity and caprice, something that hinders the advancement of the particular profession.

The critique of EBP in educational settings is directed at the idea that there is not a homology between medicine and education. In particular, education is practised in a context that severely confounds the relationship between input and output, thus questioning the relevance of the evidence from experimental studies. In addition, EBP fails to address ethical aspects of professional practice. What works will always work with respect to given purposes, and cannot be considered neutral. Also, it is claimed that, unlike medicine, education is not an intervention with clear ends and well-defined means. The relation between input and output is not a matter of causality, but is found 'in the *interpretations* of the learner, in the divers ways in which learners·make sense of the situations they encounter' (Biesta 2007, 9, emphasis in original).

Professional Practice as a Hermeneutical Experience

Due to the practical orientation of adapted physical activity, it would not be very controversial to argue that the core of professional practice is the meeting between an APA professional, the participant and the subject matter (i.e. movement activities). As outlined above, it is now argued that this meeting should be conceived of as a learning situation (Emes et al. 2002) and thus a pedagogical process (Hutzler 2007). This has certain bearings on how professional practice should be conceived, and in relation to that I will again draw on educational literature.

In *Hermeneutics and Education*, Gallagher (1992) sees learning as an integral part of an educational process that has a hermeneutical structure. Gallagher (1992, 74) states that 'learning involves an essential incompleteness of knowledge, a noncoincidence between teacher and student, a hermeneutical circularity that remains open'. With this he suggests that both teachers and learners are involved in a hermeneutical process. The student tries to understand the subject matter, and this understanding is guided by preconceptions that both enable and restrict learning. The preconceptions give the student a context to which (s)he can relate the unfamiliar, but it also limits the possible interpretations that can be made. There is no such thing as unrestricted thinking. The teacher is similarly involved in acts of understanding. (S)he is, for instance, striving to understand how to present the subject matter and how to understand the students and their interpretations of her/his pedagogical presentation. These acts of understanding are always incomplete, and this incompleteness makes learning and education an interpretational process.

The incompleteness of the educational experience also gives way to an openness towards new possibilities. Though the interpretational process is conditioned by our preconceptions, the hermeneutical structure of the process also opens up a productivity that, as Gallagher says, goes beyond all intentions. The idea of going beyond all intentions signifies that education is a process that goes beyond what can be planned in advance. It is therefore in some respect always open to the unexpected and the unfamiliar. Education as such is not primarily a deliberate human practice, but a process that happens to us. Thus, education is not reducible to the controlled activities of teachers and learners or to the methodologically defined framework of educational institutions (Gallagher 1992).

Phronesis as a Model for Professional Practice

Gallagher (1992) argues that when learning and education are understood as having a hermeneutical structure, which always entails openness and uncertainty, professional practice should be modelled on the Aristotelian concept *phronesis*. Aristotle drew a distinction between three different forms of knowledge: *episteme*, *techne* and *phronesis*. According to Dunne[4] (1993) *episteme* was considered to be 'an object-domain which is limited to necessary and eternal being, and which therefore encompassed only mathematical entities, the heavenly bodies and the divine being or first mover' (Dunne 1993, 238). This means that *episteme* concerned theoretical reasoning about laws of nature, i.e. those things that exist out of necessity, uninfluenced by human beings. Separated from the theoretical domain is the domain of practical knowledge that encompasses *techne*, which is a form of productive knowledge, regarding the capacity to make, and *phronesis*, which is practical knowledge in a stricter sense of the capacity to act. The activity of *techne* was called *poiesis* and the activity of *phronesis* was called *praxis*:

> Production (*poiêsis*) has to do with making or fabrication; it is activity which is designed to bring about, and which terminates in, a product or outcome that is separable from it and provides it with its end or *telos*. *Praxis* on the other hand, has to do with the conduct of one's life and affairs primarily as a citizen of the *polis*; it is activity that leaves no separately identified outcome behind it and whose end, therefore, is realised in the very doing of the activity itself. (Dunne 1993, 244)

An important distinction between *techne* and *phronesis* is indicated in the quote above: The activity of *techne* leaves behind a product that is separable both from its maker (i.e. the person of *techne*) and the process of making it. When it comes to *phronesis*, there is no result that can be separated and identified apart from the act; thus its end is to be found in the very process of action, i.e. in *praxis* itself. So, whereas *techne* is thought of as applying means towards the realisation of an externally defined end, *phronesis* is is an end in itself.[5]

The distinction drawn up here refers to what Dunne calls the official notion of *techne* and *phronesis* in Aristotle (e.g. as the difference between making and acting, and between actions as means towards an end and actions as ends in themselves). Nevertheless, the relations between *techne* and *phronesis* are according to Dunne not as clear-cut and ordered as they seem on first sight. An illustration of this is two problems associated with Aristotle's account of *techne*: first, in some instances the product that is left after the exercise of *techne* is not a durable and material one. This is the case in movement activities. Gymnastics is, alongside for instance playing musical instruments, described by Aristotle as a *techne*, though it does not produce a material outcome, e.g. like the table made by a carpenter would be. Secondly, in some instances a definite result that endures after the exercise of *techne* is produced, but where the actor

> rather than having disposable materials upon which he can impress a preconceived form, the *technitês* here is more readily thought of as intervening in a field of forces, or as immersing himself in a medium, in which he seeks to accomplish a propitious end. . . . What characterises these technai is a close relationship – which does not obtain in the case of the more straightforward productive technai – with the opportune (*ho kairos*) and luck or chance (*tuchê*). (Dunne 1993, 254)

On the basis of this, it would be fair to suggest, I believe, that our topic – pedagogical work with movement activities for people with disabilities – is a case that subsumes both these reservations regarding the official notion of *techne*: For one thing, movement activities do not leave a durable and material result and is thus not a *techne* in the standard sense. The more important point is that pedagogical work is, as argued above, not the straightforward application of means to an end, but should more appropriately be thought of more as an intervention in a field of forces, where the teacher to some extent must adhere to the opportune.[6]

This would seem to imply that teaching of movement activities may not be thought of as *phronesis* in the first place, but rather as a special instance of *techne*. The origin of this complication lies in Aristotle himself, who speaks of the distinction between *techne* and *phronesis* as equivalent to the distinction between *poiesis* and *praxis*, yet also speaks in some instances of *techne* as a form of *praxis*: 'by speaking of a techne whose exercise is a praxis and not a poiesis, [Aristotle] seem[s] to buck the careful alignments (between poiesis and techne and praxis and phronesis)' (Dunne 1993, 254). Does this mean that trying to base professional practice on *phronesis* rather than *techne*, as Gallagher (1992) suggested, is in vain because the distinction cannot be upheld? Not necessarily. As David Carr states, 'the distinction grounds a significant difference between technical and moral modes of practical engagement with the world' (Carr 2003, 258).

So what are the significant differences between *techne* and *phronesis* that are relevant to professional practice? *Techne* might be said to portray pedagogical work as a mechanical process with the formulation of clear and explicit goals followed by teaching as a sort of technological application of instrumental steps towards the realisation of those goals. This is what critics of EBP are resisting, namely the attempt to make teaching a practice where scientific evidence of what works should be directly applied in teaching (cf. Biesta 2007; Hammersley 2001). The practical situations of teaching, and indeed other domains that are characterised by being highly contextualised, are governed by the urgencies and necessities of practical life (Bourdieu 1990). These contexts are changing and in constant flux. It is in these situations that *phronesis* is needed:

> Faced with uncertainty and the unfamiliar, the person with *phronesis* does not appeal to ready-made universal rules that would be applied in a mechanical fashion. Rather, action is guided by a finite understanding of the actual circumstance. Instead of classifying a specific circumstance under an already devised set of laws, *phronesis* calls for application in light of the existing situation within which the actor finds herself. In *phronesis* one approaches an understanding of the universal in light of the particular, rather than the other way around. (Gallagher 1992, 153)

As opposed to the technical approach, which subsumes the particulars of the situation under a predetermined (theoretical) framework, the phronetic approach is that good actions cannot be calculated from such a framework. Instead, '*phronesis* is a habit of *attentiveness* that makes the resources of one's past experience flexibly available to one and, at the same time allows the present situation to "unconceal" its own particular significance' (Dunne 1993, 305–6, emphasis in original).

The view of professional practice as the application of science-driven evidence (i.e. as *techne*) reduces teaching to a form of managerial expertise (Carr 2003). What *phronesis* brings about is an 'understanding of teacher expertise as practical wisdom ... [and] such expertise is not primarily a matter of skill acquisition at all' (Carr 2003, 260). *Phronesis* is not a skill that we possess and then apply to the problems at hand, i.e. something external to the agent. Rather, the agent is invested in her actions, so that *phronesis* is inextricably bound up with the person one is. There can be no split 'between what we might call its *being* and its *use* (or in Gadamer's terms between its 'possession' and its 'application') in the case of phronesis' (Dunne 1993, 268, emphasis in original).

Evidence-based Practice in Adapted Physical Activity

We are now in a position to discuss EBP and EBR in APA. This discussion rests on the basic premise that professional practice in adapted physical activity is seen as having an educational rather than a medical orientation.[7] The critical examination of EBP and EBR applied to APA will therefore draw on the outline of the same topic in relation to education given above. In addition, a couple of issues specifically related to APA will be pointed out.

Earlier, it was pointed out how 'the power context' (Berliner 2002) was used as an argument against the prominence given to experimental methods in EBR. The best way of conducting EBR is reckoned to be the randomised controlled trial, where confounding factors are controlled. The setting where such research is to be carried out must be sanitised or sterilised to the highest possible degree, as a laboratory is, in order to make sure that all participants receive the same intervention. Yet the contexts where APA is practised are social settings (much like those in education) that are not in the same way immunised against the unexpected. One can therefore suspect that the situation in APA is similar to education, in that 'broad theories and ecological generalisations often fail because they cannot incorporate the enormous number or determine the power of contexts within which human beings find themselves' (Berliner 2002, 19). Further, it could also be argued that the need to control the intervention, so that all participants receive the same treatment, is in serious conflict with the basic idea of APA: physical activity must be adapted to the individual participant. Adaptations produce an intervention that is unique to the individual (Olson 2004), and this creates problems for the researcher, who then seem to be trapped between the methodological requirements of the scientific method and the basic principle of APA. It also creates problems for the reader, because it will be difficult to determine the precise nature of the intervention. Thus, transferring evidence from randomised controlled trials in APA is perhaps not impossible. Yet it is undoubtedly a very *uncertain* project.

A counter-objection to this argument is that there are other means of securing evidence that does not rely on RCT. There are other experimental methods, for instance single-subject designs (Horner et al. 2005), that can protect against the criticism outlined above and thus make sure that practitioners can be guided by scientific evidence in their practice. In any case, evidence can only show us what work*ed* in a particular setting, with a particular group of individuals (Biesta 2007). It shows us what has been possible, but it cannot show us with certainty what will work in a different context.

In addition to the problems that the power of context create for experimental researchers in education, Odom et al. (2005) argue that researchers working with people with disabilities are faced with extra complexities, as compared to educational research. For one thing there is a greater variability among the participants. Diagnostic groups often contain people with very different problems. For instance, the movement difficulties in cerebral palsy range from almost unnoticeable to profound difficulties. Also, in many illnesses and disabilities there are different stages in the development of the condition. This means that researchers either must put together groups of participants who may have the same diagnostic label, but who have different challenges that would require different adaptations, or they face the problems of small groups, where it is difficult or perhaps not even realistic to build 'power of analysis' (Odom et al. 2005).[8] We saw an example of this above, regarding the recommendations from the Norwegian SHDIR about physical activity for people with disabilities (SHDIR, 2004). Though their hierarchy of knowledge suggested that they would have preferred knowledge from RCT or other experimental designs, they ultimately had to rely on knowledge from experts' opinions. The limited number of good experimental studies was thought to come from the difficulties in researching disability in movement activities (SHDIR 2004).

In the literature on adapted physical activity, the idea of self-determination has been advocated as an important strategy to move beyond the older expert systems of service delivery, where the professional was the expert and the participant a passive recipient of services (Reid 2003). If we understand self-determination in the everyday meaning of the word, as an experience of a sense of agency, control over one's life and participation in decision-making regarding oneself, then self-determination is a call for a person-centred approach to professional practice (Emes et al. 2002). Cott (2004) draws up the history of person-centred rehabilitation. In the old fashioned paternalistic system the patient was expected to follow the doctor's orders. Later, 'a rise in consumerism in the 1970s and 1980s led to a discourse which viewed the person with chronic illness as taking the more active role in decision-making' (Cott 2004, 1411). This development is parallel to that of APA described by Reid (2003), which has lead to the present prominence given to self-determination.

According to Cott, the introduction of evidence-based medicine in rehabilitation has led to a return to the expert system, where the patient rarely has a role in the decision-making process. In the old expert system, the participant was supposed to do what the professional said, because he was the expert. With the introduction of EBP, it could be suggested that the participant again has to follow the professionals' order, not because it is the expert who says what to do, but because science says so. It is therefore pertinent to ask whether the introduction of EBP in APA is at odds with a discourse of self-determination.[9]

Reconstruction: Arguments in Favour of EBP in APA

The above criticism of the possible application of EBP to APA paints a largely negative picture of research's application to practice. Let me therefore clarify this: I believe that practice can be improved when practitioners are familiar with important and relevant research results, but as Hammersley (2001) points out, it is possible to believe that research can be of value for practice without uncritically accepting all aspects of EBP. Just the fact that I feel driven to make this qualification points to a generic problem with EBP. As Hammersley captures it, 'its name is slogan whose rhetorical effect is to discredit opposition' (Hammersley 2001, 1).

Evidence in itself is principally neither good nor bad, regardless of how rigorous the methodology employed is (Clegg 2005). What the critique of EBP points towards is the danger in treating the research/practice (or theory/practice) gap as unproblematic. EBP should be neither dismissed nor accepted at face value, but must be examined in order to understand how evidence is construed in each particular case and how it 'can give insight into the structures, powers, generative mechanisms and tendencies that help us understand the concrete world of experience' (Clegg 2005, 421).

Bredahl (2007) has questioned the relevance of some forms of research in APA. She is critical towards the lack of meaning that certain research projects and results have for the everyday lives of people with disabilities. One possible benefit of EBP is that researchers should have to orient themselves towards the challenges that practitioners face in their professional practice. Involving practitioners in the formulation and design of inquiries could make the research in APA more appropriate if this leads EBR to address those challenges actually faced by practitioners. The outcome of such collaborative research might even be more efficient because the specifications of problems are directed towards issues that practitioners find problematic. Solutions to these problems might therefore better fit the understanding of the practitioners and thus ease the transition from research to practice.

More importantly, Bredahl (2007) also encourages including people with disabilities—the people for whom professionals and researchers in APA should be working—not only as research participants but also in the formulation of research topics. If research in APA truly aims at being relevant for a practice that is evidence-based, then researchers must make 'use of the unique knowledge and insight provided by those who live with a disability and who participate in physical activity' (Bredahl 2007, 77). In this sense EBR can make the scientific work done in APA more relevant both to practitioners and participants.[10]

Wilfred Carr (2007) argues that educational research should begin with an understanding of what education is like, rather than start with an idea of what the best practice of research is thought to be. In his view, one must determine what kind of knowledge can contribute to the development of the educational practice. The question for APA is accordingly what kind of practice it actually is. Only after that question is answered can one begin to ask what kind of knowledge is needed and how researchers should go about creating relevant research. This is especially important when one tries to apply a model of professional practice imported from medicine to a field that in many other respects tries to distance itself from the medical model of disability.

Celebrating the Insecure Practitioner

One of the ideas behind EBP is that it will provide practitioners a secure ground on which to base decisions about their practice (Slavin 2002). It gives the practitioner a sense of security to be able to say that the way (s)he works is evidence-based (e.g. 'research has shown that this is the best way to deal with your problem' or 'because you have that particular disease, scientific studies recommend that you perform this type of activity'). If, however, the arguments presented above regarding the problems of employing EBP are found to be convincing, then the sense of security that EBP gives might turn out to be a chimera amply supported by the whole weight of the scientific method.

By introducing the distinction between *phronesis* and *techne* (albeit with the reservations of how distinct their really are), it is suggested that *phronesis* goes against the technology of employing a practice based on scientific results. The idea behind EBP is a technical one, where the practitioner is more like a managerial expert than a reflective practitioner (Carr 2003). What *phronesis* helps us to see is that knowledge of the universals must be balanced with sound, professional judgement of the particular case at hand. This 'requires sensitive adaptation of general social or other rules to the needs... of the right person, at the right time, with the right motive and in the right way' (Carr 2003, 257).

Aristotle held that 'it is the mark of an educated man to look for precision in each class of things just so far as the nature of the subject admits' (Aristotle 1998, 3). This tells us that it is not only a matter of determining what kind of knowledge is needed, but also a matter of determining the degree of exactness that can be expected in a given domain. In APA, the general principle is that individual solutions ought to be found for each particular participant and her/his specific difficulties with movement. As Jones (2007, 159) has pointed out in a different context, pedagogical work 'as opposed to being a reductive, knowable process that can easily be followed, is instead problematic, multifaceted and fundamentally intertwined with teaching and learning at the micro-interactive level within given situational constraints'. Consequently, each professional encounter in APA involves a degree of uncertainty. It cannot be planned in advance and must remain open to the flux of the learning situation.

The insecurity that I celebrate does not amount to a lack of knowledge. Instead of being ignorant, the insecure practitioner has knowledge of the universals. At the same time, (s)he is also aware that this knowledge must be balanced with a sound appreciation of the particulars of each case. Accepting the insecurity faced by practitioners of APA requires that we must recognise that the kind of deliberation and action that is needed in their practice involves understanding in addition to knowledge. Understanding is practical-moral activity that is concerned more with engaging with that which is to be understood, than grasping the content of it (Schwandt 1999).

Further, recommending a healthy portion of insecurity does not mean that practitioners should become paranoid or paralysed in their actions: It does not amount to a throwing one's hands up in despair. Accepting and working with insecurity both grants and requires an openness towards the unfamiliar and unpredictable. As a positive term, the insecure practitioner is constantly learning by being 'drawn out of himself towards his own possibilities and is remade by his experience' (Gallagher 1992, 189). This learning involves a changed self-understanding or character formation (Carr 2003), which is of a very different kind than the learning achieved through objectively evaluating the effects of one's intervention. Though it is not suggested that the latter holds no importance, it is clear that such evaluative information is external to the professional practitioner as an agent.

Phronesis, which necessarily involves the self of the practitioner, is learned through practicing *phronesis* (e.g. in order to be brave, I have to do brave deeds), so that the self-transformation of the insecure practitioner is part of a 'practice-promoting-practice' (Carr 2003, 259). It could be suggested that the outcome of insecure practices is not accumulation of experience in order to become more secure, but rather developing ways of handling the inescapable insecurity. This is a positive outcome for the insecure practitioner, and an important one too.

Conclusion

The point of using 'the insecure practitioner' has been to get a lens through which we can come to better appreciate that the flux of learning situations cannot be controlled by EBP. To the contrary, the idea of the insecure practitioner suggests that in a time of increasing technologisation of professional practice, some more tentativeness is needed in order to be open to possibilities that go beyond the notion of *techne*.

In medicine, from where EBP emanates, there is an understanding that evidence of what works must be balanced with the independent judgement of professional expertise: Evidence-based medicine is 'about integrating individual clinical expertise and the best external evidence' (Sackett et al. 1996, 71). Evidence is but one, and certainly not the only, factor driving clinical practice (Biesta 2007). On the basis of the critical discussion of EBP in relation to APA, I maintain that it is important for APA professionals to be granted the same degrees of freedom, so that they are not only supposed to apply evidence of what works to their practice. There must be an open space in professional practice where the practitioner is allowed to navigate between the universals and the particulars according to his or her professional judgement. This space opens up the possibility of engagement with the unpredictable and unfamiliar. Insecurity need not be a paralysing condition that disables the practitioner. Rather, through meeting the unfamiliar with a productive insecurity, the practitioners are involved in a process of transforming their self-understanding.

ACKNOWLEDGEMENTS

The author would like to thank professor Kjetil Steinsholt and the editors for helpful comments on the manuscript. This article is part of a larger project funded by the a grant from *Helse og Rehabilitering*.

NOTES

1. Here it must be pointed out that in the APA literature education is almost exclusively connected to the instruction of school-aged children (cf. Porretta et al. 1993; Sherrill 2004). However, as Morisbak (1988, 73) pointed out, an educational approach is to be understood more broadly encompassing organised physical activity not only in 'schools, [but also in] sports competitions, recreational activities and remedial/corrective therapies'.

2. This hierarchy is identical to the one developed by the Oxford Centre for Evidence-based Medicine (Odom et al. 2005). Note also here that on level four one leaves the secure foundation of evidence and enters the dubious terrain of opinions.

3. It should be noted that due to the lack of scientific evidence, the recommendations actually given by SHDIR draw to a large extent on experiences from experts in the field (i.e. level four). In addition to lack of scientific evidence, the report also states that the large variation in how different disabilities affect the individual 'makes a clear approach difficult' (SHDIR 2004, 9). This important point will be discussed below.

4. In order to understand the concept *phronesis*, I will mainly draw on Joseph Dunne's seminal book *Back to the Rough Ground*, which is a philosophical exposition of Aristotle's distinction between *techne* and *phronesis* motivated from problems in the educational domain, not too distant from the challenges regarding EBP.

5. Dunne notes that seeing something as an end in itself is somewhat problematic because it operates within the rational logic of means to ends. The full significance of *phronesis* is according to Dunne not to be grasped 'unless we see that it involves nothing less than what Gadamer calls a "fundamental modification" of the means-end framework' (Dunne 1993, 262).

6. This does not mean that pedagogical encounters are totally subjected to chance. However, 'the play of chance is simply ineliminable', so that what is required is a 'flexible kind of dynamism.... [T]his is the meaning of *kairos*; one's active intervention has skilfully awaited until one's polyvalent materials – be they the wind and the waves in play upon one's boat or the changing humors in the sick body – are at their most propitious, i.e. are most able to help, or at least able to hinder, the accomplishment of one's end' (Dunne 1993, 256).

7. Even if this premise is not universally accepted, and APA is still conceived of as a medical practice (as it indeed sometimes will be), there will still be at least a marginal room for the critical approach offered here. For instance Svenaeus (2000; 2003) has discussed the non-technical nature of medical practice, and the need for the general physician to exhibit *phronesis*.

8. Implicit in this argument is the idea that research in special education, and in APA, uses medical diagnostics as the groups or labels whereby research participants are divided into to intervention and control group. With regard to APA, one can ask how research done in a medical model of disability can inform a practice that is supposed to move away from the medical model.

9. This matter is more complicated: One could say that there is good and bad self-determination, much like there is good and bad paternalism. Respecting the autonomy of the participant is of course crucial, but as Loewy argues, a stark autonomy where the participant is left to make all the choices is to 'abandon [the participants] to their own autonomy' (Loewy 2005, 446). This means that, at worst, too much emphasis on autonomy and self-determination is a form of professional abdication, jeopardising the good of the participants. Balancing between stepping back and letting the participant make decisions (self-determination), and stepping in and assuming responsibility when needed (good paternalism) is an ethical issue that has received little attention within APA, but one that merits some closer examination.

10. Of course, it might be argued that this form of collaborative research, tending towards action research, fails to address an underlying problem with EBR, namely whether the questions one is concerned with at all are 'best approached via any sort of empirically or experimentally conceived research' (Carr 2001, 465).

REFERENCES

ARISTOTLE. 1998. *The Nicomechean Ethics*, trans. David Ross, Oxford: Oxford University Press.

BERLINER, D.C. 2002. Educational research: The hardest science of all. *Educational Researcher* 31 (8): 18–20.

BIESTA, G. 2007. Why 'what works' won't work: Evidence-based practice and the democratic deficit in educational research. *Educational theory* 57 (1): 1–22.

BOURDIEU, P. 1990. The scholastic point of view. *Cultural Anthropology* 5: 380–91.

BREDAHL, A.-M. 2007. Participation of people with disabilities in adapted physical activity research. *Journal of the Brazilian Society of Adapted Motor Activity* 12 (1): 74–9.

————. 2001. Educational philosophy, theory and research: A psychiatric autobiography. *Journal of Philosophy of Education* 35 (3): 461–76.

————. 2003. Rival conceptions of practice in education and teaching. *Journal of Philosophy of Education* 37 (2): 253–66.

CARR, W. 2007. Educational research as a practical science. *International Journal of Research and Method in Education* 30 (3): 271–86.

CLEGG, S. 2005. Evidence-based practice in educational research: a critical realist critique of systematic review. *British Journal of Sociology of Education* 26 (3): 415–28.

COTT, C.A. 2004. Client-centred rehabilitation: client perspectives. *Disability and Rehabilitation* 26 (24): 1411–22.

DEPAUW, K.P. 1997. The (in)visibility of DisAbility: Cultural contexts and 'sporting bodies'. *Quest* 49: 416–30.

————. 2000. Social-cultural context of disability: implications for scientific inquiry and professional preparation. *Quest* 52: 358–68.

DUNNE, J. 1993. *Back to the Rough Ground. Practical Judgement and the Lure of Technique.* Notre Dame, IN: University of Notre Dame Press.

EMES, C., P. LONGMUIR and P. DOWNS. 2002. An ability-based approach to service delivery and professional preparation in adapted physical activity. *Adapted Physical Activity Quarterly* 19: 403–19.

FEUER, M.J., L. TOWNE and R.J. SHAVELSON. 2002. Scientific culture and educational research. *Educational Researcher* 31 (8): 4–14.

GALLAGHER, S. 1992. *Hermeneutics and Education.* New York: SUNY Press.

GRENIER, M. 2007. Inclusion in physical education: From the medical model to social constructionism. *Quest* 59: 298–310.

HAMMERSLEY, M. 2001. Some questions about evidence-based practice in education. Available online at http://www.leeds.ac.uk/educol/documents/00001819.doc, accessed: Oct. 2007.

HORNER, R.H., E.G. CARR, J. HALLE, G. MCGEE, S.L. ODOM and M. WOLERY. 2005. The use of single-subject research to identify evidence-based practice in special education. *Exceptional Children* 71 (2): 165–79.

HUTZLER, Y. 2006. Evidence based practice and research in adapted physical activity: Theoretical and data-based considerations. *Journal of the Brazilian Society of Adapted Motor Activity* 11 (1): 13–24.

————. 2007. SWOT analysis of adapted physical activity: A rehabilitation perspective. *Journal of the Brazilian Society of Adapted Motor Activity* 12 (1): 48–57.

JONES, R. 2007. Coaching redefined: An everyday pedagogical endeavour. *Sport, Education and Society* 12 (2): 159–73.

LOEWY, E.H. 2005. In defense of paternalism. *Theoretical Medicine & Bioethics* 26: 445–68.

MORISBAK, I. 1988. Adapted physical activity: An overview of the field. *Scandinavian Journal of Sport Sciences* 10 (2–3): 73–8.

ODOM, S.L., E. BRANTLINGER, R. GERSTEN, R.H. HORNER, B. THOMPSON and K.R. HARRIS. 2005. Research in special education: Scientific methods and evidence-based practices. *Exceptional Children* 71 (2): 137–48.

OLSON, D.R. 2004. The triumph of hope over experience in the search for 'what works': A response to Slavin. *Educational Researcher* 33 (1): 24–6.

PORRETTA, D.L., J. NESBIT and S. LABANOWICH. 1993. Terminology usage: A case for conceptual clarity. *Adapted Physical Activity Quarterly* 10: 87–96.

REID, G. 2003. Defining adapted physical activity. In *Adapted Physical Activity*, edited by R.D. Steadward, G.D. Wheeler and E.J. Watkinson. Edmonton, AB: University of Alberta Press: 11–25.

REID, G. and H. STANISH. 2003. Professional and disciplinary status of adapted physical activity. *Adapted Physical Activity Quarterly* 20: 213–29.

SACKETT, D.L., W.M.C. ROSENBERG, J.A.M. GRAY, R.B. HAYNES and W.S. RICHARDSON. 1996. Evidence based medicine: What it is and what it isn't. *British Medical Journal* 312: 71–2.

SCHWANDT, T.A. 1999. On understanding understanding. *Qualitative Inquiry* 5 (4): 451–64.

SHDIR. 2004. *Fysisk aktivitet for mennesker med funksjonsnedsettelser – Anbefalinger*, ['Physical activity for people with disabilities– recommendations']. Oslo: Sosial- og helsedirektoratet.

SHERRILL, C. 2004. *Adapted Physical Activity, Recreation, and Sport. Crossdisciplinary and Lifespan*. Boston, MA: McGraw Hill.

SHERRILL, C. and K.P. DEPAUW. 1997. Adapted physical activity and education. In *The History of Exercise and Sport Science*, edited by J.D. Massengale and R.A. Swanson. Champaign, IL: Human Kinetics: 39–108.

SLAVIN, R.E. 2002. Evidence-based education policies: Transforming educational practice and research. *Educational Researcher* 31 (7): 15–21.

SVENAEUS, F. 2000. *The Hermeneutics of Medicine and the Phenomenology of Health*. Dordrecht: Kluwer Academic Publishers.

———. 2003. Hermeneutics of medicine in the wake of Gadamer: The issue of phronesis. *Theoretical Medicine & Bioethics* 24: 407–31.

Øyvind Førland Standal, Norwegian School of Sport Sciences, Postboks 4014, Ullevål Stadion, 0806 Oslo, Norway. E-mail: oyvind.standal@nih.no

THE 'I' OF THE BEHOLDER: PHENOMENOLOGICAL SEEING IN DISABILITY RESEARCH

Christina Papadimitriou

In this paper I explicate what it means to see phenomenologically for an able-bodied researcher in the field of disability, and how this seeing yields a non-reductionistic understanding of the phenomenon of disability. My aim is to show how in this context, I, as a human and social scientist can use phenomenological methodology for both collecting and interpreting data. Though phenomenological philosophy can provide the basis of social scientific epistemology, it does not lend itself easily to a single specific or programmatic social scientific methodology. I offer possible ways of using phenomenological theory, methodology and techniques in order to understand the experience of a person with physical disability learning to use a wheelchair. I use data from a clinical encounter between a physical therapist (PT) and an adult with Spinal Cord Injury (SCI) in an inpatient rehabilitation hospital in Midwestern United States in order to flesh out phenomenological seeing. I conclude with implications for qualitative researchers who use phenomenological methods to inform their work.

Resumen

En este artículo explico lo que significa fenomenológicamente el ver para un investigador sin discapacidades dentro del campo de la minusvalía, y como este ver produce un entendimiento del fenómeno de la discapacidad no-reduccionista. My objetivo es mostrar cómo en este contexto, yo, como una científica humanista y social puedo utilizar la metodología fenomenológica para ambas, la recopilación y la interpretación de datos. Aunque la fenomenología filosófica puede proporcionar las bases para la epistemología científica social, no se presta fácilmente a una metodología bien única y específica bien programática social y científica. Ofrezco posibles maneras de utilizar la teoría, metodología, y técnicas fenomenológicas para entender la experiencia de una persona con discapacidad física que aprende a usar una silla de ruedas. Utilizo datos de un encuentro clínico entre un terapeuta físico (TF), y un adulto con una lesion de la columna vertebral [Spinal Cord Injury (SCI)] en un hospital de rehabilitación de pacientes internos en la región central de los Estados Unidos para detallar el ver fenomenológico. Concluyo con las consecuencias para los investigadores qualitativos que utilizan métodos fenomenológicos a la hora de conducir su trabajo.

Zusammenfassung

In diesem Artikel führe ich aus, was es für einen nichtbehinderten Forscher heißt, mit phänomenologischem Blick auf das Feld der Behinderungen zu schauen, und wie fruchtbar dieser Blick für ein nicht-reduktionistisches Verständnis des Phänomens Behinderung ist. Mein Ziel ist es, zu zeigen, wie ich mir als Mensch und Sozialwissenschaftler in diesem Zusammenhang zum einen für die Datensammlung und zum anderen für die Interpretation der Daten die phänomenologische Methode zunutze machen kann. Obwohl man die philosophische Phänomenologie als Grundlage der sozialwissenschaftlichen Epistemologie betrachten kann, so eignet sie sich nicht so einfach als singuläre oder programmatisch sozialwissenschaftliche Methodik. Ich biete verschiedene Anwendungsmöglichkeiten phänomenologischer Theorie, Methodologie und Techniken an, um die ersten Erfahrungen eines Behinderten mit einem Rollstuhl verstehen zu können. Ich nutze hierzu Daten von Sprechstunden von Erwachsenen mit Rückenmarksverletzungen (Spinal Cord Injury = SCI) mit dem Physiotherapeuten bei stationärer Behandlung in einem Reha-Krankenhaus im Mittleren Westen der USA. Diese Daten dienen dazu, die phänomenologische Betrachtungsweise zu veranschaulichen. Abschließend benenne ich Implikationen, um qualitativ Forschenden, die sich phänomenologischer Methoden bedienen, Informationen zu liefern.

摘要

本文從現象學的觀點，闡釋一個健全的身體如何從事失能研究的領域，以及此種觀點如何針對失能現象產出非化約的觀點。我的目標是企圖展示作為一個人和社會科學家，如何在「我」的脈絡裡，運用現象學方法來收集和解釋資料。雖然現象學可以提供社會科學的基本知識論，但是它本身並非簡單的有助於成為一個單獨特殊、或大綱式的社會科學方法論。我提供運用現象學理論、方法論及技術的可能途徑，來了解身體失能者學習使用輪椅的經驗。所使用的資料，是來自臨床上，介於身體治療師，和位於美國中西部復健醫院的脊隨受傷者，來呈現現象學的觀點。我以暗示性的結論，來告知使用現象學方法的質性研究者之工作。

Introduction

This essay is a continuation of themes explored in an article on conceptual and methodological concerns in the study of physical disability (Papadimitriou 2001). There I chose to focus on making the research process transparent in an effort to offer qualitative researchers interested in disability and persons with disabilities a way of thinking and doing phenomenologically-informed research. By using the term 'phenomenologically-informed', I wish to point to an important distinction between philosophical phenomenology and sociological phenomenology. In philosophical writings and research, phenomenology is seen as the search for general (invariant) structures or features of human experience (for example, Husserl 1913, 1962; Merleau-Ponty 1945, 1962; Schutz 1962; Zaner 1971, 1988; Toombs 1992). In social scientific writings, phenomenology can be used to explicate and understand the meaning-making practices that are taken for granted by actual social agents while engaging in specific social contexts (Frank 1985, 1988; Goode 1994; Waksler 1995; Wendell 1996; Winnance 2006b, 2007). In explicating how agents co-create and co-produce an intersubjective world, I include ethnomethodological understandings of agents' accounts (Garfinkel 1967; Sacks 1989).

Qualitative health researchers struggle to find methods that offer rigour, validity, trustworthiness, quality (e.g. Adami and Kiger 2005; Rolfe 2006) and interpretative strength (e.g. Diekelmann 2001; Ironside 2001, 2006; Smith 2006). Current trends in qualitative research have also focused on reflexivity regarding the research and writing processes (Diekelmann 2001, Smith 2006, Savin-Baden 2004, Doucet 2008, among many others). I cannot address all these issues in this paper. What I offer instead is an account of how I have used phenomenological methodology and methods[1] to analyse field data from a clinical encounter. Since it is not the purpose of this paper to review phenomenological theory, explain its concepts or debates, I assume some familiarity with phenomenological terms and will limit my use of jargon-laden terminology.

For investigators and readers interested in wheelchair sports and adapted physical activity, the vignette that follows affords an appreciation of how wheelchair users develop embodied skills during their medical rehabilitation, which they then take for granted as they become wheelchair sportspersons. Furthermore, by opening up the research process, it is hoped that social scientific investigators in the field of sport and disability learn about potentially valuable uses of phenomenological seeing in their own work.

Phenomenology, First-person Writing and Embodiment

Phenomenology prioritises lived experience over mechanistic and reductionistic accounts of experience and embodiment that dominate positivist epistemology and theory-laden research methodology. It thus offers an alternative to perspectives that theorise experience *a priori* and/or assume dualistic conceptualisations between mind and body, and subject and object (Husserl 1913, 1962; Heidegger 1926, 1962; Merleau-Ponty 1945, 1962). By doing so, the lived immediacy of human action and interaction may become apparent and thus available for investigation in ways that theory-based approaches often obscure.

Phenomenological writings have offered us many examples of the importance of lived experience in understanding illness and disability within wider social, cultural, emotional, interpersonal and political contexts (for example, Kestenbaum 1982; Kleinman 1988; Leder 1990; Toombs 1992, 1995; Paterson and Hughes 1999; Williams and Bendelow 1999; Winance 2006, 2007; Hughes 2007; Hodge 2008.). In this way, third-person perspectives such as quantitative positivistic social science have been shown to be inappropriate postures for the study of human experience and behaviour since they theorise and interpret behaviour in ways that are incapable of accounting for the local, situated and lived experience of an interpersonal world.

A phenomenologically-informed study starts with lived experience and with embodied beings. It is thus opposed to views of the human subject as mechanistic objects among others. Phenomenology seeks to transcend the subject-object, mind-body dichotomies that positivist positions foster. For instance, with respect to the mind-body dichotomy, phenomenologists argue that rather than having a body, we *are* our bodies and that our experiences and meanings are grounded in our active corporeal and inter-corporeal involvement in the world (Merleau-Ponty 1945, 1962; Crossley 1996, 28). This involvement in the world happens because embodied beings form a part of the world that they open onto. This also means that they open onto each other. It is meaningful behaviour that opens them to each other, not their sheer visibility as embodied beings (Crossley 1996, 30), nor their capacity to perceive and organise sense data. In this sense, human interaction is a dialogue between self and other within an intersubjective (meaningful) ground, not a raw physical world. Furthermore, existence is fundamentally dialectical and ambiguous (Merleau-Ponty 1945, 1962, 198) and always and inevitably culturally immersed (Csordas 1994). Actions, ideas, choices are not the property of individuals but of the dialogue among embodied beings out into which and through which they exist.

Using phenomenological methods, the researcher can uncover the meaning-making structures of phenomena such as a clinical encounter that are invisible to third-person perspectives which rely on positivist understandings (viz. most medical, developmental, political explanations of disability). Historically, there have been various attempts to decipher phenomenological methods, such as the *epoché*, bracketing and reduction, for (social) scientists to use (for example, Spiegelberg 1965; Psathas 1973; van Manen 1990, 2001; Toombs 1992; Moustakas 1994). I find that there is still a fair amount of openness regarding how a researcher may use phenomenological methodologies to approach her subject matter. Several sociological and anthropological perspectives have attempted to use phenomenology to inform their methodologies, such as ethnography, case histories, narrative studies, first-person accounts and grounded theory, among others. What I offer here are possible insights into ways that researchers doing phenomen-ologically-informed ethnographic research may come to do so more self-critically. I will concentrate on three major aspects of this training: observation, documentation and interpretation of field data.

I have elsewhere (Papadimitriou 2001) offered a detailed account of certain theoretical and conceptual biases in the study of disability and discussed the merits of phenomenologically-informed sociological studies of disabled embodiment. In that article, I offer further ways that I have used phenomenology in my research in order to achieve what I termed a 'least able bodied' attitude[2] with my research subjects (adults with Spinal Cord Injury [SCI] and other physical disabilities) through the use of 'bracketing' and through empathic understanding.[3] Following the writings of disability activists and scholars such Charlton (1998), Linton (1998), Shakespeare (2006), Watson (2002) and others, I have argued for seeing disability as a form of diversity rather than of deviance, as it has tended to be represented by normative medical, psychological and sociological perspectives. I concluded that as researchers of disability, we needed to move away from focusing on *dis*-ability (that is, inability, dependence, deviance, incompetence) towards an appreciation of difference. As such diversity and normality should not be seen as opposites but located along a continuum of the humanly possible ways of existing. Disabled embodiment, in this sense, is a form of *difference* in the double sense of the word: both unique and contentious. It is unique in the sense that it is a particular, specific and idiomorphic aspect of one's life-world. It is contentious in the sense that, in an 'ableist' society, ability is unequally stratified along normative (ableist) lines and thus disabled persons must contend with unfair discrimination and hegemonic agendas. Some writers take this point further and suggest that disability has transgressive or emancipatory potentials (Oliver 1984, 1996; Mitchel and Snyder 1997; Seymour 1998), and thus challenge dominant assumptions about beauty, autonomy and competence.

The value of a phenomenologically-informed perspective is that it can attend to both aspects of difference that disability may present. Phenomenological writings have been criticised for being apolitical, merely descriptive or subjective (Finkelstein 1980; Abberley 1987, 1992; Oliver 1992). Yet these criticisms stem from the social model's (Oliver 1992) insistence on a structural analysis of disability (Paterson and Hughes 1999, 601). As such, they fail to appreciate the impact of concepts such as lifeworld, embodiment, lived experience and intersubjectivity. Thus they also fail to appreciate the power of everyday encounters to produce oppression through normative, embodied practices (Paterson and Hughes 1999; Hughes 2007; Winance 2007).

In what follows I will present a description of a clinical encounter in the form of an ethnographic vignette, a descriptive record taken from field notes in which a physical therapist (PT) and an inpatient adult with Spinal Cord Injury (SCI) practise a transfer from the patient's wheelchair to a matted surface during the patient's physical therapy session. The goal of this transfer is for the patient to become more independent in his use of the wheelchair. Being able to transfer without assistance is a target that this client is expected to achieve during his rehabilitation stay, and once he has mastered it, he can move on to learning further skills that will lead to greater independence in activities of daily living. I then explain how I documented, attended to, analysed and interpreted the vignette. This clinical encounter that I present and analyse comes from a larger ethnographic field-study I conducted of rehabilitation centres, disability activism and sports programmes for adults with SCI and other physical disabilities in the mid-western United States. I do not offer a detailed analysis of the encounter, as that can be found elsewhere (Papadimitriou 2008).

'It Was Hard But You Did It': An Ethnographic Vignette

Roy is a 28-year-old SCI patient (Latino) who wore a brace to support the top part of his body and a knee-immobiliser, a metal device that locked his knees in a straight position. In this rather constricted embodiment, Roy wheeled into the physical therapy room looking for his physical therapist. Susan (PT, Caucasian, able-bodied, early 30s) summoned him, and with a half-smile Roy greeted her by a brief hand wave. He wheeled closer and situated himself near the mat on which Susan was sitting. Susan and a physical therapist aide quickly transferred him onto a matted exercise bed (about two feet off the ground). I assumed the role of a volunteer assistant. Roy knew who I was, and we simply smiled at each other acknowledging each other's presence.

Susan had already explained to me that during this therapy session Roy was expected to transfer from the bed to his wheelchair by himself, without bending his knees or his back and without using a sliding board (an assistive device typically used in wheelchair transfers). It was primarily his arms and hands that were to be used in order to accomplish this task, which was designed to train him in bed-to-chair transfers.

Susan was seated at the end of a bed across from Roy, who also was seated. Susan brought Roy's wheelchair closer to him and to the bed, checked that the chair brakes were locked and freed the wheelchair cushion from the seat belt and Roy's belongings. She then looked at him and said in a strong and determined voice: 'Ready?' Roy answered softly and hesitantly 'I think so', and without further ado, Susan moved his legs closer to the wheelchair. Susan was doing what Roy could not (yet?) do for himself. I was placed behind him in a 'just in case' way, that is, my body was there 'just in case' Roy fell backwards so that I could balance him or hold him.

Roy lifted up his upper body with the use of his arms, shoulders and hands. I was still standing behind him and was now holding his wheelchair. Susan and Roy looked at each other briefly, sternly, but said nothing. Roy seemed to know what he needed to do and so did Susan. The absence of a sliding board to help him transfer became apparent to Roy and me. There was an empty space between the bed and the chair; there was nothing there to support or assist him. With one hand, Susan held his legs and moved them a bit closer to the wheelchair, while her other hand was behind him supporting his back.

Roy lost his balance and fell backwards, but since my body was there, he did not physically hurt himself. My guarding positioning proved useful. Roy seemed alarmed by this unsuccessful attempt to transfer.

'I am sorry about that, it won't happen again,' Susan said immediately.

She looked around and saw another therapist, who must have been observing us, and made an 'oops' face. Roy remained silent and pulled himself back down, relaxing his shoulders. He seemed to be catching his breath when Susan uttered: 'Push with your hands to come closer'.

Roy obeyed the suggestions, but then said: 'I can't do more.'

'Yes you can, you are doing fine.'

Susan was holding him from his torso brace this time, I had my hand ready to catch him just in case he slid back again, and Roy pushed with his hands and shoulders. Roy was now sitting partly on the wheelchair and partly on one wheel. Susan moved his legs, and Roy moved his body toward the seat of his chair. Susan placed his legs on the leg rests, looked at him and said: 'How was that?'

'Hard!' Roy replied softly.

'It was hard but you did it,' said Susan.

Roy remained silent; he seemed to be reflecting on what he had just done. He seemed tired. Susan interrupted the silence and explained: 'Let me tell you why it was hard. It was hard because you did most of the work. I did not help so much, which means that you are doing better. When I don't do as much and you do all the work, it is not as hard for me, but it is harder for you. But this means that you are improving.'

'Oh, OK,' Roy said.

'Yeah, so when you hear me say "I am not holding you" or something it means that you are doing most of the work and not me…as I have been. So the less work I do, the better you are,' she said.

Roy listened and nodded. After about ten or 15 seconds of silence Susan said in a playful voice: 'OK, we're done. You can leave…come on…go go go.'

Roy laughed and playfully responded: 'Oh now you tell me to go. OK, I am leaving.' And he started to wheel away from us.

'Go have lunch,' she said. 'See you tomorrow.'

'See you tomorrow' he said as he was already almost out of the door.[4]

Phenomenological Seeing and Training the 'I'

The expression 'training the "I"' means training the researcher to see through phenomenological lenses. The wordplay here between 'eye' and 'I' is intended to underscore the priority of the intersubjective experience of being a person-in-the-world (expressed as one's 'I', i.e. one's self) properly understood and the subjective experience of seeing (usually through one's eyes).

Phenomenologists such as Spiegelberg (1965), van Manen (2001), Gendlin (1962) and Moustakas (1994), among others, have all offered their versions of 'the way to phenomenology'. Spiegelberg (1965), for instance, offers seven steps to the phenomenological method. In this paper I do not attempt such as a comprehensive treatment. I concentrate rather on an exploration of phenomenologically-informed ethnographic research in the field of disability.

In a phenomenologically-informed ethnographic study there are three moments for which a properly trained 'I' is necessary for phenomenological seeing: (1) observation; (2) documentation through the production of a written record; and (3) interpretation of encounters/data. In each moment the researcher needs to eschew third-person, objective, and theory-laden perspectives in favour of a stance that remains open to an 'appreciation for and an attunement to the fullest possible ways meanings are at play in any situation and especially, what makes action possible, shared and able to be related to, and how those are produced in situations.' (David A. Stone, personal communication, 2007) The order of these three moments reflects my own 'way to phenomenology' and may be in conflict with other phenomenological treatments (e.g. Spiegelberg 1965).

It is important in this instance to locate myself as a researcher before I begin the explanation of the three moments. The biographical position of the researcher—such as one's gender, age, ethnicity, class, religion, ability/disability, professional status, education and other dimensions—affects research relationships and the collection and interpretation of data (Hammel 2004). When I began collecting the data presented in this article I was 26 years old and a graduate student at Boston University's department of sociology. I stayed in the field for 18 months. I am Caucasian, tall, average weight, female, of Greek origin (not an American citizen at the time) and with a slight but noticeable accent in my spoken English. In the rehabilitation setting, where the data presented herein were collected, I blended easily with therapy staff (physical and occupational therapists and many aides) most of whom were young, female, able-bodied, and Caucasian. My 'Greekness' often became one of the first points of conversation (patients and staff could see and read my name badge and thus recognise my ethnicity, or would try to locate my accent) and it served as an 'ice-breaker' in many instances with staff, patients and families. As a student and researcher, my position was relatively familiar to staff and patients since there were many other students, faculty and doctors who were doing research in the institution. Though I have tried to stay critically reflective about how my biographical positioning may affect my research relationships, data collection etc., I was not always aware of how others perceived me.

The three moments that I discuss next are only analytically distinct. In reality they often blend together. As hermeneutic writers remind us, interpretation takes place at every stage of the research process. In what follows, I try to separate the three moments for purposes of clarity and presentation, but note that the tools of phenomenology, the *epoché*, reduction, bracketing, self-reflection and empathy, are all at play in each of the three stages of the process.

First moment: Observation

In observing, whether as a participant observer or simply as an outside observer, a phenomenologically-informed researcher must assume a non-judgemental attitude. That is, the researcher must avoid appearing to be judging participants or their activities in any way while at the same time staying engaged with them. This includes observing and listening attentively while exhibiting minimal facial expressions. In other words, the researcher's embodied affect can be described as being present, open, neutral and careful. This is best practiced with the phenomenological *epoché*.

The phenomenological *epoché* is a process whereby the researcher must bracket, put aside and suspend prior suppositions in order to allow for a viewing of the phenomenon as it is given to (not as it understood by) the researcher. Husserl (1913, 1962) explains that the *epoché* is meant to suspend our engagement with the world through the natural attitude. The term 'natural attitude' refers to everyday life biases that we know in advance or assume but which are external to the phenomenon. The process of setting aside presuppositions and biases, and thus allowing for experiences to be presented 'just as they show themselves', provides a new vantage point for the researcher. It should be readily evident how this differs from the approaches a theory-laden sociology or psychology would take to a situation under study. The *epoché* requires sustained attention, concentration and patience in order to see what interferes with the description of the phenomenon. The *epoché*, though rarely achieved in perfection, allows for the clearing of biases by marking them as judgements superimposed upon the phenomena.

Biases, judgements and assumptions may be physical (see Husserl's ball example, 1913/1962, or Gestalt writers), but they are also social, practical, emotional, political and so on. For example, Roy's body as described earlier in the vignette and his overall embodied presence (metal halo bolted on his scalp and knee immobiliser) brought forth an array of able-bodied/ableist biases that I had not realised I held. For one, the brace and knee immobiliser made him look a bit non-human, more cyborg-like to me. In a typical able-bodied fashion, I felt pity, awe and fear upon meeting him. Roy's particular embodiment scared me because I assumed that he must have been uncomfortable, in pain, limited in function and ability—generally, he appeared 'damaged goods'. Upon seeing him, therefore, I ascribed characteristics (ability, feelings etc.) that were based on (1) my own assumptions of either how I would feel if I were 'in his shoes'; or (2) how he looked physically which allowed me to assume that he was less well-off than non-injured, non-disabled persons (like myself). These assumptions and presuppositions imply that I saw him as inferior (i.e. pity) but also as a hero because of this persistence in getting better in spite of his limited bodily function (i.e. awe). I did not see Roy in himself, as it were; rather, I superimposed ableist assumptions based on Roy's external/physical characteristics. These biases reflect cultural assumptions regarding personal autonomy, independence, self-determination and so on as individual (not social/structural) problems. From this standpoint, impairment signifies disorder (Davis 1995) and as such is not 'normal' (Swain et al. 2003, 23). From a deviance perspective, persons with disabilities may be seen as violating cultural norms of appearance, beauty and autonomy and thus are set apart as 'other'. Livneh (1982) and Hahn (1988) explain that these violations may raise an 'aesthetic anxiety' in non-disabled persons. In other words, the ableist 'anxiety' is that 'a disability could interfere with [a person's] functional capacities necessary' (Hahn 1988, 42) to pursue a satisfactory life, which may trigger negative reactions and social stigma toward persons with disabilities. Sociological and psychological studies on attitudes toward persons with disabilities (severe or otherwise) show that visible deformities and disability evoke powerful feelings such as distress, anxiety, fear and pity, in the non-disabled (Goffman 1963; Fabrera and Manning 1972; Ainlay et al. 1986; and for a different perspective see Cahill and Eggleston 1995). Such perceptions have been criticised by disability activists and scholars for their insistence on uncritically assuming that disability is a catastrophic and tragic event (Oliver 1990). Using an individualistic model of perceiving and understanding disability, persons with disabilities are assumed to be victims of their circumstances, suffering, dependent on others for assistance, incompetent and unproductive, rather than recognising that limitations are social and cultural in nature rather than merely personal (Fine and Asch 1988; Hahn 1988; Oliver 1990, 1996; Albrecht 1992).

By seeing Roy as 'damaged', limited and suffering, I was superimposing a 'tragic' or medico-psychological model onto his existence that he never confirmed nor denied, but that I had uncritically invoked upon just seeing him. What I needed to do was see Roy without a restrictive ableist lens.[5] By using the technique of bracketing, I needed to set aside my assumptions that he was less well off than me just because he physically appeared a particular way and that his life was tragic because of his traumatic spinal cord injury. Feeling pity for him (and implicitly good about my own physical condition) was indeed clouding my ability to observe and see him for who he is, for who he could be and become or how he may want to be seen.

How could I, the phenomenologically informed, politically progressive researcher, possibly be so biased? Asking this question was possible because of my commitment to understanding Roy's lifeworld phenomenologically, i.e. without prejudging it or interpreting it from a theory-laden perspective. Because phenomenology allows for the critical examination of research conventions and practices, it was possible for me to be reflexive about my own assumptions and thus expose my biases. I became attentive to these biases for future encounters and especially for the documentation and analysis phases. Once on the surface and reflexively addressed, pre-understandings and biases offer an opportunity for researchers (and by extension the research community) to recognise that they are a part of the subject-matter that they try to explore as much as the research subjects from whom they receive consent forms and whose behaviour they are expected to observe and analyse. Through the *epoché*, I began to develop the 'least able-boded attitude' mentioned earlier (Papadimitriou 2001)—an attitude where I would check for presuppositions and biases, such as an inappropriate pitying attitude towards Roy. In this new attitude, Roy appeared as neither limited nor a super-hero, but rather as a man who was reconstructing his lifeworld. I was able to better listen and see him rather than presume who or how he was.

Another technique that aims at helping the researcher practise avoiding labelling or pre-conceptualising participants' behaviours and can be practised outside the field is the exercise of non-judgemental writing. For example, researchers can try to describe black-and-white artists' photographs using simple, precise words to describe in detail how the lighting and colour gradations create particular moods. In doing so, researchers become aware that everyday and commonsensical assumptions influence our interpretation of expressions since we are always already situated in cultural and meaningful contexts. In my case, I was able to separate personal, reflective, conceptual and descriptive notes from each other and keep separate records of them. Exercising this technique allowed me a greater interpretative openness and perspectival neutrality. The phenomenological 'I' was thus open to and therefore able to see beyond the physical actions taking place in space and time, aware of the multiplicity of perspectives taking place in a human interaction and of how meanings are enacted, negotiated and produced in social/cultural situations; and most importantly, the 'I' is open to the lived experiences of participants as well as to the one's own professional, personal and cultural biases.

Second Moment: Documentation

After observing, participating and writing field notes, the next step is to produce written documentation of the data. The purpose of documentation is to create a record of the data so they can be interpreted. One such form of documentation is a vignette. The key to a successful vignette is its ability to permit the researcher and subsequent readers to have a clear view of the encounter that allows them to feel 'I was there'; a view that encourages continuous exploration of further and deeper meanings; and makes possible a view of things 'just as they showed themselves'. It is important to remember that while a vignette strives for descriptive accuracy and minimal interpretation, it is not 'raw data', as perhaps a video recording of this clinical encounter might be thought of. The construction of a textual description of the data can be assisted by another phenomenological method, the phenomenological reduction. Max van Manen (2001, 461) eloquently explains that:

> the phenomenological reduction tries to grasp the intelligibility that lets the world 'be' or come meaningfully into existence in different experiential modalities.... [I]t is indeed less a technique than a 'style' of thinking and orienting, an attitude of reflective attentiveness to what it is that makes life intelligible and meaningful to us.

The phenomenological reduction is related to the *epoché* and refers to the task of constructing a reflective description of the experiences at hand. This task has the researcher describe the phenomenon at hand by writing reflectively, documenting changes in seeing the phenomenon by asking questions such as 'Is this my own perception of what is going on, or the participants'?'; 'How is this meaningful to me? How do I experience it?'; 'How is this meaningful to the participants? How is that evident to me?'; 'If I look again, what do I see?' In traditional phenomenological terms, this 'task requires that [the researcher] look and describe; look again and describe; look again and describe;...descriptions that present varying intensities; ranges of shapes, sizes, and special qualities; time references; and colors all within the experiential context' (Moustakas 1994, 90–1). By looking at his or her own presuppositions, the researcher becomes self-reflective and hopefully able to distinguish between self and other, between pre-judgements or pre-understandings and what the phenomenon/the other offers. Each new looking may create a further awareness of the phenomenon and new perceptions and 'angles' may become available. As such the goal is that the reduction will facilitate clear seeing.[6]

For example, my first attempts at documenting and interpreting the clinical encounter were dominated by questions/thoughts such as: 'why is Susan pushing Roy so much, so hard? Why doesn't she give him a break? She seems unduly hard on him. She should apologise more. It was not acceptable that he fell backwards, what if I hadn't been there? Isn't she being a bit distant here? I cannot appreciate her affect. Why is Roy so passive and accepting of her behaviour and this situation?' The problem with these thoughts is that they come from a distanced third-person perspective. My training had been heavily influenced by the early Chicago School ethnographers who worked with the presupposition that a sociologist ought to side with the underdog (in this case the patient). Additionally, critical and political perspectives of medicine, such as Illich (1976) and the disability writings of Oliver (1984, 1990, 1992) among others, informed my judgements of the physical therapist as an agent of social control, a rehabilitation professional representing/embodying an oppressive medical model—that is, a view whereby the PT exercises power and controls the situation. Therefore, from an uncritical and third-person perspective, early versions of this vignette read like an example of the power and control that medical staff have over patients, casting the patient as the passive receiver of care, thus offering a picture of rehabilitation as a series of actions leading to prescribed goals. At best, such a vignette would have portrayed the aforementioned encounter as a learning exercise or drill, perhaps an ordinary clinical encounter, a brief and not particularly significant moment in Roy's overall rehabilitation.

This practice of developing the vignette also brought me face to face with my own emotions of loss, sadness and fear. Using *epoché* and bracketing did not mean that I was protecting myself from these feelings. Rather, through this practice, I was able to open my life-world to include the other's perspective without imposing pre-determined categories.[7] This practice is not a way of saying that I am detaching myself from my subject-matter, nor is it a claim that I am being 'objective' in a positivist way. In bracketing, the experience endures; it is the stance that changes. In becoming more open to the world of the other (persons with disability), I discovered my own biases and limitations. Leaving aside the natural attitude by using the phenomenological *epoché* and reduction and thus assuming 'an attitude of reflective attentiveness' is especially important for a non-disabled researcher studying disability because of the unequal power relations that exist between disabled and non-disabled people (Stone and Priestley 1996) and between researcher and research subjects.

Third Moment: Interpretation

The third moment is the interpretation or analysis of the encounter described in the vignette. In phenomenological philosophy, the goal of analysis is to allow the essence of the phenomenon to show itself *as itself*, to ask, in other words, how does this phenomenon appear within a horizon of lived experience as what it is and not something else? In phenomenologically-informed ethnography, the goal of the analysis is to allow what is essential in the situation or encounter to show itself—in other words, how does this situation, encounter or series of actions appear as the meaningful situation that it is within a horizon of lived experience? And so, in analysing this therapeutic encounter, I was looking for how the co-constitution of meaning and the co-creation of intersubjective understanding among two actors was accomplished.

By interactional work and the co-creation of meaning I mean actors' embodied social (not physical) actions during their encounters with others[8] (in this instance therapists and patients) that may be used to establish, communicate and negotiate their social position, status, expectations, boundaries etc.. In clinical encounters such as the one described here, this work is predicated upon the establishment of trust, care and commitment, which are, of course, not simply 'given', but must be enacted and accomplished relationally. This interactional work is what becomes visible through phenomenological seeing and training.

As an individual researcher, the phenomenological *epoché* and reduction helped me by forcing me to repeat: 'How do I know?' and 'Can I prove it with evidence from within?' in order to identify additional prejudgements and biases in interpreting the phenomenon. For example, when I concentrated on 'why did the PT act this way?' I was asking a causal question. It was not until I shifted my focus to 'how do her actions affect the patient, her therapy plan, the general transformation that the SCI adult is undergoing?' that I could see what was essential in the meaning-making that took place within the encounter. I was able to concentrate on the process of caring. So it is not that the *epoché* offers a neutral way of seeing (as the positivists would have it), but rather it allows lived experience to present itself without prejudgements and prescriptive assumptions—that is, moving away from explanatory descriptions and analyses to an emphasis on experience as lived.

To put prior assumptions and suppositions aside, I used the phenomenological *epoché* and reduction described earlier. I wrote and edited interpretations of this vignette many times, as I would attempt to see the phenomenon from many angles. It took me at least eight readings of this vignette, the guidance offered by several people's feedback, and an extended examination of my own biases before I could provide what I hope is a rich and nuanced interpretation.[9]

And so, in analysing the vignette through phenomenological seeing, what I see is a committed PT attempting to turn Roy's efforts into successful accomplishments. I see Susan doing this when she apologises and reassures him that she will not allow any more backward falls, and then coaxes him to continue by offering a new way (hands closer to chair) of pushing himself off the chair. By moving away quickly from the unsuccessful attempt and on to a new try, Susan reinforces her commitment to helping Roy achieve his goal. Susan's behaviour can be seen as a technique that succeeds in re-directing Roy's attention away from failure and towards success. But this teaching achieves more than that: it shows her commitment to working with Roy and reinforces that together they can achieve a successful transfer. By telling him that he can 'do more', she is not being unduly tough or insensitive, she is pushing Roy to go beyond his perceived abilities and trusting him to do so with her assistance and care. She is thus once again showing her commitment to his rehabilitation and affirming her interest in helping him. Together, Susan and Roy show commitment to working together, listening to each other, accepting each other's roles, and a motivation to work hard, trust in each other and in their relationship—in short, they are engaged in the co-creation of a common ground of understanding and meaningful action.

All of this is typically taken for granted by the participants. This means, importantly, that the process is almost entirely invisible to both the participants *and* to investigators exploring either qualitative or quantitative approaches that rely on participants' reports of (or insights into) their actions and practices (such as surveys or interviews). Their taken-for-granted actions are of vital importance for all this interactional work to be possible because they point to the co-creation of a trustworthy relationship and intersubjective understanding between PT and patient that permits clinical sessions to be effective (see also Mattingly 1998 for a similar point among occupational therapists and patients), and identity to be constituted. When Susan explains to Roy why this was hard to do ('because you did most of the work'), what she is doing is offering an insider's explanation: when therapists do less, it means patients are improving. In this role as translator,[10] Susan decodes Roy's behaviour and turns it into success, progress and hard work. When, how and to what degree she does so are not pre-given or pre-determined based on theoretical knowledge or social positions; rather they are constituted in action and interaction (Winance 2007). The details of this work are available through phenomenological seeing as described in this paper.

Concluding Remarks

In this paper I have attempted to clarify phenomenological seeing for the purposes of doing field research in the area of disability with particular reference to wheelchair users. There are certainly various ways of 'doing phenomenology', and I do not claim that this is the only or best way. This is *a* way that can inspire qualitative researchers in the area of disability to use phenomenological methodology and methods to study their subject matters. To examine the world of disability (be it in the clinic or in everyday life) through phenomenological methods means:

> to suspend judgment, to direct attention to modes 'of appearing', to acknowledge the multiplicity of perspectives (including one's own), and to recognize the socially con-structed nature of knowledge and reality is to clarify one's perception of the world in which one lives, in which others live, and the worlds that we inhabit together. (Waksler 2001, 84)

It is important to remember that even after such reflective clearing and appreciation of phenomena, interpretation is never complete. Typically, in traditional, positivist-informed scientific endeavours, a researcher's 'findings' and analyses are taken as though there are definitive. What phenomenologically-informed enquiry suggests is that enquiry is never complete and that 'the possibility of discovery is unlimited' (Moustakas 1994, 95). There is certainly a selection process that takes place—that is, the researcher needs to select and emphasise certain themes and not others—and thus interpretation is hermeneutic in nature. Further, as Spiegelberg also argues (1965), what distinguishes phenomenology from other methods is not its steps, but its challenge to reductionism/positivism, its opposition to explanatory hypotheses, its insistence on direct evidence and its 'determined attempt to enrich the world of our experience by bringing hitherto neglected aspects of this experience' (ibid., 700).

What I have argued is that by using phenomenological methods such as the *epoché*, reduction, bracketing, self-reflection and empathy, the researcher is able to recognise biases, put them aside, revisit the phenomenon, recognise different standpoints, value and respect the evidence presented and move toward an interpretation of the phenomenon at hand as it presents itself rather than through *a priori* theoretical lenses. Presuppositions appear limiting, annoying and embarrassing at first, difficult to set aside; but they are also valuable as possible themes and perspectives. In addition to my ableist assumptions, my political and activist inclinations in seeing the medical establishment as an agent of social control primarily limited my ability to see what was going on between PT and patient beyond the general and abstract notions of medicalisation, hegemony and/or power-lessness of patients. In assuming a third-person perspective, I was not able to appreciate the situated accomplishments and meaning-making practices of therapist and patient. At the same time, however, these same presuppositions helped me be open and accepting of disability politics and activism perspectives, which in the mid-1990s were at their peak in the USA, the Americans with Disabilities Act (ADA) having been passed in 1990. From a disability activism perspective I could incorporate an understanding of how rehabilitation of adults with SCI may address the physical aspects of disability, while often missing the longitudinal, political and sexual aspects. As such, activist perspectives needed to be included but without losing the micro-processes that constitute the actual clinical encounter and affect one's general being-in-the-world as a patient and wheelchair user. As a phenomenologically-informed sociologist applying the aforementioned methods, I realised I needed to incorporate the political (structural or macro) with the local (actual or micro) and in doing so to bracket the local in order to see the structural aspects of living with disability while remaining appreciative of the local and particular.

NOTES

1.   There is some confusion regarding the terms methodology and methods. Methodology is related to epistemology in that it refers to 'how knowledge can be developed and how research ought to proceed given the nature of the issue it seeks to address.' (Carpenter 2004, 9) Methods refer to techniques or tools that researchers can use to collect and manipulate data. Methods derive from chosen methodologies, and can also cross different methodological approaches. Examples of methods include interviews, focus groups, participant observation, observation, questionnaires etc. The two terms are not interchangeable (Carpenter 2004).

2.   This is a phrase inspired by Nancy Mandell's article 'The least-adult role in studying children', in Waksler 1991.

3.   As adumbrated by Frank (1985) and Stein (1964) before him.

4.   This description has previously appeared in Papadimitriou 2008.

5.   I have described elsewhere (2001) how I 'cleared myself out of the way' through the use of empathic acts and psychotherapy. See also Frank 1985, for similar techniques.

6.   See Spiegelberg 1965, 690–4, for an explanation and critique of reduction.

7.   For an example of the impossibility of complete bracketing, see Papadimitriou 2001.

8.   In this instance, I am influenced by the writings of Goffman, symbolic interactionists, ethnomethodologists and conversation analysts, all of whom have in varying ways produced detailed analyses of 'interactional work'.

9.   Though a full analysis of this vignette can be found elsewhere (2008), the reader may benefit from a short summary of interpretative findings. For Roy, the SCI patient, several features of his overall rehabilitation process and particular learning became apparent through the analysis of the vignette. Some such features include: regaining self-confidence, independence and physical strength; establishing the limits of his abilities; transcending his perceived limits; surrendering control of his body; cooperating with his therapist; falling backwards is possible, though he did not get hurt; recuperation is a slow, painful and difficult experience; progress happens in small steps, not all at once; and so forth. In phenomenological terms, these aspects of Roy's acute rehabilitation form his re-embodiment experiences in his effort to reconstruct a sense of self post-injury. For Susan, the PT, this clinical encounter points to her coaxing and supporting the efforts of the client; pointing to and explaining/translating that her patient has progressed; knowing when to push, apologise and congratulate him; establishing trust; showing her

commitment to his recuperation. Susan both creates and translates meaning during this encounter.

10.   This is a clinical way of interpreting behaviour and it is the dominant one in rehabilitation hospitals. It is important here to remember the unintended consequence of this translation process – that is, that patients become dependent on staff's interpretations of their abilities, while their own lived understandings become secondary or even unimportant. Some writers (Phillips 1985, 45; Finkelstein 1991; Oliver 1993; Carpenter 1994, 615; Oliver and Sapey 1999; French and Swain 2001) see this as a form of paternalism where staff are seen as knowers: i.e., as arbiters of need, and agents of social control.

REFERENCES

ABBERLEY, P. 1987. The concept of oppression and the development of a social theory of disability. *Disability, Handicap and Society* 2 (1): 5–20.

———. 1992. Counting us out: A discussion of the OPCS disability surveys. *Disability, Handicap, and Society* 7 (2): 139–55.

ADAMI, M.F. and A. KIGER. 2005. The use of triangulation for completeness purposes. *Nurse Researcher* 12 (4): 19–29.

AINLAY, STEPHAN C., GAYLENE BECKER and LERITA M. COLEMAN. 1986. *The Dilemma of Difference: A Multidisciplinary View of Stigma*. New York and London: Plenum Press.

ALBRECHT, G. 1992. *The Disability Business: Rehabilitation in America*. Newbury Park, CA: Sage Publications.

ALBRECHT, G.L., K.D. SEELMAN and M. BURY, eds. 2001. *Handbook of Disability Studies*. London: Sage.

CAHILL, E. SPENCER and ROBIN EGGLESTON. 1995. Reconsidering the Stigma of disability: Wheelchair use and public kindness. *The Sociological Quarterly* 36 (4): 681–98.

CARPENTER, C. 1994. The experience of spinal cord injury: The individual's perspective – implications for rehabilitation practice. *Physical Therapy* 74 (7): 614–28.

———. 2004. The contribution of qualitative research to evidence-based practice. In *Qualitative Research in Evidence-Based Rehabilitation*, edited by K.W. Hammel and C. Carpenter. Edinburgh: Churchill Livingstone.

CHARLTON, I. JAMES. 1998. *Nothing About Us Without Us: Disability Oppression and Empowerment*. Berkeley, CA: University of California Press.

CROSSLEY, NICK. 1996. Body-subject/body-power: Agency, inscription and control in Foucault and Merleau-Ponty. *Body & Society* 2 (2): 99–116.

CSORDAS, THOMAS J., ed. 1994. . *Embodiment and Experience: The Existential Ground of Culture and Self*. Cambridge: Cambridge University Press.

DAVIS, L. 1995. *Enforcing Normalcy: Disability, Deafness, and the Body*. New York: Verso.

DIEKELMAN, N. 2001. Narrative pedagogy: Heideggerian hermeneutical analyses of lived experiences of students, teachers, and clinicians. *Advances in Nursing Science* 23 (3): 53–71.

DOUCET, A. 2008. 'From her side to the Gossamer Wall(s)': Reflexivity and relational knowing. *Qualitative Sociology* 31 (1): 73–87.

FABRERA, HORACIO JR. and PETER K. MANNING. 1972. Disease, illness, and deviant careers. In *Theoretical Perspectives on Deviance*, edited by R.A. Scott and J.D. Douglas. New York and London: Basic Books.

FINE, MICHELLE and ADRIENNE, ASCH, eds. 1988. *Women with Disabilities: Essays in Psychology, Culture, and Politics*. Philadelphia, PA: Temple University Press.

FINKELSTEIN, V. 1980. *Attitudes and Disabled People*. New York: World Rehabilitation Fund.

———. 1991. Disability: An administrative challenge? In *Social Work: Disabled People and disabling Environments*, edited by M. Oliver. London: Jessica Kingsley.

FRANK, GELYA. 1985. 'Becoming the Other': Empathy and biographical interpretation. *Biography* 8 (3): 189–210.

———. 1988. On embodiment: A case study of congenital limb deficiency in American culture. In *Women with Disabilities: Essays in Psychology, Culture, and Politics*, edited by Michelle Fine and Adrienne Asch. Philadelphia, PA: Temple University Press.

FRENCH, S. and J. SWAIN. 2001. The relationship between disabled people and health and welfare professionals. In *Handbook of Disability Studies*, edited by G.L. Albrecht, K.D. Seelman and M. Bury. London: Sage.

GARFINKEL, H. 1967. *Studies in Ethnomethodology*. Englewood Cliffs, NJ: Prentice-Hall.

GENDLIN, E. 1962. *Experiencing and the Creation of Meaning*. Glencoe: Free Press.

GOFFMAN, ERVING. 1963. *Stigma: Notes on the Management of Spoiled Identity*. Engelwood Cliffs, NJ: Prentice-Hall.

GOODE, DAVID. 1994. *A World Without Words: The Social Construction of Children Born Deaf and Blind*. Philadelphia, PA: Temple University Press.

HAHN, H. 1988. The politics of physical differences: Disability and discrimination. *Journal of Social Issues* 44: 39–47.

HAMMEL, K.W. 2004. Using qualitative evidence to inform theories of occupation. In *Qualitative Research in Evidence-Based Rehabilitation*, edited by K.W. Hammel and C. Carpenter. Edinburgh: Churchill Livingstone.

HAMMEL, K.W. and C. CARPENTER, eds. 2004. *Qualitative Research in Evidence-Based Rehabilitation*. Edinburgh: Churchill Livingstone.

HEIDEGGER, M. 1926/1962. *Being and Time*, translated by J. Macquarrie and E. Robinson. New York: Harper & Row.

HODGE, N. 2008. Evaluating Lifeworld as an emancipatory methodology. *Disability & Society* 23 (1): 29–40.

HUGHES, B. 2007. Being disabled: Toward a critical social ontology for disability studies. *Disability & Society* 22 (7): 673–84.

HUSSERL, E. 1913/1982. *Ideas: General Introduction to Pure Phenomenology*, translated by F. Kersten. The Hague: Martinus Nijhoff.

ILLICH, IVAN. 1976. *Medical Nemesis: The Expropriation of Health*. New York: Pantheon Books.

IRONSIDE, P.M. 2001. Creating a research base for nursing education: An interpretive review of conventional, critical, feminist, postmodern, and phenomenological pedagogies. *Advances in Nursing Science* 23 (3): 72–87.

———. 2006. Using narrative pedagogy: Leaning and practicing interpretive thinking. *Journal of Advanced Nursing* 55 (4): 478–86.

KESTENBAUM, V. 1982. *The Humanity of the Ill: Phenomenological Perspectives*. Knoxville, TN: University of Tennessee Press.

KLEINMAN, ARTHUR. 1988. *The Illness Narratives: Suffering, healing and the human condition*. New York: Basic Books.

LEDER, DREW. 1990. *The Absent Body*. Chicago and London: University of Chicago Press.

LINTON, SIMI. 1998. *Claiming Disability: Knowledge and Identity*. New York: New York University Press.

LIVNEH, H. 1982. On the origins of negative attitudes toward people with disabilities. *Rehabilitation Literature* 43: 338–47.

MANDELL, NANCY. 1991. The least-adult role in studying children. In *Studying the Social Worlds of Children: Sociological Readings*, edited by C.F. Waksler. London: The Falmer Press.

MATTINGLY, C. 1998. *Healing Dramas and Clinical Plots: The Narrative Structure of Experience*. Cambridge: Cambridge University Press.

MERLEAU-PONTY, MAURICE. 1945/1962. *Phenomenology of Perception*, translated by C. Smith. London: Routledge & Kegan Paul.

MITCHEL, T.D. and L.S. SNYDER. 1997. *The Body and Physical Difference: Discourses of Disability*. Ann Arbor: The University of Michigan Press.

MOUSTAKAS, C. 1994. *Phenomenological Research Methods*. Thousand Oaks: Sage.

OLIVER, M. 1984. The politics of disability. *Critical Social Theory* 4 (2): 21–32.

———. 1990. *The Politics of Disablement*. London: Macmillan.

———, ed. 1991. *Social Work: Disabled People and disabling Environments*. London: Jessica Kingsley.

———. 1992. Changing the social relations of research production. *Disability, Handicap, and Society* 7: 101–14.

———. 1993. Disability and dependency: A creation of industrial societies. In *Disabling Barriers – Enabling Environments*, edited by J. Swain, V. Finkelstein, S. French and M. Oliver. London: Sage.

———. 1996. *Understanding Disability: From Theory to Practice*. New York: St Martin's Press.

OLIVER, M. and B. SAPEY. 1999. *Social Work with Disabled People*. London and Basingstoke: Macmillan.

PAPADIMITRIOU, C. 2001. From dis-ability to difference: Conceptual and methodological issues in the study of physical disability. In *Handbook of Phenomenology and Medicine*, edited by S. Kay Toombs. London: Kluwer Academic Publishers.

———. 2008. 'It was hard but you did it': The co-production of 'work' in a clinical setting among spinal cord injured adults and their physical therapists. *Disability & Rehabilitation* 30 (5): 365–74.

PATERSON, K. and B. HUGHES. 1999. Disability studies and phenomenology: The carnal politics of everyday life. *Disability & Society* 14 (5): 597–610.

PHILLIPS, M.J. 1985. 'Try harder': The experience of disability and the dilemma of normalization. *Social Science Journal* 22: 45–57.

PSATHAS, GEORGE, ed. 1973. *Phenomenological Sociology: Issues and Applications*. New York: Wiley.

ROLFE, G. 2006. Validity, trustworthiness and rigour: Quality and the idea of qualitative research. *Journal of Advanced Nursing* 53 (3): 304–10.

SACKS, H. 1989. *Harvey Sacks Lectures 1964–1965*, edited by Gail Jefferson. London: Kluwer Academic Pulbishers.

SAVIN-BADEN, M. 2004. Achieving reflexivity: Moving researchers from analysis to interpretation in collaborative inquiry. *Journal of Social Work Practice* 18 (3): 365–78.

SCHUTZ, A. 1962. *The Problem of Social Reality*, vol. 1 of *Collected Papers*. The Hague: Martinus Nijhoff.

SHAKESPEARE, T. 2006. *Disability Rights and Wrongs*. London: Routledge.

SEYMOUR, WENDY. 1998. *Remaking the Body: Rehabilitation and Change*. London: Routledge.

SMITH, S. 2006. Encouraging the use of reflexivity in the writing up of qualitative research. *International Journal of Therapy & Rehabilitation* 13 (5): 209–15.

SPIEGELBERG, H. 1965. *The Phenomenological Movement: A Historical Introduction*, vol. 2, 2nd edn. The Hague: Martinus Nijhoff.

STEIN, EDITH. 1964). *On the Problem of Empathy*, translated by E.W. Straus. The Hague: Martinus Nijhoff.

STONE, E. and M. PRIESTLEY. 1996. Parasites, pawns and partners: Disability research and the role of non-disabled researchers. *British Journal of Sociology* 47: 496–716.

SWAIN, J., S. FRENCH and C. CAMERON. 2003. *Controversial Issues in a Disabling Society*. Buckingham: Open University Press.

SWAIN, J., V. FINKELSTEIN, S. FRENCH and M. OLIVER. 1993. *Disabling Barriers – Enabling Environments*. London: Sage.

TOOMBS, S. KAY. 1992. *The Meaning of Illness: A Phenomenological Account of the Different Perspectives of Physician and Patient*. London: Kluwer Academic Publishers.

———. 1995. The lived experience of disability. *Human Studies* 18 (1): 9–23.

———, ed. 2001. *Handbook of Phenomenology and Medicine*. London: Kluwer Academic Publishers.

VAN MANEN, M. 1990. *Researching Lived Experience: Human Science for an Action Sensitive Pedagogy*. London, Ontario: Althouse Press.

———. 2001. Professional practice and 'doing phenomenology'. In *Handbook of Phenomenology and Medicine*, edited by S. Kay Toombs. London: Kluwer Academic Publishers.

WAKSLER, FRANCES C. 1991. *Studying the Social Worlds of Children: Sociological Readings*. Boston: The Falmer Press.

———. 1995. Introductory essay: Intersubjectivity as a practical matter and a problematic achievement. *Human Studies* 18 (1): 1–7.

———. 2001. Medicine and the phenomenological method. In *Handbook of Phenomenology and Medicine*, edited by S. Kay Toombs. London: Kluwer Academic Publishers.

WATSON, N. 2002. Well, I know this is going to sound very strange to you, but I don't see myself as a disabled person: Identity and disability. *Disability & Society* 17 (5): 509–27.

WENDELL, SUSAN. 1996. *The Rejected Body: Feminist Philosophical Reflections on Disability*. London: Routledge Press.

WILLIAMS, S.J. and G. BENDELOW. 1999. *The Lived Body: Sociological Theories, Embodied Issues*. London and New York: Routledge.

WINANCE, M. 2006. Pain, disability and rehabilitation practices. A phenomenological perspective. *Disability & Rehabilitation* 28 (18): 1109–18.

———. 2007. Being normally different? Changes to normalization processes: from alignment to work on the norm. *Disability & Society* 22 (6): 625–38.

ZANER, RICHARD M. 1971. *The Problem of Embodiment: Some Contributions to a Phenomenology of the Body*, 2nd edn. The Hague: Martninus Nijhoff.

———. 1998. *Ethics and the Clinical Encounter*. Englewood Cliffs, NJ: Prentice-Hall.

Christina Papadimitriou, Rehabilitation Institute of Chicago, Center for Rehabilitation Outcomes Research (CROR), 345 E. Superior Street, Chicago, IL 60611, USA.
E-mail: cpapadimit@ric.org

THE REMARKABLE LOGIC OF AUTISM: DEVELOPING AND DESCRIBING AN EMBEDDED CURRICULUM BASED IN SEMIOTIC PHENOMENOLOGY

Maureen Connolly

Autism spectrum disorder (ASD) is a wildly heterogeneous lived experience of stressed embodiment. Many children, youths and adults with ASD are unable to access meaningful, relevant physical activity programmes because of the complexities associated with their behavioural, emotional and communicative idiosyncrasies. This paper describes an approach to designing, implementing and evaluating a movement-education-based embedded curriculum which was developed using semiotic phenomenology as a theoretical framework for observations, description and analysis of lived experiences of ASD.

Resumen

El trastorno del espectro del autismo (TEA) [Autism spectrum disorder (ASD)] es una muy heterogénea experiencia vivida del cuerpo en tensión. Muchos niños, jóvenes y adultos con TEA son incapaces de acceder a programas de acticidad física significativos y pertinentes a causa de las complejidades asociadas con sus idiosincracias de comportamiento, emocionales, y comunicativas. Este artículo describe un enfoque para diseñar, poner en práctica y evaluar un currículo incorporado basado en la educación del movimiento que fue desarrollado utilizando la fenomenología semiótica como un armazón para la observación, descripción y análisis de las experiencias vividas del TEA.

Zusammenfassung

Zur Autismusspektrumstörung (ASS) zählt eine Fülle heterogener körperbezogener Erfahrungen. Viele Kinder, Jungendliche und Erwachsene sind aufgrund der Komplexität ihrer verhaltens-, emotions- und kommunikationsbezogenen Eigenheiten nicht in der Lage, in sinnvoller Weise an entsprechenden Bewegungsprogrammen teilzunehmen. Dieser Artikel beschreibt einen Ansatz zur Formung, Implementierung und Bewertung von Lehrplänen im Hinblick auf Bewegungserziehung. Dieser Ansatz wurde mithilfe semiotischer Phänomenologie als dem theoretischen Rahmenkonzept zur Beobachtung, Beschreibung und Analyse der gelebten/praktischen Erfahrung von ASS entwickelt.

摘要

自閉症是廣泛的不同生活經驗的壓力體現。許多患有自閉症的小孩、年輕人及成人，無法使用有意義的、恰當的身體活動計劃，是因牽涉到複雜的、情緒的、行為的、溝通的個人特質。本文描述一種徑路，來設計、實施和評鑑奠基於嵌入式課程的活動教育，其理論架構是建立在使用符號現象學，作為觀察、描述和分析自閉症的生活經驗。

Introduction

The movement-education-based embedded curriculum I have developed and implement in an ongoing way has emerged out of my 30 years working with children, youth and adults with autism spectrum disorder (ASD), and in particular the past ten years working with a stable cohort within an environment where I can train and facilitate an instructional staff. Buttressed by empirical, anecdotal, comparative and research literature sources, I employ semiotic phenomenology as a theoretical framework for understanding and describing lived experiences of ASD. I will here discuss implications of this theoretical framework for physical activity programming with persons with ASD.

In this paper I offer what I believe to be an alternative, complementary approach to understanding and describing lived experiences of ASD and embodied expressions of these lived experiences. I have arrived at this point of proposing an alternative approach to understanding and describing after more than three decades of working with children, youth and adults who manifest the accepted profile of ASD, the last ten years spent in intense, systematic observation, analysis, and programming with a consistent group over time.

ASD is a wildly heterogeneous condition, and everyone living with ASD manifests an idiosyncratic profile, albeit within the broad parameters of accepted features associated with ASD. This being said, I base my curricular model in the dominant tendencies and qualities I have observed over the years (most of which are consistent with the literature) as I have constructed movement profiles on the children, youth and adults with whom I have worked—and from whom I have learned and continue to learn. My paper will unfold in the following sequence: (a) a background section which will include a summary overview of the premises of movement education and similar overview of ASD and the more prevalent and traditional—as well as emerging—approaches to managing it. In the ASD overview I will also include material on sensory integration and conceptual models of learning, since familiarity with this subject matter is important for context; (b) a section describing and discussing the theoretical frameworks I have utilised and what they have allowed me to notice, interrogate, propose, develop, evaluate and refine; and (c) a section describing and discussing my methodology for developing and monitoring the embedded curriculum, including background on movement profiling, habits of body informing the curricular model and descriptions of actual environments and activity programmes and their consequences in the lives of persons with ASD.

Background

Movement Education

Movement education is an approach to the body which influences teaching, learning and attitude in physical/bodily-based programmes. It is based on the premises that there are overarching 'themes' of the moving body—body, space, quality, (effort) and relationship—which are always present, regardless of the movers, the context or the activity (Laban 1949, cited in Connolly 1993). These 'existential' movement themes allow the teacher to plan activities which are *inclusive*, i.e., which operate at a *conceptual* planning level. Examples might be 'sending' as an activity rather than perfecting the mature pattern of the overhand throw, or 'stability' rather than learning a handstand balance. This is not to say that overhand throwing and handstands do not happen in movement education settings—they most certainly do; but the emphasis is on understanding, contextualising, developing and refining movement patterns that are relevant and meaningful to the learners at their own skill levels; the emphasis is not on everyone in the class doing the same thing, at the same time, in the same way. A thematic or conceptual approach to designing and presenting tasks allows for an array of 'correct' responses and the opportunity to refine movement patterns and broaden the movement repertoire. Movement education also has high efficacy as a therapeutic intervention. Persons who experience bodily stress as a result of crisis, trauma, chronic pain, depression or anxiety can learn muscle relaxation and re-patterning techniques which allow them a modest to significant degree of autonomous management of their stress. In addition to relaxation and re-patterning, movement profiles (developed out of systemic and prolonged observation/analysis) can identify dominant, underdeveloped and absent components in a functional and expressive movement repertoire, thereby allowing for individualised programming in under-developed and absent areas of neuro-physiological and expressive development.

This kind of movement-education-based approach is especially powerful for individuals with developmental delays and/or dramatically idiosyncratic movements and behaviour habits. There is room for the 'unusual' or 'unmanageable' body habits or behaviours, possibilities for expanding beyond the existing habits and behaviours, and opportunities for neuromuscular integrative activities to assist in the challenges posed by delayed, missed or under-resourced motor—as well as other developmental—milestones. Movement education, with its strong links to concept understanding at the *bodily*, as well as linguistic level, makes it an ideal complement for programmes whose focus is interactive/relational development. The blending of cognitive, social, emotional and bodily-based activities provides an environment which holds great promise for adaptation, resourcefulness, adventure and meaning making.[1]

ASD and Approaches to Managing It

The current definition of ASD, although refined and broadened over the years, remains remarkably consistent with the features observed in Kanner's (1943) original group of children. Three general categories of behavioural impairment are common to all or most persons who have ASD:

1. A qualitative impairment of reciprocal social interaction;
2. A qualitative impairment in the development of language;
3. Restricted, repetitive and stereotyped patters of behaviour, interests and activities.

These three categories are further refined through consideration of delays or atypical functioning in at least one of the following areas, with onset prior to age three years: (1) social interaction; (2) language as used in social communication; or (3) symbolic or imaginative play.

Asperger's Syndrome and pervasive developmental disorder (PDD) have also been introduced as diagnoses for milder cases which may be on an autistic continuum but are not believed to meet the full criteria of ASD. In addition, persons with ASD commonly have unusual responses to sensory stimuli that can be exaggerated or diminished and positive and negative (depending on context) (Talay-Ongan and Wood 2000; Bellini 2004; Canavera et al. 2005).

Theories abound as possible explanations for this complex way of being in the world; among the most widely consulted are Hobson's (1991) affective developmental theory, Baron-Cohen's (1988, 1989) cognitive theory of mind approach, and Josef Perner's (1991) distinction between the theory of mind and the capacity for meta-representation. Each of these theories serves to illuminate and interrogate the others, and the research— and research debates—continue. In addition, investigation is ongoing regarding less explored psychological and neurological bases for ASD and their possible intersections. Notable among these include Burnette et al.'s (2005) inquiry into weak central coherence and its relation to theory of mind and anxiety in autism; Dykens and Hodapp's (2000) work on genetic causes of developmental disability and Shasty's (2003) molecular genetics of autism spectrum. Contemporary debates fuelled by MRI technologies also acknowledge the complexity of brain adaptation—i.e. are the changes noted in the various sites causing or responding to ASD?

My examination of the literature has allowed me to develop immense respect for the persistence, creativity and findings of cognitive, affective, perceptual, psychological and neurological frameworks. It has also allowed me to notice the relative absence of investigation grounded in embodied (i.e., somatic or 'lived body') or semiotic approaches and frameworks.

Management, Programming and Intervention

While there have been accounts of 'recovery' from ASD, it is more likely than not that most people living with the condition work with strategies of management rather than cure. Chronic illness types of management models are the most prevalent, emphasising support to the child, youth or adult and family; 'treatment' of or interventions into problematic characteristics and complications when possible; and intensive and ongoing efforts to improve the overall functional status of the person with ASD. Evidence suggests that such approaches (based on current knowledge of what works with ASD) can lead to improved functioning and adaptation in many cases and to improved family coping abilities and quality of life in most.

According to the prevailing wisdom, the most important aspect of management, both at the home and in the educational environment, is implementation of an effective behavioural training programme. The details of such programming vary with individual cases, but the specific techniques are drawn from behavioural modification principles of behavioural psychology. The general goal is to use specific types of reinforcement to encourage desirable behaviours and reduce undesirable behaviours. It generally is agreed that positive reinforcement, as opposed to punitive approaches, most often is effective at promoting improvement in skills.

Categories of enablers used in behavioural approaches include consistent routines and schedules, knowledge of expectations, de-sensitisation processes, rehearsal strategies, stimulus cues, environmental adaptations, augmentative communication, peer advocates and motivational procedures. The greatest success occurs when these efforts are started at an early age and used consistently both in the home and in the school or programme site(s). For most children and youths with ASD, educational management typically emphasises development of social skills and communicative language, the long-term goal being a functional and comfortable placement in a least restrictive environment.

Children with ASD generally do best when daily routine and schedule are highly predictable, and when they are well prepared for any variations in routine. The educational plan will also include helping the child gradually learn to accept greater levels of variation and unpredictability.

Many specialised programmes for the treatment of children with ASD have attempted to incorporate these principles. Several widely known and well-documented examples include Dunlap and Fox's (1996) work on early intervention strategies, Krantz and McClannahan's (1999) strategies for integration and transition, Barbara and Mitchell-Kvacy's (1994) excellent articulation of positive behavioural support approaches, and a number of institutionally-based programmes, including Division TEACCH, developed by Schopher, Mesebov and associates at the University of North Carolina, the Indiana Resource Centre for Autism, and Lovaas and associates in California. Other approaches include pharmacological management—increasingly seen as limited—nutritional and vitamin interventions and more unconventional therapies such as facilitated communication and auditory integration training. In any approach that is taken, family support and advocacy—including stress and conflict management, respite and counselling—are critical components.

Most of the programming and interventions developed for persons with ASD are based in behavioural models, largely because behaviour is the most visible and unnerving manifestation of ASD. Aversion techniques—sometimes quite extreme—positive reinforcement strategies, altering the physical environment and varying task variables are among the approaches employed to control, address or eliminate undesirable behaviours and/or repetitive non-functional behaviours (Carr et al. 1996; Koegel et al. 1996; Ghezzi et al. 1999).

Physical activity and exercise programmes are among more recent approaches to addressing behaviours of ASD (Reid et al. 1983; Miller and Miller 1989; Reid et al. 1991; Levinson and Reid 1993; Kaufman 1994). These studies point to the significance of physical activity for reducing negative behaviours and improving quality of life. Other studies within the same area of concern focus more on the intensity and vigorousness of the activity (Elliot et al. 1994; Todd and Reid 2006) and on embodied strategies of meaning for the person with ASD (Connolly and Craig, 2001; Pan and Frey 2006; Carr and

Owen-DeSchryver 2007). The curriculum I have developed considers intensity, as well as *type* and *quality* of movement. The details and significance of these factors will be discussed further in the concluding section of this paper as well as considerations, timing, frequency and markers of effectiveness.

Sensory Integration

Sensory or sensorimotor integration is defined in the cognitive science and disability/rehabilitation literature as the organisation of sensory information for practical use. This organisation occurs within the brain and spinal cord (the central nervous system—CNS), and is often referred to as central processing. Intrasensory and intersensory integration are outcomes of both sensorimotor and perceptual motor training. Intrasensory integration refers to improved function within one sensory system; intersensory integration refers to improved function across sensory systems.

Ten modalities provide sensory input that must be organised and processed by human subjects. These are touch and pressure, kinaesthetic-proprioceptive, vestibular, temperature, pain, smell, taste, vision, audition, the common chemical sense (e.g., eyes burning when peeling an onion). Each modality has a special type of sensory receptor (end organ) that is sensitive only to certain stimuli, and each has a separate pathway from the sensory receptor up the spinal cord to the brain. Sensory systems especially important to motor learning are tactile and deep pressure, kinaesthetic, vestibular and visual. When these systems exhibit 'delayed' or 'atypical' functioning, motor development and/or learning is affected.

Perceptual-motor (P-M) learning is acquiring knowledge about the self and the environment through the integrated processes of sensation, perception and action that occur during spontaneous or teacher/parent-guided movement exploration. P-M learning includes processes of memory, cognition, perceptual-motor skills, sensorimotor integration, perception/decoding and attention. These processes overlap and blend together to constitute central processing.

During the first two years of life, sensory integration usually 'happens' automatically. It develops without the conscious involvement of the developing child, and most of us experience sensory integration (if we bother to think about it at all) as a necessary (albeit taken for granted) feature of being in the world as a concordant (stable, healthy, productive) entity. Likewise with perceptual-motor development, the development 'happens' between the ages of two and seven and we take the gifts of this development as typical and natural.

ASD can be manifested as profound disruptions in sensory integration and perceptual-motor functioning, especially executive control/central processing challenges, curiously amplified responses to sensory input and the dys-integration of sensory and perceptual-motor functioning itself.

Children and adults with autism must live in the world without the taken-for-granted, already established, invisible functioning of sensory integration and perceptual-motor development. The lived experiences of children and adults with such ongoing disruptions compel a deeper examination of normalising narratives of social control, commodity exchange and bodily/behavioural codes (i.e., the politics of sensory integration) and the expectations of ongoing concordance and 'normal functioning'.

Conceptual Models of Learning

A developmental continuum is a way of describing where a person is located along a series of developmental states or milestones. For example, self-care skills: if a child is able to dress himself or herself, and attend to his or her own toileting and personal hygiene, then this achievement places that child at a particular location along a continuum of self-care and independence skills. If these skills are learned by age three to five, then the child is probably on a par with so-called 'typical' child development; if these skills are not in place by age eight, or 12, or 18, then significant interventions and assistance are needed in order for the person to participate in the activities of daily living (ADL) with choices, equity and dignity. Another example might be conflict resolution skills or decision-making skills. Usually we see the beginnings of mature development in these areas by pre-adolescence, but there are many instances of adults in their 20s, 30s and beyond who have not developed healthy conflict resolution or decision-making strategies. Likewise physical development follows a similar progression—particular motor experiences and patterns are seen as significant milestones in healthy neurological development.

When considering the concept of a developmental continuum, several overarching principles must be taken into account:

1. The dimensions of development are interdependent and intertwined; this means that physical, emotional, cognitive and social development are dependent on each other and contribute to each other, and that programming interventions must be integrated across the dimensions if we are to see significant outcomes in any of the dimensions.
2. A developmental continuum is age- and ability-inclusive; this means that persons with and without disabilities exhibit various extremes of the *same developmental area*. For example, language development: a child with ASD may have little or no language development by age five, whereas children without developmental delays may exhibit fairly proficient speech patterns and vocabulary by that age. By contrast, children who grow up in under-resourced environments (without books, ongoing nurturing interaction/conversation or significant adult attention) may also show delayed or skewed language and concept development. Aggression and impulse control are other areas where neuro-physiological or environmental influences may contribute to similar manifestations of developmental delay. And it is certainly the case that a person does not have to manifest extreme degrees of behaviour in order for an intervention to be appropriate.
3. It is never too late to begin programming/interventions for developmental issues; later interventions into established habits can be challenging but persistence within a meaningful, dignified, relevant programming environment usually results in modest to significant improvements.

Not only do I work within a shared understanding of a developmental continuum along which any and all learning can occur, I also work within conceptually driven models of learning—that is to say, I believe there are deep concepts which apply to many kinds of learning and I am more interested in teaching these concepts than in re-enforcing single events which may have no transfer to other events or situations. For example, the concept of 'shape' is a deep one, which cuts across many kinds of learning. If I understand the shape of my foot, then I can find the correct shape for my shoe; if I understand how 'round' works, then I will be able to manage buttons and buttonholes, hats, cereal bowls, lids on jars and bottles and so forth. If I understand up, down, right and left, then I will realise that I have a top and bottom half to my body, as well as a left and a right side; I will understand stairs, elevators, high and low, tall and short; I will cross the mid-line of my body, making more complex neurological processing possible. These kinds of learning transfers do not occur when I learn in a context of disconnected, arbitrary or unrelated skills and activities.

Exploring Alternative Theoretical Frameworks

Before providing the necessary thumbnail sketches of the several non-behavioural frameworks I employ, I must emphasise that the bodily-based understandings and interventions I have developed are offered as *parallel* and not oppositional discourses. I employ many of the features already described in my own programmes, but they are facilitated, and, I believe, enhanced through bodily-based movement education programming.

I work within a complex blending of a number of theoretical frameworks. I primarily identify as a semiotic phenomenologist, heavily influenced by the theoretical work of Maurice Merleau-Ponty (1962) and Richard Lanigan (1988) and the more applied semiotic phenomenological work of Tom Craig (1997, 1998, 2000) and Jackie Martinez (1999). I would be remiss if I did not also acknowledge the edited collection *Semiotics and Disability* (Rogers and Swadener 2001) and especially the essay on the 'Miller Method' by Christine Cook. I should also disclose my own ideological posture and postcolonial biases as well as my years of training in Laban-based movement education, overlaid on three decades of training and practice within physical education and adapted physical activity with the neurological, biomechanical and motor control frameworks therein.

In its most naively articulated form, phenomenology is the study of lived experiences or meaning structures as they reveal themselves to an (embodied) consciousness. Phenomenologists attempt to suspend the 'natural attitude' or already assumed 'truths' or 'givens' about the everyday world. With this bracketing technique (i.e., the placing of one's so-called certainties in brackets) phenomenologists try to experience phenomena as if they had not been encountered or accounted for. In this way the eidetic features or meaning structures of phenomena which might be missed because of presumption or assumption can be encountered and perceived. A common method used within this reductive aspect of phenomenological analysis is free imaginative variations, whereby the understanding of phenomena is pushed to its extreme limits of existential possibility. This allows phenomenologists to consider features and interpretations that might be dismissed as preposterous by the constraints of more traditional approaches.

Further, since consciousness is necessarily embodied, the phenomenological body is constructed as subject/object. This serves to highlight the tension between having and being a body (Lyon and Barbalet 1994). In his book, *Phenomenology of Perception*, Merleau-Ponty (1962) developed a conception of human embodiment which attempted to transcend mind-body dualism. He grounded perception in the experienced and experiencing body. The world as perceived through the body was, for Merleau-Ponty, the ground level of all knowledge, for it is through the body that people gain access to the world. Human perception of everyday reality depends upon a 'lived body' (Bendelow and Williams 1995)—that is, a body that simultaneously experiences and creates the world. This expresses the essential ambiguity of human embodiment as both personal and impersonal, objective and subjective, social/cultural and natural. In the process of inquiry, phenomenologists work though a recursive and embodied process of description, reduction and interpretation all the while taking into account the *Lieb*—animated living through the experiential body (body for itself)—and *Korpor*, the objective exterior institutionalised body (the body in itself).

Invoking the semiotic aspect of semiotic phenomenology means locating the lived body within the codes and signs of a given culture. The body is located at the nexus of lived experience and culture, a portal, a site, an experience. Lanigan's (1988) semiotic phenomenological analysis adds a cultural dimension to the aforementioned phenomenological process of description, reduction and interpretation. It considers the norms and inscriptions of a culture, the body as sign (of political discourse) and the sign systems that hold these together. This analysis necessitates a semiotic and phenomenological examination of the contexts—large and small—that constitute culture and that constrain choices. Lanigan encourages strategies of *choice of context* as opposed to working only within contexts of choice (i.e., where the choices or interpretations are already predetermined by the context). This is an especially helpful framework for studying disability, pain and other forms of stressed embodiment which typically are studied within already established contexts. It is also a more culturally and contingency sensitive approach which acknowledges the complex ways in which ASD, as a 'carnal property' (Paterson and Hughes 1999), is culturally produced and productive.

Semiotic phenomenological approaches are politically postcolonial in their ideology critique and also resonate with infusion- and inclusion-based and cultural/social minority perspective approaches (Sherrill, 1994; Sherrill and Williams, 1996; Sherrill and DePauw 1997). In addition, they allow for an interrogation of tokenistic and/or ablest-driven efforts at integration at all costs, approaches that are coming under critique from an increased presence of disability studies scholars and theorists.

Lived experience accounts are also considered significant data/capta for semiotic phenomenological approaches, hence I have included insider accounts of ASD from Temple Grandin (1986, 1995), Donna Williams (1992; Williams-Venables 1995) and Raun Kaufman (1994) in the development of my analysis and appreciation of ASD, and in the development of an embedded curriculum based in habits of body generated or disclosed by stressed embodiment.

I have also included conversations with the children, youths and adults with ASD with whom I have worked, especially over the past ten years, and conversations with parents, workers and consultants. And, because I am a movement educator, I cannot neglect the observations and analyses of movement I have conducted, again particularly with my cohort of the past ten years. Martha Graham, a movement educator and dancer, claimed that 'movement never lies—it is a barometer telling the state of the soul's weather for all who can read it' (Graham 1997, cited in Connolly and Lathrop 1997). My experience certainly bears this out, I have chosen to suspend cultural norms and inscriptions regarding appropriate behaviour—especially as they relate to embodied expressions of lived experience characteristic of people with ASD – and have chosen to accept these embodied expressions as serious sites of somatic exploration and understanding.

Approaching ASD this way has allowed me to ask embodied questions. For example, Grandin's and Williams's autobiographical writing reveals the intensely stressful experience of sensation from the perspective of the experiencer. Auditory, visual and tactile sensations can be particularly distressing by virtue of how intensely they are manifested for the person with ASD. Further, sensory integration is often a problem for persons with ASD, so there is the constant stress of managing sensation as separate corridors of existence, with the potential for each one to interfere with any or all of the others. I propose that this management of the taken-for-granted is exhausting and anxiety-producing, but it is also 'normal' or 'familiar' for persons with ASD. Because this way of being in the world calls for an ongoing state of readiness (or bracing against the world), it is not surprising that many persons with ASD manifest extreme muscle tension (and possibly concomitant pain) but since this is also 'normal' or 'familiar' it is seldom spoken of by those who are verbal, and difficult to access in those who are non-verbal. Touch is a powerful modality for muscle tension assessment and treatment, but focused observation is equally helpful in locating tension sites. Once located, a tension site can be considered both a doorway and a pathway. It is a way into understanding expressions of distress, and it is a journey into very unfamiliar, usually deep, embodied experience.

Sensation may also be amplified for persons with ASD. As someone with an extremely broad auditory range, I can testify to the distress I feel when I hear (or sense) certain sounds or pitches of sounds. Often others around me do not hear what I hear. This is a frequent event for persons with ASD. They 'receive' across a remarkably broad sound and sight spectrum. When they cover their ears or pull at their ears, or scream or exhibit other signs of distress, I choose to believe it might be in response to an experience of intense and uncontrollable sensory stimulation. When one sensation becomes the focus of attention, it is also possible that it is also serving as filter for or respite from the chaos of non-integration of sensation. According to Grandin, Williams, Kaufman, Vanden-Abeele (2001) and others, many persons with ASD have an over-aroused or 'wild' nervous system. When this is coupled with 'high stim' environments (motion, smells, patterns, sounds, to name a few), one can almost predict levels of embodied overload that have to find an outlet (i.e., that will be processed for an embodied response appropriate to the internal 'logic').

Working semiotically and phenomenologically has allowed me to ask questions such as: If I cannot feel my skin as a boundary between me and the world, what might I do to create some awareness of that boundary? What if this were a fluctuating experience? What if I discovered strategies to make myself present to myself—might I repeat them? Or the converse: if my skin feels everything, what might I do to protect myself? What surfaces or textures might be more soothing? Or: how do I process my body's physiological responses to emotion? Or: how might I manage one activity when so much is happening simultaneously? How do I know what separates one experience from another?

If I am working from the premise that the lived body is the site of meaning-making, then many behaviours associated with ASD can be seen as embodied solutions to existential, neurological, sensory or motor trauma or crisis rather than outbursts of deliberate deviance.

For example, if I do not know where my body ends and the world begins, one solution might be to use nudity against definite textures or in intense temperatures; another solution might be craving pressure, another might be self-biting. Furthermore, some sites of the body may be highly sensitised to stimulation in some persons with ASD (such as the mouth or fingertips, or head or nose), so these sites may emerge as 'first responses' to a 'loss' of self.

Highly sensitised skin feels even the slightest stimulation, so definite or soothing surfaces, textures or contrasting types of pressure might provide relief. Fixations can be strategies for stillness: when a whole world is in motion, achieving some form of stillness is helpful for self-locating. Structure and ritual can contain or 'rein in' an indeterminate, messy blending of space, time and tasks. I have found it helpful to create singular events with distinct beginnings and endings so that an eventual sequence of events can unfold without undue anxiety associated with trying to prevent or discern overlap.

My observations, interactions and ongoing semiotic and phenomenologically grounded interrogations of the embodied expressions of persons with ASD have led me to some tentative and ongoing 'working premises':

1. That the expressions that are developed and/or displayed to me are logical solutions based in an embodied intentionality that need not be based in a pre-established array of neurological 'givens'—i.e., I choose to experience the children, youths and adults in my programmes as geniuses trying to solve problems (usually *without* context-sensitivity or meta-knowledge) rather than deviants trying to annoy me;
2. The more extreme behaviours are manifestations of more extreme terror or unmanageability and my efforts have to go towards identifying or locating the source of the distress in addition to treating the distress;
3. Interventions that are bodily-based, dignified, contrasting and physically exhausting (i.e., intense gross motor activity) can be effective if they are imagined from the perspective of the person with ASD;
4. Most of the people I have worked with have an uncanny sense of my motives and feelings; they are remarkable barometers—with and without language. This compels me to be authentic; and
5. If I believe in the authenticity of embodied expression, then I must base my programming and interventions on it. This means rethinking the norms and inscriptions of cultures based in largely deterministic/behaviourist and productivist values and processes. And I must continue to return to the body as my source, my gut-check, my self-examination. Thus:

> When one is oneself uprooted, what is the point of talking to those who think they have their own feet on their own soil? The ear is receptive to conflicts only if the body loses its footing. A certain imbalance is necessary, a swaying over some abyss, for a conflict to be heard. Yet when the foreigner—the speech—denying strategist—does not utter his conflict, he in turn takes root in his own world of a rejected person whom no one is supposed to hear. The rooted one who is deaf to the conflict and the wanderer walled in by his conflict thus stand firmly, facing each other. It is a seemingly peaceful coexistence that hides the abyss: an abysmal world, the end of the world (Kristeva 1991, 17).

My experiences with persons with ASD over the past several years make it impossible for me to perpetuate a charade of peaceful coexistence which hides the abysses and wonders of lived experiences of ASD. Our strangeness to each other need not be the end of a shared world. We have to move to a place of learning from each others' differences (and embodied experiences) rather than creating hierarchies of legitimacy which exclude (or reprogramme) those who not fit within the narrow parameters of what is considered to be the 'norm'.

For persons with ASD—who can live anywhere along simultaneously occurring and/ or clashing neurological, existential, sensory, perceptual and relational continua—the body *is* a sign of political discourse. Perhaps the willingness—and courage—to embrace our own experiences of uprootedness might be a helpful, humane and embodied strategy for reimagining what counts as 'common ground'.

Methodology for Developing an Embedded Curriculum

A few comments are called for on the strategy of embedded curriculum. The overall structure and content are based in the findings observed over time (ten years) and across contexts (a highly heterogeneous group and a variety of activity settings) and consistent with the neuro-physiological literature. Nevertheless, what I have developed is also necessarily customised to the idiosyncrasies of each person participating in the various movement programmes. The behavioural and attention challenges are immense and require creative teaching and facilitation. One of the tendencies that has been noted as prevalent is the relative absence of midline crossing in the children and youth. Typically, children begin midline crossing as infants (e.g. two hands grabbing one foot) and continue on with thousands of repetitions over the years. Developmentally, I cannot expect to make up for the loss of these repetitions; however, I can set an environment where midline crossing happens regardless of the activity that is scheduled. Likewise, I cannot expect children to engage in high repetition of midline crossing on demand or command. Instead, I must make it inevitable and unavoidable within the activity they are doing. Examples include pulling with two hands on a rope, pushing with two hands on a stick, deliberate cross-body reaching for objects. In this way midline crossing is embedded and does not have to be requested.

Embedding the movement patterns that need attention allows me to work from a lived body perspective within a cultural system of signs and honour the insider's stories and experiences as expressed through autobiographies, biographies, anecdotes, observation and analysis and, increasingly, blogs and other digital media (e.g., Second Life).

The curriculum content and processes have developed over time and are adaptable to each participant's needs. There are, however, habits of body that have consistency across heterogeneity and these form the core of the embedded curriculum. These habits of body are the findings of years of observation and analysis based in Laban movement principles and employing a process of movement profiling for each participant involved in a movement program. The profiles are based in the movement education template (see Appendix) which considers a variety of subcategories within the existential movement themes of body, space, effort/quality and relation—i.e., in lived (perceptual) as well as experienced (sensory) contexts. A summary description of movement profiling follows.

When it comes to observing movement—especially idiosyncratic habits of body— 'seeing it' means more than simply looking. Laban movement analysis offers a non-mechanistic, adaptable, body-friendly approach to observing human movement across contexts and ability levels. Developed by the Austro-Hungarian dancer, choreographer and movement theorist Rudolf Laban, movement education thematic analysis has been used in performance, competition, rehabilitation, training and workplace settings since the

1930s. The beauty of the analytic method is that it provides a framework for observation, a language for description, a notation system for preserving the movement and a logic for therapeutic and/or pedagogic intervention.

The framework is a deceptively simple matrix of existential themes of movement: *body*, *space*, *quality* and *relation* (Laban 1949). Within each of these thematics are features or components which allow for more detailed and individualised breakdown of the overarching theme. For example, within a consideration of *body* one would engage in a deeper consideration of shape, function, body-part responsibilities, symmetry and asymmetry, weight transfer, balance, locomotion and gesture, among others. A consideration of SPACE would compel examination of personal and general use of and awareness of space, directions, pathways, levels, near and far extensions, planes of movement and so forth. If one observed a mover (over time and across context) avoiding or demonstrating distress in the low level, one could anticipate the long-term developmental, strategic and neurological effects of this avoidance, and plan an appropriate intervention.

Movement profiling allows a teacher, coach or therapist to observe a mover over time and across contexts using the features and components of each theme to develop a 'movement fingerprint', such that not only dominant patterns become apparent, but also missing features become apparent. Here, one can plan interventions, use the dominant patterns to facilitate the interventions and then do a follow-up profile to assess the effect of the intervention on the movement repertoire. Since movement-education language is conceptual and non-pejorative, it can be used in any situation with any mover of any movement capacity.

The movement profile, developed out of Laban movement education analysis, can function as a pedagogic, evaluative, pre-post comparative, training and therapeutic tool. It complements other measurement modalities, and can be easily taught to coaches, parents, teachers and other interested professionals.

Habits of Body (Dominances and Absences in the Movement Repertoire)

The following represents a summary of the most consistent habits of body noted from the observations and analysis (i.e., movement profiling).

Dominances in the movement repertoire: fine, sudden movement; limbs kept near the body; flexed spine; same-side or no-arm action; toe walking; uneven gait; balance and balance-regain issues; pathway drifting; uneven skill development.

Absences in the movement repertoire: midline crossing; firm movement; extension of spin and hip; running gait; landings with control; gradual deceleration; contralateral arm-leg movement; weight transfer variety; contrast.

General or less specific habits of body include consequences of seemingly absent or underdeveloped sensory integration and motor milestones (including anxiety, distract-ibility, need for structure, problematic problem solving and decision-making); fixations—including 'codes', metaphors, objects; stimming; over-aroused nervous system; sensory hyper-sensitivities (especially in the 'built' environment); vestibular and perceptual issues; absent, underdeveloped or unevenly developed gross motor activity, especially involving intense exertion in a firm, sustained time/weight register; underdeveloped, hyper-developed or selectively developed body awareness.

Ingredients in the Embedded Curriculum

The embedded curriculum at work in my movement programmes is made up of environmental, content, process and instructional components. I shall describe each of these in the following paragraphs.

Environment

I aim to create an environment low in excess stimulation, which also allows for maximal involvement of the body with the absences from the movement repertoire. Thick, absorptive surfaces compel sustained foot contact with the floor, reduce speed of movement and force firm weight qualities in the large muscles. Unstable surfaces (inclines, declines, absence of perpendicularity and flatness) and obstacles compel ongoing balance loss and regain, controlled and cushioned falls, vestibular and kinaesthetic adjustments and dorsi-flexion at the foot (the heels forced into the surface by virtue of the surface itself assists in reducing toe-walking). Dim or subdued lighting and few or no patterns on walls or floors reduce distractions from extraneous visual stimuli. Contrast in height, task function and inside/outside and/or wet/dry allow for definite 'felt' separations between one type of activity or task and another and allow for activity sequencing to be achieved with more distinctiveness in the attributions and identifiers/signifiers (i.e., the semiotics of each space). Heavy and non-bouncy objects require more gross motor activity for lifting, compel sustained time and firm weight qualities and reduce noise. Many possible entries and exits and the movement equipment stations compel problem-solving and the potential for avoidance, parallel and interactive play. Typical equipment includes thick and heavy mats, heavy props, medicine balls, non-bounce balls and other manipulables, trampolines (large and small), blankets, towels, ropes, scooters, games equipment, fine motor props and toys, containers for toys, equipment set-ups that can be got inside of, parachutes, mattresses, cushions, ladders, trestles and benches, stacking boxes.

Content and Process

Movement programmes, whether they are in a once-a-week, daily or 'summer camp' intensive format, are necessarily structured and predictable, with visual schedules, social stories, scripting and re-directing as significant processes. There is a high level of attunement for body signs of frustration, anxiety and tension and dignified intervention for calming (for example, deep pressure is helpful for many tactile stressors). Time-based activities have distinctive tactile and visual markers for beginnings, middles and endings. Typical activities include body awareness work on core-distal relationships; spinal flexion and extension and assisted flexibility; pushing, pulling, dragging, lifting and carrying; mid-line crossing via gripping, climbing and various forms of reaching across the body to the opposite side; activities that compel intense gross motor activity and result in muscle fatigue; landings from a variety of heights; weight transfers and weight bearing on various combinations of body parts (other than hands and feet).

Instructional Strategies

Participants with ASD typically do not initiate play or activity episodes and, once engaged in an activity, do not conclude or exit episodes well. For this reason—and others (e.g. lack of impulse control, self-injury) facilitation must be ongoing, vigilant, attentive with a neutral and calm demeanour, no sense of urgency and an even, somewhat emotionally flat and lower-volume voice.

When involving students in my movement programmes, I work with direct instruction or as low a teacher-learner ratio as possible on concept learning, which impacts across the dimensions of physical, cognitive, emotional and social development. The outcome goals are relatively simple:

1. Identify the strengths and weaknesses in a person's developmental repertoire, and then use appropriate and dignified interventions to refine the strengths and address the weaknesses in ways which make it possible for the person to interact in meaningful ways with developmentally and/or age compatible peer groups;
2. Continue to refine the programme intervention so that continued development occurs across the developmental dimensions in ways which are consistent with the person's profile;
3. Involve a support team in the developmental process in ways which enhance the ongoing development of the members of the team.

The Gymnasium Space and Pedagogic Intentionality

Each participant has an individualised programme and this program is housed in the larger context of gymnasium spaces and activity areas designed specifically to address the tendencies within ASD which seem to cut across the heterogeneity of each individual living with ASD. I believe our groundedness in a phenomenological orientation enables us to design spaces which are 'insider'-driven and autism-friendly. Further, it allows me to suspend my assumptions and codes of 'normalcy' and preconceptions of what *ought* to happen so that I can imagine what *needs* to happen in order to provide a healthy environment as I move towards expanding the movement and social repertoires of my participants.

The gymnasium is deceptively regular in appearance—an inviting activity space for young children—yet it is a strategic space with a deliberate pedagogical rationale where equipment and space are specifically arranged for the developmental needs of the children who will dwell there for the duration of the planned activity or programme. As has been previously mentioned, the equipment and small apparatus are configured and used in ways which acknowledge the lived experiences of ASD and which provide opportunities to expand the movement repertoires (or limit horizons). Several examples of linkages between ASD lived experience and embedded curriculum follow:

1. Mats on the floor to soften the noises made by balls, small apparatus, and feet. Noise can be a frightening stimulus for many children with ASD and can progress to a level of making participants literally sick or moving to various degrees of panic.

2. Minimal perpendicular/vertical structures since these tend to be overly compelling for children who are over-selective with vertical and horizontal tracking.
3. Practically no flat surfaces—mostly inclines, declines and changes in level and texture of surfaces so that vestibular, tactile and kinaesthetic systems can be stimulated simultaneously.
4. Ropes, bean bags, and squeezable objects compel firm, sustained gripping action—a necessary contrast to the fine, sudden, flicking actions that tend to dominate the movement repertoires of many children with ASD.
5. Heavier than usual balls and other objects to stimulate large muscle activity. Sustained action against a resistance involves the neuromuscular system in ways that contrast the usual movement patterns of the activities of daily living in ASD. Also, many children are either hypotonic or hypertonic, and need intense and consistent neuromuscular stimulation.
6. Variety and open space within the larger space allows for motion to be spread out over a larger surface area. Too much motion or 'busy-work' in one area can be over-stimulating and distressing for children with ASD.
7. Portable movement tasks—i.e., no matter where children are working, the focus is on developing sustained time and firm weight qualities, kinaesthetic awareness of body parts relative to each other and the body core, tactile awareness of deep pressure and body boundaries, vestibular activities which compel balance regain, and large muscle activity which calls upon consistent neuromuscular involvement.

When a programme intervention works, it works conceptually and it works across the developmental dimensions. For example, when I do physical programming involving intense and vigorous gross motor activity, the child experiences a different kind of neuromuscular involvement in the activity; this usually results in fatigue—real fatigue, not simply the cumulative distress of being in the world—and the child sleeps through the night. Parents continually remark on the improved sleep patterns following these physical programmes and the ripple effects, including parental sleep and the fact the child is more alert and attentive in morning, exhibits less unmanageable behaviour at night and is at ease in learning tasks, to name a few. Further, gross motor activity stimulates more focused cognitive learning and more manageable social skills programming (since the child is calmer).

Observed outcomes in the movement programme participants include: real fatigue and real sleep; improvements in fitness and strength and expansion in the movement repertoire, hence improvements in self-sufficiency and activities of daily life; improvements in motor milestones; reduction in 'stimming'[2] behaviours; improvements in redirection and self-selection of preferred modes of relaxation; some improvements in social read, activity initiation, parallel and partner play. A welcome outcome for parents, workers and teachers is an increased awareness of early signs of distress, hence earlier implementation of appropriate interventions.

Larger Outcomes and Consequences

The ASD population is quite diverse, in so far as it is also homogeneous in its disability base. The families with whom I work are located variously across the developmental dimensions: high, medium and low economic status; graduate, university, professional, high-school or grade-school educations; high, moderate and low involvement in their children's lives and programming.

The factor that seems to stand out as common across these families who are living with a person with a disability is stress—there are high levels of stress based in uncertainty, guilt, scheduling, funding, programmes, schools, interpersonal communication and time management, to name a few of the contributing factors. This stress can and does manifest itself in pain, insomnia, forgetfulness, depression, anxiety, irritability, despair, intensities of emotion and a variety of related illnesses (migraines, ulcers, heart disease, G-I disorders, respiratory disorders). When I introduce a programme intervention for the person with a disability, it often creates a ripple effect, and other aspects of family life are also affected.

When the parents are involved in aspects of programming, the child benefits from the ongoing, consistent application and reinforcement of concepts over time and across contexts, but the parents also benefit. They learn focus, planning, attending, listening and observing skills; they learn how to give appropriate feedback; they learn balance and priority in their own lives; they learn more effective stress management; and they learn to be more reflective about their own behaviours.

Meaningful movement programmes such as the embedded curriculum described in the paper also have incalculable professional development, policy development, pedagogic and scholarly benefits, including:

1. continued provision of a necessary service based in physical activity;
2. opportunities to study and increase understanding of persons with ASD;
3. opportunity for inter-agency liaison;
4. heightened profile of ASD in the community;
5. expanded movement and social skills repertoires in programme participants;
6. movement profiles are portable to schools and specialised programs as benchmarks for evaluation of progress;
7. increased exposure to ASD for young professionals in training;
8. increased potential for transdisciplinary work (especially across disciplines using markedly differing methodologies, i.e., semiotic phenomenology and neurophysiology);
9. appreciation for scholarship and pedagogy with a basis in narrative, lived experience and robust observation.

Concluding Comments

Patti Lather (1991) sees socially conscious research leading to theory-building with a difference: that is, theory that is generated out of the everyday world and in conjunction with people living in their everyday worlds. In Lather's words:

> For praxis to be possible, not only must theory illuminate the lived experience of progressive social groups, it must also be illuminated by their struggles. Theory adequate to the task of changing the world must be open-ended, non-dogmatic, speaking to and grounded in the circumstances of every day life. It must, moreover, be premised on a deep respect for the intellectual and political capacities of the

dispossessed. This position has profound substantive and methodological implications. (Lather 1991, 55)

The basic ingredients of such approaches include the 'informants' as active agents in the construction and validation of meaning out of their own experiences (e.g. accounts, life-world descriptions), the questioning of the 'given' or 'natural' in a dialogic enterprise, and a focus on fundamental contradictions which demonstrate how 'ideologically frozen understandings' (Comstock 1982, 384) are not able to serve the interests of the people involved. Gradual and more courageous forays into ideology critique call for prolonged engagement and many entry points as participants move to a negotiation of meaning beyond the descriptive level, which necessarily includes negotiation with consciousness, unconsciousness and false consciousness in self and others, not to mention the often shattering acknowledgement of the carnal, heterogeneous body.

It is the authentic engagement with the carnal, heterogeneous bodies of the children, youth and adults with ASD that I have worked with that forms the basis of the embedded curriculum. This engagement has been made viable as a scholarly praxis using semiotic phenomenology as both orientation and methodology.

A few contemporary phenomenological theorists (most notably Maurice Merleau-Ponty) grant a legitimacy to the lived body, inextricably intertwined with inter-subjective, communicative, expressive projects of lived relation. Indeed, in his *Phenomenology of Perception* Merleau-Ponty critiques perceptual faith as a habitual unreflexivity based on a subject-object epistemology within a pre-established standpoint in which subjects perceive the world from a detached and distant perspective (Merleau-Ponty 1962, 13–14). To counter this naive notion, Merleau-Ponty proposes a concrete subject as the existential 'lived body' (*corps propre*) that must not be bracketed *out* but rather taken *in* as the starting point of all phenomenological analysis. However, in spite of what body-friendly educators (and researchers) see as the enlightened embrace of actual bodies in some phenomenological work, in the main, much phenomenological work is committed to (and premised on) the ontological self-givenness of the so-called 'objective body'.

Merleau-Ponty (in *The Cogito of Phenomenology of Perception*) presents a critique of an ideology of rationality as being unable to go beyond itself, by virtue of its having to use its own internal criteria to continue to validate its own concordances. According to Merleau-Ponty, all that one has to do to get out of this loop is to 'recognise these phenomena which are the ground of all our certainties. The belief in an absolute mind, or in a world in itself detached from us is no more than a rationalisation of this primordial faith' (1962, 409).

Moving away from the ground of all our certainties requires a human-science approach which is both bodily based and culturally (and, often times, politically) sensitised. Lanigan's (1988) semiotic phenomenology provides a helpful theoretical framework for exploring embodied contingency (e.g. the stressed embodiment of ASD) by combining phenomenological explication of the freedom of individual expression with semiotic analysis of the field of culturally sedimented perception. Here, I can work carefully with the expressive bodies of programme participants as they disclose through words, codes, movement, habit and gesture how they live with and through autism spectrum disorder. Here, I can honour their bodily expressions by creating and adapting a curriculum that is responsive to them while at the same time building bridges to a shared community and culture. Ultimately, it is the body I must take seriously as my guide and my muse. In Merleau-Ponty's words:

> If the subject *is* in a situation, even if he is no more than a possibility of situations, this is because he forces his ipseity into reality only by actually being a body, and entering the world through the body. In so far as, when I reflect on the essence of subjectivity, I find it bound up with that of the body and that of the world, this is because my existence as subjectivity is merely one with my existence as a body and with the existence of the world, and because the subject that I am, when taken concretely, is inseparable from this body and this world. The ontological world and body which we find at the core of the subject are not the world or body as idea, but on the one hand, the world itself, contracted into a comprehensive grasp, and on the other hand, the body itself as a knowing body. (1962, 408)

The embedded curriculum articulated in this paper is a project of reading movement and honouring bodies. Such a project is theoretically defensible through a semiotic phenomenology of the experience of the body coupled with a consciousness of choice, and it is experientially constituted by a phenomenological and semiotic sensibility grounded in the actual bodies we—all of us—live.

NOTES

1. A detailed outline of the Laban grid used in profile development can be read in Appendix A.
2. 'Stimming' … stimming is any repetitive, usually gestural or movement-based behaviour exhibited by a person with autism which the observer assumes has no purpose or which appears to the observer to provide a form of escape from an undesired situation for the person engaging in the stimming.

REFERENCES

BARBARA, L.M. and A.A. MITCHELL-KVACY. 1994. Positive behavioural support for students with developmental disabilities: An emerging multi-component approach for addressing challenging behaviours. *School Psychology Review* 23: 263–78.

BARON-COHEN, S. 1989. Social and cognitive deficits in autism: Cognitive or affective? *Journal of Autism and Developmental Disorders* 18: 379–402.

―――. 1988. The autistic child's theory of mind: A case of specific developmental delay. *Journal of Child Psychology and Psychiatry* 30: 285–97.

BELLINI, S. 2004. Social skill deficits and anxiety in high functioning adolescents with autism spectrum disorders. *Focus on Autism and Other Developmental Disabilities* 19 78–86.

BENDELOW, G. and S. WILLIAMS. 1995. Transcending the dualisms: Towards a sociology of pain, *Sociology of Health and Illness* 17: 139–55.

BURNETTE, C., D. CHARAK, J. MEYER, P. MUNDY, S. SUTTON and A. VAUGHAN. 2005. Weak central coherence and its relation to theory of mind and anxiety in autism. *Journal of Autism and Developmental Disorders* 35: 63–73.

CANAVERA, K., D. EVANS, F. KLEINPETER, E. MACCUBIN and K. TAGA. 2005. The fears, phobias and anxieties of children with autism spectrum disorders and down syndrome: comparisons with developmentally and chronologically age matched children. *Child Psychology and Human Development* 36: 3–26.

CARR, E.G. and J.S. OWEN-DESCHRYVER. 2007. Physical illness, pain and problem behaviour in minimally verbal people with developmental disabilities. *Journal of Autism and Developmental Disorders* 37 (3): 413–24.

CARR, E.G., C.E. REEVE and D. MAGITO-MCLAUGHLIN. 1996. Contextual influences on problem behaviours in people with developmental disabilities. In *Positive Behavioural Support*, edited by L.K. Koegel, R.L. Koegel and G. Dunlap. Baltimore, MD: Brookes.

COMSTOCK, D. 1982. A method for critical research. In *Knowledge and Values in Social and Educational Research*, edited by E. Bredo and W. Feinberg. Philadelphia, PA: Temple University Press.

CONNOLLY, M. 1993. Respecting children's voices: Shared sentiments in the work of Waksler, Lather and Laban. *Human Studies* 16: 457–567.

CONNOLLY, M. and T. CRAIG. 1999. Your body tells me stories: Living pain, flirting madness, transforming care, *Narratives of Professional Helping* 5 (4) (Disability and Diversity): 16–26.

———. 2001. Stressed embodiment: Doing phenomenology in the wild (Invited essay in 25th anniversary issue of *Human Studies*). Dordrecht: Kluwer.

CONNOLLY, M. and A. LATHROP. 1997. Maurice Merleau-Ponty and Rudolf Laban – an interactive appropriation of parallels and resonances. *Human Studies* 20: 27–45.

CRAIG, T. 1997. Disrupting the disembodied status quo: Communicology in chronic disabling conditions. Unpublished doctoral dissertation, Southern Illinois University at Carbondale.

———. 1998. Liminal bodies, medical codes. In *Semiotics 1997* (Proceedings of 22nd annual meeting of the Semiotics Society of America). New York: Peter Lang Publishing.

———. 2000. A funny thing happened on the way to renown: On the concrete essence of chronic illness and the intercorpoeal weight of human suffering. Paper presented in the panel Articulating Phenomenologies of Embodied Speaking Subjects', annual meeting of Society for Phenomenology and the Human Sciences, Pennsylvania State University, 5–7 Oct.

DALRYMPLE, N. 1992. *Helpful Responses to Some of the Behaviors of Individuals with Autism.* Bloomington, IN: Indiana Resource Center for Autism, Indiana University.

DUNLAP, G. and L. FOX. 1996. Early intervention and serious problem behaviours: A comprehensive approach. In *Positive Behavioural Support*, edited by L.K. Koegel, R.L. Koegel and G. Dunlap. Baltimore, MD: Brookes.

DYKENS, E.M. and HODAPP, R.M. 2000. Applying the new genetics. In *Genetics and Mental Retardation Syndromes*, edited by E.M. Dykens, R.M. Hodapp and B.M. Finucane. Baltimore, MD: Brookes.

ELLIOT, R.O., A.R. DOBBIN, G.D. ROSE and H.V. SOPER. 1994. Vigorous aerobic exercise versus general motor training activities: Effects on maladaptive and stereotypic behaviours of adults with both autism and mental retardation. *Journal of Autism and Developmental Disorders* 24 (5): 565–76.

GHEZZI, P.M., W.L. WILLIAMS and J.E. CARR, eds. 1999. *Autism Behavioural – Analytic Perspectives.* Reno, NV: Context Press.

GRANDIN, T. 1995. *Thinking in Pictures.* New York: Vintage.

GRANDIN, T. and M. SCARIANO. 1986. *Emergence: Labeled Autistic.* Novato, CA: Arena Press.

HOBSON, R.P. 1991. What is autism? *Psychiatric Clinician, North America* 14: 1–17.

KANNER, L. 1943. Autistic disturbances of affective contact. *Nervous Child* 2: 217–50.

KAUFMAN, R. 1994. *Son-rise: The Miracle Continues*. Tiburon, CA: H.J. Kramer.

KOEGEL, L.K., R.L. KOEGEL and G. DUNLAP, eds. 1996. *Positive Behavioural Support*. Baltimore, MD: Brookes.

KRANTZ, P.J. and L.E. MCCLANNAHAN. 1999. Strategies for integration: Building repertoires that support transitions to public schools. In *Autism Behavioural – Analytic Perspectives*, edited by P.M. Ghezzi, W.L. Williams, and J.E. Carr. Reno, NV: Context Press.

KRISTEVA, J. 1991. *Strangers to Ourselves*, trans. Leon S. Roudiez. New York: Columbia University Press.

LANIGAN, R. 1988. *Phenomenology of Communication*. Pittsburgh, PA: Duquesne University Press.

LATHER, P. 1991. *Getting Smart – Feminist Research and Pedagogy with/in the Postmodern*. New York: Routledge.

LEVINSON, L. and G. REID. 1993. The effects of exercise intensity on the stereotypic behaviors of individuals with autism. *Adapted Physical Activity Quarterly* 10 (3): 255–68.

LOVAAS, I. 1981. *The Me Book*. Austin, TX: Pro Ed.

LYON, M.L. and J.M. BARBALET. 1994. Society's body: Emotion and the somatization of social theory. In *Embodiment and Experience: The Existential Ground of Culture and Self*, edited by T.J. Csordas. Cambridge: Cambridge University Press.

MARTINEZ, J. 1999. *Phenomenology of Chicana Experience and Identity*. New York: Roman and Littlefield.

MERLEAU-PONTY, M. 1962. trans. Colin Smith. *Phenomenology of Perception*. Englewood Cliffs, NJ: The Humanities Press.

MILLER, A. and E.E. MILLER. 1989. *From Ritual to Repertoire: A Cognitive-developmental Systems Approach with Behaviour-disordered Children*. New York: John Wiley and Sons.

PAN, C. and G.C. FREY. 2006. Physical activity patterns in youth with autism spectrum disorders. *Journal of Autism and Developmental Disorders* 36 (5): 597–606.

PATERSON, K. and B. HUGHES. 1999. Disability studies and phenomenology: The carnal politics of everyday life. *Disability and Society* 14 (5): 597–610.

PERNER, J. 1991. *The Representational Mind*. Cambridge, MA: MIT Press.

REID, G., D. COLLIER and M. CAUCHON. 1991. Skill acquisition by children with autism: Influence of prompts. *Adapted Physica Activity Quarterly* 8: 357–66.

REID, G., D. COLLIER and B. MORIN. 1983. The motor performance of autistic individuals. In *Adapted Physical Activity*, edited by R. Eason, T. Smith, and F. Caron. Champaign, IL: HKP.

ROGERS, L.J. and B.B. SWADENER, eds. 2001. *Semiotics and Disability – Interrogating Categories of Difference*. Albany, NY: SUNY Press.

SCHOPLER, E. and G.B., MESIBOV, ed. 1987. *Neurobiological Issues in Autism*. New York: Plenuum Press.

SHASTY, B. 2003. Molecular genetics of autism spectrum disorder. *Journal of Human Genetics* 48 (10): 495–501.

SHERRILL, C. and K.P. DEPAUW. 1997. Adapted physical activity and education. In *History of Exercise and Sport Science*, edited by J.D. Massengale and R.A. Swanson. Champaign, IL: HKP.

SHERILL, C. and T. WILLIAMS. 1996. Disability and sport: Psychosocial perspectives on inclusion, integration, and participation. *Sport Science Review* 4 (1): 42–64.

SHERILL, C. 1994. Least restrictive environments and total inclusion philosophies: Critical analysis. *Palaestra* 10 (3): 25–35.

SZATMARI, P. 1991. Asperger's syndrome: Diagnosis, treatment, and outcome. *Psychiatric Clinician, North America* 14: 81–93.

TALAY-ONGAN, A. and K. WOOD. 2000. Unusual sensory sensitivities in autism: a possible crossroad. *International Journal of Disability, Development and Education* 47 (2): 201–12.

TODD, T. and G. REID. 2006. Increasing physical activity in individuals with autism. *Focus on Autism and Other Developmental Disabilities* 21 (3): 167–76.

VANDEN-ABEELE, J. 2001. Training, sport and dance for persons having a disability – person centered and action-oriented dynamic approach. Paper presented in conjunction with the Active Living Alliance for Canadians with a Disability, 12th annual forum, Brock University, St Catharines, Ontario, 14–18 June.

WILLIAMS, D. 1992. *Nobody Nowhere: The Extra-ordinary Autobiography of an Autistic*. New York: Times Books/Random House.

WILLIAMS-VENABLES, D. 1995. Non-firings, over-firings, and mis-firings: The confusing case of making sense of emotions. *MAAP Newsletter* 1: 3–5.

Maureen Connolly, Physical Education and Kinesiology, Faculty of Applied Health Sciences, Brock University, 500 Glenridge Avenue, St Catherines, ON L2S 3A1, Canada. E-mail: mconnoll@brocku.ca

APPENDIX
Movement concepts

Body Awareness	Space Awareness	Effort	Relationships
1. Basic body function: bend, curl, stretch or twist	**1. Personal space – kinesphere:** a) 3-dimensional cross	**1. Qualities:** a) weight – firm (strong) – fine (light) – heavy	**1. With objects:** a) manipulative – send/receive/ retrain
2. Body parts can: a) bend, curl, stretch or twist b) lead an action c) be used symmetrically or asymmetrically	b) diagonals c) planes **2. General space:** a) levels – high/ medium/low	b) time – sudden (fast) – sustained (slow)	b) nonmanipulative – obstacle/ extension/ target/apparatus **2. With people:** a) alone
3. Weight bearing: a) support (body parts taking weight) b) transference of weight c) balance – counterbalance – counter-resistance – counter tension	b) pathways – air – floor (straight, angular curved, twisted) c) extensions – large, small, near, far d) directions	c) space – direct (straight) – flexible (wavy) d) flow – bound (stoppable) – free (ongoing) **2. Emphasize one element**	b) alone in a mass c) partners, small groups, large groups (cooperatively/ competitively) copy question/ answer
4. Body actions: a) locomotion b) elevation c) turns d) gestures e) inversion	**3. Space words:** over, under, around, near, far, towards, away from, onto, into, above, below	**3. Emphasise two elements** **4. Basic effort actions:** **3 elements** a) thrust-sudden/ firm/direct b) slash-sudden/ firm/flexible	match action/ reaction mirror dance together contrast travel with unison lead/follow conversation
5. Body shapes: pin, wall, ball, screw **6. Symmetrical and asymmetrical use of the body** **7. Motion and stillness**	**4. Using space:** explore, penetrate, fill, surround, replace **5. Spatial mass**	c) flick-sudden/ fine/flexible d) dab-sudden/ fine/direct e) press-sustained/ firm/flexible f) wring-sustained/ firm/flexible g) float-sustained/ fine/flexible h) glide-sustained/ fine/direct	cannon send/ receive take turns merge/disperse meet/part near/far passing dance to linking d) Intergroup relationships

ETHICAL ASPECTS IN RESEARCH IN ADAPTED PHYSICAL ACTIVITY

Anne-Mette Bredahl

This paper discusses some of the ethical aspects in research in Adapted Physical Activity (APA). It indicates some of the ethical challenges related to the choice of research problem to be investigated, and the treatment of participants, not least when working with people who are in some ways in a more vulnerable life situation. Drawing also on experiences as a researcher with a disability, the challenges and potential benefits of involving people with disabilities in APA research is critically discussed.

Resumen

El artículo trata sobre los aspectos éticos en la investigación de la actividad física adaptada (AFA) [Adapted Physical Activity (APA)]. Indica algunos de los desafíos éticos relacionados con la elección del problema de investigación a ser indagado y el tratamiento de los participantes, todo lo más importante cuando se trabaja con personas que, de algunas maneras, están en una situación más vulnerable. Basándome también en mis experiencias como investigadora con una discapacidad, trato críticamente los desafíos y beneficios potenciales a la hora de involucrar a gente con discapacidades en la investigación de la AFA.

Zusammenfassung

Dieser Aufsatz diskutiert einige ethische Aspekte der Forschung in Bezug auf Bewegung, Spiel und Sport in Prävention, Rehabilitation und Behinderung (APA = adapted physical activity). Es werden ethische Herausforderungen hervorgehoben, die sich aus der Auswahl des Forschungsgegenstandes und der Behandlung der Teilnehmer ergeben. Insbesondere ist zu berücksichtigen, dass sich die Teilnehmer zum Teil in einer verletzlicheren Lebenssituation befinden. Unter Bezug auf Erfahrungen als Forscher mit Behinderten werden die Herausforderungen und möglichen Vorteile der Einbindung von Behinderten in die APA-Forschung kritisch diskutiert.

摘要

本文在於討論一些研究適應體與活動中所產生的一些倫理課題層面。這顯示出一些對研究選擇上的倫理課題挑戰，以及對參與者的處理方式，不只限於

與一些在較脆弱生活中的人們之工作關係。本文也針對殘障研究者的經驗來
仔細探討適應體育活動所涉入的殘障人士所面對的挑戰與潛在利益。

Introduction

Adapted physical activity (APA) is a cross-disciplinary body of knowledge centred on making physical activity possible for people who experience difficulties with movement (Reid 2003, 20). It is a young and interesting field of research with many topics yet to be explored. Having worked in the area since 1993[1] and participated in international conferences in APA, however, I have been surprised by the apparent lack of discussion and questioning of ethical aspects of the research. With a background as a trained clinical psychologist, I have been 'brought up' in a tradition where ethical aspects should always be considered.[2] Now, working in the field of research and APA, I find that ethical considerations are often overlooked, or at least seldom discussed openly and in a committed way.

Ethicists of science look at science as a process, as a form of socially organised human activity. Scientific activity has assumptions, consequences and functions that demand ethical and political assessment and legitimisation (Tranøy 1986). It is this ethical assessment and legitimisation, where research carried out is seen as part of a bigger picture, that I want to promote here within the debate concerning APA research. As expressed by McNamee, ethics should be in the heart of sport as a practical activity, and every topic in sport necessarily has an ethical dimension, often of considerable significance (McNamee et al. 2007).

In the field of APA good and useful research is being done where the aim and justification is obvious; in some research in APA it seems more unclear, and the same applies with regard to treatment of participants and other ethical issues. In some studies it appears as if researchers have not given these aspects the attention that I believe they deserve. Instead, ethical aspects sometimes seem to be treated more like useful technical reminders of how to conduct research and as 'having to pass an ethical committee', ensuring that the research is 'not harmful to the research subjects' and that the statistical significance of the results is of great importance to the study. This is a somewhat harsh stance, and I will seek to illustrate and discuss it critically through examples in this article.

Reid (2000) indicates in his article 'Future directions for inquiry in APA', that there have been few philosophical papers in APA—which is unfortunate, since ideology plays an important part in APA. He finds that ethical considerations have to be one of the future's main areas for development in APA; and writes that 'A careful study of ethics will assist adapted physical activity to critically evaluate accepted rules and practices. A value system, thereby created, in conjunction with databased experience and experiment, will guide intervention' (Reid 2000, 370). While Reid's remarks were written in 2000, the topic has still received very little attention in *Adapted Physical Activity Quarterly* (*APAQ*), the main journal in the field. In fact, when searching through the articles published in the journal since then, it has not been possible to find any articles that have ethical issues as their main topic.

In research in APA it has also been surprising to discover the lack of participation of researchers who themselves have a disability.[3] It is noticeable seen in the light of approaches promoted by the disability rights movement, where the necessity of involvement of people with disabilities in the research that concerns them is strongly advocated (Barton 1996; Charlton 2000; Johnstone 2001). Bridges (2001), however, indicates that it is not a matter of 'outsiders' (not from the group in focus for the research) not being able to make valuable and ethical sound research; still the lack of involvement is striking as APA research and statements today often seem to promote inclusion.

I am well aware that ethics in research is a comprehensive topic, yet rather than providing answers I want to indicate some of the ethical challenges in research in APA, make some suggestions and, most of all, invite a debate on the matter.

Choosing Topics for Research in APA

Can choosing topics for research in APA research be seen as an ethical challenge? To what degree does a study need to have an obvious purpose or aim to solve a problem? It could be projects such as: 'Fitness of Black African early adolescents with and without mild mental retardation' (Onyewadume 2006) or 'The ideal relation of extensor and flexor muscles of the knee as the target of rehabilitation programs' (Tsaklis et al. 1998). Do we have a special obligation when researching with human participants? Of course there is a wide span of the types of research and I am well aware of the distinction between therapeutic and non-therapeutic research (McNamee et al. 2007), where the first (potentially) aims directly to benefit participant(s), which is not the case or aim in the latter. Precisely how well the type and the aim of the research is communicated to potential participants, without overestimating the potential outcome of the research, is also an ethical consideration. Haywood (1977) also stresses how there are types of studies that have already been researched enough, for instance studies comparing people with disability with those without. While researching the developmental challenges of growing up with a visual impairment and the possible benefits of participation in physical activity (Bredahl 1997), the article with the title 'The effect of regular exercise programmes for visually impaired and sighted schoolchildren' (Blessing et al. 1993) appeared. The 60 youngsters in the study (half of them with visual impairment) completed a physical test, then subsequently a 16-week training programme, and finally were retested. The results were hardly surprising: the students who had trained became fitter, whether they were visually impaired or not. It might not seem fair to single out this particular project, as it is not unique in kind; nor am I criticising the way in which this particular study was carried out. It made me wonder, however, precisely what assumptions lay behind the study. Moreover, what were the researchers actually trying to examine or test, as it has already been demonstrated numerous times that physical training makes people fitter. It is not the design of the study that I question, as the same study could have been interesting if it had been carried out with a different group of participants—people with multiple sclerosis or muscular dystrophy, for instance. These diagnoses affect people in a way that would make it interesting to investigate whether or not participants would benefit from a particular form of physical training, or perhaps whether it actually had an opposite effect. Acknowledging my limited understanding of physiology, I do not, however, find any justification for a hypothesis that training would *not* affect muscle strength and oxygen uptake simply due to a lack of vision.

This might not seem like an ethical problem. As Haywood (1977) emphasises, however, when researching with human participants it is an ethical consideration for researchers to reflect upon to what degree the project is likely to be meaningful to society or to the participants, and also whether the resources we use and the effort we ask of the participants is worth it with regard to the possible results of our projects.

Mentioning projects like the ones above is not meant as examples to demonstrate that quantitative or medically-based research is not meaningful or important. There are many examples of such research, but also examples of research that could benefit from a greater dialogue with practitioners and athletes. At one APA conference, for instance, a wheelchair basketball player presented the problem: 'We use normal height basketball hoops when playing wheelchair basketball. The hoops used are constructed to fit two-metre-tall men, who are able to jump. When we sit in a wheelchair and are not able to jump, the height of the hoops excludes many players with more severe injuries from the play.' He raised the question: *What hoop height is optimal for including the most players without losing the characteristics of the game?* Unfortunately the scientific committee of the conference turned down his paper, and he had to settle for a poster presentation (Mills 1998). The issue he raised, however, was a question that researchers could look into from a biomechanical perspective in order to find answers that could make a difference by helping to solve a problem raised by an athlete who had experienced a practical problem in his sport. This could be seen as an example where a closer dialogue between researchers and people with disabilities might benefit both the researchers in finding interesting topics for research and the people it aims to assist more than what might often happen today.

Treatment of Participants

Another ethical concern that I wish to raise is the treatment of participants in research. It is a concern shared across medical and social research traditions, and an issue that always should concern us as researchers. This not least when researching with participants, as in APA, who in some ways could be seen as vulnerable. Although the meaning of a study such as the one mentioned concerning youngsters with visual impairment above could be questioned, it is not likely to have been harmful to its participants. I find, however, that in order not to do 'harm', it is important for researchers not only to consider the risk of physical injuries to the participants but also to consider the risk of psychological stress, and to make sure that the participants in the study are treated with dignity (Resnik 1998; Drowatsky 1996). By 'dignity' I mean treating participants with respect and not making them participate in anything pointless or humiliating. Although in much research, the treatment of participants in research appears to be taken seriously, I have listened to presentations of research projects at APA conferences, where participants did not seem to be treated with dignity. Frankly, this research could have been done just as well with rats.

Consider the example of researching reaction time with a Down syndrome population (Tranda et al. 1998). The aim of the project was to test whether people with Down syndrome could improve their reaction time. To test this, participants were asked to practice pressing a button repeatedly over a three-week period, and their reaction times and improvements were measured. The study concluded that it could be demonstrated that the participants had improved their reaction time.

On hearing the presentation, I asked about the purpose of the study, and whether the results potentially could be of benefit for the participants, for people with Down syndrome in general or to professionals working with people with Down syndrome. The presenter, however, did not understand my question, and repeated that the aim was to test whether people with Down syndrome, by practising pressing a button for three weeks, could improve their reaction time. According to the presenter, however, this would not make any difference in the participants' everyday lives. I consider a project such as the one described above to be ethically questionable. Not because of the way in which the study was designed, as it could have been relevant if presented as a part of a larger complex issue, or possibly if it had been carried out with a different target group. If, for instance, the study had concerned elite-level fencers, some milliseconds might potentially have made a difference to their performances.

Some might argue that it is solely up to participants to decide whether they want to participate in any type of project. I do not discourage such arguments; I would, however, question how clear the purpose of the study was to the participants and I would also emphasise the authority of the position of being a researcher holds while recruiting participants.

The ethics of this study seen even more questionable, since the participants (here with Down syndrome) might not fully understand the purpose of the study or what their participation implied. A challenge when working with a group of such participants is to make sure that the participants understand the meaning of the project, and also understand the meaning of 'informed consent', which includes the right to withdraw from a project one does not wish to participate in any more (Ervik 1998; Bannerman et al. 1990; Reid et al. 1993; Stineman and Musick 2001).

This project might not have been directly harmful to its participants, yet for both the participants themselves and for the purpose of accumulating knowledge for society, I would say that the results had a very limited use. Which raises questions about the responsibilities of organisers of conferences and editors of journals: to what extent are ethical considerations raised when selecting studies for presentations? Some might suspect that the research in a project such as the one above is more concerned with providing an opportunity to produce and present a paper at an international conference than it is with ethical issues and the treatment of its participants.

When I relate my experiences of witnessing such questionable projects to my colleagues in Norway, they find it hard to believe. Their surprise and doubt are supported by the fact that an ethical committee in Norway would not be likely to approve such projects.

One could say that the example mentioned above is just a matter of poor research; however in research by well-established researchers also I find a lack of discussion of more fundamental ethical questions. One example is the highly regarded set of studies with the aim of providing training programmes to enable babies with Down syndrome to walk earlier than they normally would (Ulrich et al. 2001). The research shows that participation in a daily training programme hastens the babies' ability to walk by an average of three months, which means they walk at an average age of 21 months. I do not doubt the results or the sincere effort put into the study; there are, however, some more fundamental questions I find it relevant to raise such as: why is it important to walk earlier? An answer such as 'to walk closer to what babies normally do' is not sufficient. It is not that these children would never be able to walk, so is one perhaps just pushing a skill that would come in due time? From my point of view it would be relevant to examine questions such as: what are the meanings of walking? Does earlier walking provide the child with opportunities that it otherwise would not have had? And is it possible to see any difference later on in life between children who did and did not participate, a difference that possibly could be linked to the project?[4] It could also be interesting to look at how the family as a whole was affected. Was having to train the disabled child every day worth the effort for the family as a whole in order to speed up the child's process of learning how to walk? Ethical considerations like these might strengthen the study.

Involvement of People with Disabilities in APA Research

The involvement of, and influence by, the people who are the focus for studies is often a challenge in research. In the field of APA today I find that the voice of people with disabilities has been heard only to a very limited extent, and they have not often had the chance to actually influence the topics being researched. This remains the case in spite of the fact that inclusion is often stated to be central in the APA approaches. Consider, for example, the following: 'It is about advocacy in physical activity and promoting self-advocacy in people with a disability. ... It is an attitude about *including rather than excluding people*, but we can acknowledge a number of activity settings' (Reid 2003, 20, *my emphasis*).

Whether the lack of involvement of people with disabilities in the research can be seen as an ethical question, is open for debate. Consider, by contrast, the articulation of ethics in Aristotle's writings, as a practical discipline rather than a theoretical one: ethics is not reducible to right statements but rather instantiated in one's actions and character. Under this description, the conduct of APA research must be seen to promote inclusion not just in theory, but also in practice; I find the lack of involvement of people with disabilities in research remarkable.

At APA research conferences, for instance, very few of the participants have had a disability themselves.[5] By participants I mean being researchers or students who actively take part in the presentations and discussions at the conference. During the conferences people with disabilities typically have only got the chance to show themselves when 'entertaining the guests' by showing their skills in practical sport, dance or music. The fact that they contribute in this way is valuable, as it reminds conference participants of central issues and helps to set a frame for the presentations and discussions. People with disabilities, however, need not only to be seen or heard but, also, to a greater extent, to be listened to in the research of APA, to be *involved* in it. By 'involvement' I mean to participate in conducting the research or, just as importantly, to provide inspiration by revealing relevant and interesting research topics.

APA, however, is not the only area dealing with issues that relate to people with disabilities that is struggling when it comes to the practical representation of the researched in research. In 2007, for instance, I participated in a Nordic conference in special education on 'inclusion'. Interestingly, not a single presenter in the three-day conference had personal experience with being included and being in need of special adaptation to make participation possible. Quite thought-provokingly, the organisers also failed to provide the requested electronic version of the programme (readable to visually impaired participants); neither did they provide a hearing loop to the other disabled participant. Challenged on this, the organisers replied that they had not imagined that any disabled person would participate. As I see it, however, 'inclusion' is about participating and feeling welcomed, not about having to 'fight for your right' to get access and get the adaptations needed. Examples like these support the contention that there is still far to go in order to put theory and good intentions into practice.

I re-confirm the widespread view that current researchers, the research conducted and the potential participants in research in both special education and APA could all benefit from a greater involvement of researchers with disabilities. So why are so few people with disabilities involved in research in APA?

Challenges in Involving People with Disabilities in APA Research

The Challenge of Being Biased

One of the arguments that might be raised against involving people with disabilities in research could be that they could be too personally involved and therefore have difficulties being professional or objective in their research. When researchers research topics they have personal experience with, it is always relevant to consider the risk of 'going native' – that is, losing one's critical or professional distance as a researcher (Tregaskis and Goodley 2005; Kvale and Brinkmann 2008). In some research traditions, biases are seen as a problem because they can affect the possibility of being 'objective', that is, being neutral and 'free from bias'. In research traditions such as German critical psychology (Holzkamp 1983; Tolman 1994) and phenomenology (van Manen 1990; Spinelli 2005), this is viewed differently: when doing research it is not a matter of being biased or not, but a question of being aware of which biases one has in order to take them into account. As emphasised by Husserl, researchers are not and cannot be objective or neutral, and therefore 'objectivity' cannot be seen as a prerequisite for doing good research (Spinelli 2005).

The challenge of being biased is an issue often raised with regard to qualitative research. Yet to do quantitative or experimental studies, however, does not eliminate the fact that researchers have biases. Subjectivity is present in the topics we choose, and the methods we choose to use: both are influenced by our presuppositions. For any researcher, interest in the topic is an important prerequisite for doing good research, but also requires that we are on guard and check our findings, no matter the method we use. To check the findings is also part of doing good and ethically defensible research.

To be a researcher with a disability, it is important to be aware that one's personal experiences might differ greatly from the experiences of the participants in one's research. These are challenges, however, that are shared with all other researchers, with or without disabilities, and no matter what we research.

To be Biased and to be in a Unique Position

In research concerning 'disability', being biased, by having a disability and having experiences in participating in APA, could also be seen as giving the researcher a unique position, when trying to understand the participants' situations and statements. Tregaskis and Goodley (2005) emphasise how being a researcher with a disability researching issues related to disability holds challenges, but also how it can be of help in the phase of collecting and analysing research data.

Today, however, research in APA is carried out almost exclusively by able-bodied researchers.[6] As Bridges (2001) indicates, the fact that a person does not him- or herself have a disability does not mean that he or she cannot do good, valuable and ethically sound research, and I would add the following corollary: just as being a researcher with a disability does not dispose him- or herself to 'go native'.[7] It is a pity that the field of APA does not make fuller use of contributions from colleagues who both have the professional background and personal experience of disability. There are parallels in this discussion with arguments raised by early feminist researchers (e.g. Bjerrum Nielsen 1995) and also in the disability rights movement (Barton 1996; Charlton 2000; Johnstone 2001). Both approaches challenge traditional research and question whether research about women should rather be carried out by women, and whether research concerning people with disabilities should be carried out by people who themselves have disabilities.

As Bridges (2001) indicates, however, the discussion risks supporting the assumption that research can only authentically be carried out by someone who is in a highly similar situation to the persons the research concerns or, stronger, that the subject of the research is uniquely situated in epistemological terms. He argues that the position is not logically tenable, let alone desirable. It might not always be practical, easy or even possible if, for example, the research concerns children, people with learning difficulties or with dementia. Involving participants such as those is not impossible, but might demand that researchers need to use different methods, such as, for instance, certain research being done in developmental psychology researching infants (Stern 2000; Gopnik et al. 2000). I would not advocate that it is necessary for researchers to have a disability in order to do good and relevant research concerning disability; at the same time, however, I think that researchers who themselves live with a disability (just like living a life as a woman or a man) tend to gain insights into the challenges a disability can create and can contribute with more perspectives on the issue. This could include, for example, experiences of being visibly different from others, or being in need of assistance more often than most others, or experiences of not being treated with dignity. Experiences like these might be of value also during the process of finding relevant topics for research.

The importance of involving the people the research concerns and the 'nothing about us without us' approach, as emphasised by Charlton (2000), does not seem to have influenced the practice of research in APA to any great extent yet. If we look to other fields today, there is a greater awareness of the importance of involvement of the groups the research concerns. Research concerning women is done by both men and women, as well as research concerned with ethnic minorities tending not to be carried out solely by researchers belonging to the ethnic majorities.

Although the involved researchers might be both qualified and eager to do good research, if nobody from the group under investigation is involved, however, it seems appropriate to ask: 'Why not?'

Practical Barriers in Going into Research as a Disabled Researcher

The fact that few people with disabilities are involved in research has not only to do with prejudices, lack of interest or qualifications, but also with practical hindrances in society. Hindrances against participation have been extensively explored and described in the social model of disability (Swain et al. 1992; Hales 1996; Oliver 1996; Charlton 2000).

Not only have researchers with disabilities to overcome disabling barriers, they have to fight them constantly. This applies whenever attempting to gain access to a school or university, applying for a job, getting the necessary technical and practical support or getting access to knowledge necessary in order to do the job. I, for instance, began my career as a staff member at university by having to wait ten months for my adapted computer to arrive so I could start to work. My sighted colleague waited for a week for his non-adapted one. As a visually impaired researcher it is a challenge to get access to literature in a readable format, as access is being restricted by copyright protection. Quite paradoxically, even to obtain a copy of the existing electronic version of *Protection of Human Subjects with Disability: Guidelines for Research* (Stineman and Musick 2001) has so far been impossible or probably illegal.[8]. One could also ask whether to deny certain groups access to available information because of disability might be viewed as an ethical problem. Experiences such as these have, in addition to generating a great deal of frustration, provided important knowledge and inspiration to continue the research relating to disability and APA.

Inclusion in Practice in APA Research

If the field of APA research were to make better use of the knowledge and insight provided by those who live with a disability and who have experience with participating in physical activity, some hard choices need to be made.

To what extent can those of us in the field of research in APA today say that we, for instance, encourage gifted students with disabilities to go into research; that we select students with disabilities to attend conferences; and that we make an effort to give the floor equally to researchers with disabilities? Attracting more people with disabilities to become involved in APA research does not occur only through resolutions on equal rights passed by the World Health Organisation and the United Nations; it occurs mainly through the daily choices that each of us make locally. Attitudes are not the most important thing; it is *actions* that make a difference. If researchers in APA truly want to advocate inclusion, they should support the resolutions by including people with disabilities in the field to a greater extent than is the case today. This would help show both people with disabilities and society at large that people with disabilities have opinions and contributions that are valuable and should be taken seriously.

Involvement of People with Disabilities is Slowly Improving

No doubt matters can improve, of which there are several encouraging examples. In 2006 the board of the International Federation of Adapted Physical Activities (IFAPA) decided to appoint a person to be disability community liaison—ensuring that there will always be at least one person at the board at any time who besides being a professional also has a disability. At the same time, the board was made aware of the difficulties in accessing the IFAPA homepage to people with visual impairment, and an immediate decision was made and the money granted to carry out the necessary adaptations. This is an example of a barrier that was not erected deliberately to exclude people, but was due simply to a lack of awareness. It can also serve as an illustration of how collaboration can help improve matters.

Just as the extent of a disability is affected by society's willingness to allow for the participation, this goes for the field of research in APA as well. The International Symposium in Adapted Physical Activity (ISAPA) in Brazil 2007 was the first ISAPA ever to also offer the conference programme in an electronic format, while none of the previous organisers had made the effort.

Prior to the ISAPA 2007 the organisers invited me as a keynote speaker at the Brazilian APA conference.[9] To me this was an honour, while for many of the participants it was a new experience to meet a researcher who had a disability, was also an athlete and who had contributed to research in APA. In the studies, many had focused more on how to be of help to people with disabilities, and had less experience of being taught by them. To actually give the floor to researchers with disabilities at conferences can be viewed as an ethical choice, and can be one way to change perceptions and build bridges between professionals, athletes and researchers with and without disabilities.

As a researcher I was also different in the way that I presented research based on qualitative methods, while the conference have traditionally been dominated more by medical, physiological and sociological approaches. Studies based on qualitative methods potentially give the participants a chance to raise their voices and to be listened to. I am, however, all too aware that it is not the method but equally the topics chosen that might benefit from the participation of researchers with disabilities. I am also aware that this does not guarantee better research or a greater amount of research *with* and not only *on* people with disabilities, but I think that it increases the chances.

The Future of Ethical Aspects in APA Research

In this article I have indicated the apparent lack of discussion of ethical issues in research in APA, and given some examples of the challenges and its consequences. I have also called attention to the ethical dilemma that the lack of involvement of people with disabilities in APA research presents, and discussed some of the benefits that research in APA could gain from a greater involvement of people with disabilities.

When Loland (1992) writes about sport sciences being a young field that consists of very different approaches, from biomechanics to phenomenology, this applies to APA as well. In fact, one could say that APA is an even younger field. Perhaps the fact that APA is a young field has meant that the emphasis has been put on its establishment and legitimisation as a science, with more focus on the natural sciences and the technicalities of research, rather than on giving attention to, and debate on, ethics in research.

APA being a relatively new field of research, like other (young) fields, continuously constructs and reconstructs itself. This means that the choices that researchers make, the conferences they hold and the journals that publish their findings play an important part in this construction (Loland 1992). To develop good ethics in research is a joint responsibility, but researchers and organisers of research conferences have a central role in establishing good and reflected practices, which should also be reflected in the acceptance of papers for presentations at conferences.

To improve the involvement of people with disabilities, however, require choices and encouragement by people already involved in research. My claim is that a greater involvement of people with disabilities would contribute to both the internal and external validity of research in APA. If we want to change things, however, we must be willing to change practice to allow for participation, both in society and in the field of research in APA.

When I look to the future of research in APA, I am optimistic. I do not see the lack of involvement as an active, deliberate exclusion of people with disabilities by those without but more as a bad practice based on old and unreflective habits. This might be seen as an academic difference, as it results in the same practice: very few people with disabilities are involved in research in APA. Although the current researchers do not *actively* refuse involvement of people with disabilities in research, I, on the other hand, do not see many making an extra effort to involve them. I believe that those of us who do research with any minority group have an ethical obligation to make an extra effort, both in order to make a statement and to benefit the researched and the research itself.

I have no doubt that the existence and visibility of the Paralympics has inspired new athletes to participate in physical activity. The Paralympics shows that there is a variety of ways to do sport and also what is possible for people with disabilities to participate in and to achieve. In the same way a better representation of people with disabilities in research will demonstrate that disability is not a hindrance to contributions in research. Such contributions can be varied, as it is with participation in physical activity and sport. Not everybody has the capacity, the talent, the will or the desire to become a Paralympian, let alone to win a gold medal. Similarly, not everyone, disabled or not, has the capacity, talent, will or wish to become a researcher. Those who do, however, ought to be encouraged and welcomed. The involvement of people with or without disabilities in research in APA is not a matter of an 'either/or' but of how to develop a better 'both/and' through greater collaboration, and join together the efforts of researchers with a variety of qualifications, interests and experiences, which also includes having disabilities.

A greater involvement of people with disabilities might also help call attention to ethical issues in research, such as ensuring that participants are being treated with dignity. This assumption is, among others, supported by my experiences in attending gatherings with other people with disabilities. Even at the highly competitive Paralympics, I have often experienced participants being attentive to each others' needs, for instance a Russian athlete with one arm who helped a French blind athlete who was lost, or an American athlete in a wheelchair who was immobilised being pushed by a Chinese visually impaired athlete.

A greater involvement of people with disabilities in research might enhance the possibility of research looking into more important and relevant issues. As the example of the wheelchair basketball player illustrates, there are many problems out there in the world waiting to be explored and researched, from a variety of approaches, jointly.

A greater involvement of people with disabilities into research on different levels; as formulators of topics for research, as researchers and as members of ethical committees, will, of course, not solve all ethical problems in APA, but might improve some and will be a step in the right direction. Not least of all, I think it would benefit the necessary discussion of important ethical issues in research in APA.

ACKNOWLEDGEMENT
An earlier version of this paper was published in the proceedings of The International Symposium in Adapted Physical Activity (ISAPA), Rio Claro, Brazil, 2007.

NOTES

1. As my academic journey into the area of APA is influenced by my personal experiences as a visually impaired person, as a once clumsy kid and later as a Paralympic athlete, it seems appropriate to mention in this context my multifaceted engagement with APA.
2. This is not to say that psychological intervention cannot be ethically questionable; of course it can be, but at least it is open for ethical debate and expected to be so.
3. For the scope of this article I will use a broad definition of the term 'disability', understood as relating to individuals who have physical, sensory or mental challenges to a degree that require some adaptation to make participation in physical activity possible.
4. Whether it had to do with the actually walking or the interaction with an adult during the project is a further question.
5. Confirmed to me through personal correspondence with Claudine Sherrill, founder and former president of IFAPA (January 2008). She also confirmed that this fact has not often been questioned or documented in writing.
6. Confirmed through personal correspondence with Claudine Sherrill, January 2008.
7. Uncritically surrender to the host norms.
8. As reported by the librarian at my university, after contacting the publisher!
9. Sociedade Brasileira de Atividade Motora Adaptada (SOBAMA) 2005, Rio Claro, Brazil.

REFERENCES

BANNERMAN, D.J., J. SHELDON, J.A. SHERMAN, and A.E. HARCHIK. 1990. Balancing the right to habilitation with the right to personal liberties: The rights of people with developmental disabilities to eat too many doughnuts and take a nap. *Journal of Applied Behavior Analysis* 23: 79–89.

BARTON, L., ED. 1996. *Disability and Society*. London: Longman Ltd.

BJERRUM NIELSEN, H. 1995. Kvinneforskning som et kritisk korrektiv [Feminist Research as a critical corrective]. *Kvinneforskning* 4: 40–8.

BLESSING, D.L., D. MCCRIMMON, J. STOVALL and H.N. WILLIFORD. 1993. The effect of regular exercise programmes for visually impaired and sighted schoolchildren. *Journal of Visual Impairment & Blindness* 87: 50–2.

BRANTLINGER, E. 2005. Qualitative studies in special education. *Exceptional Children* 71 (2): 195–207.

BREDAHL, A.-M. 1997. *Kan man løbe fra problemene? Om udvikling synshandicap, og fysisk aktivitet* [Can You Run and Leave Your Problems Behind You? Development, Blindness and Physical Activity]. København: Hans Reitzels Forlag.

BRIDGES, D. 2001. The ethics of outsider research. *Journal of Philosophy of Education* 35 (3): 371–86.

BRINKMANN, S. and S. KVALE. 2005. Confronting the ethics of qualitative research. *Journal of Constructivist Psychology* 18: 157–81.

CHARLTON, J. 2000. *Nothing About Us Without Us: Disability Oppression and Empowerment*. London: University of California Press.

DROWATSKY, J.N. 1996. *Ethical Decision Making in Physical Activity Research*. Champaign, IL: Human Kinetics.

ERVIK S.N. 1998. Forskningsetikk [Research ethics]. *Nordisk tidsskrift for spesialpedagogikk* 3: 146–54.

GOPNIK, A., A.N. MELTZOFF and P.K. KUHL. 2000. *The Scientist in the Crib: What Early Learning Tells Us about the Mind*. New York: HarperCollins.

HALES, G., ed. 1996. *Beyond Disability. Towards an Enabling Society*. London: Sage.

HAYWOOD, H.C. 1977. The ethics of doing research … and of not doing it. *American Journal of Mental Deficiency* 81 (4): 311–17.

HOLZKAMP, K. 1983. *Grundlegung der Psychologie*. Frankfurt/Main: Campus.

JOHNSTONE, D. 2001. *An Introduction to Disability Studies*. London: David Fulton Publishers.

KVALE, S. and S. BRINKMANN. 2008 (in press). *InterViews: Learning the Craft of Qualitative Research Interviewing*, 2nd edn. London: Sage.

LOLAND, S. 1992. The mechanics and meaning of alpine skiing. Methodological and epistemological notes on the study of sport technique. *Journal of Philosophy of Sport* XIX: 55–79.

MCNAMEE, M., S.P. OLIVIER and P. WAINWRIGHT. 2007. *Research Ethics in Exercise, Health and Sport Sciences*. London and New York: Routledge.

MILLS, A.J. 1998. Comparison of shoot styles between 8ft 10ft baskets in wheelchair basketball. Presentation at third European Conference in APA, Thessaloniki Greece.

OLIVER, M. 1996. Defining impairment and disability: Issues at stake. In *Exploring the Divide*, edited by C. Barnes. Leeds: The Disability Press: 29–54.

ONYEWADUME, I.U. 2006. Fitness of Black African early adolescents with and without mild mental retardation. *APAQ* 23: 277–92.

REID, G. 2000. Future directions on inquiry in Adapted Physical Activity. *Quest* 52: 369–81.

———. 2003. Defining adapted physical activity. In *Adapted Physical Activity*, edited by R.D. Steadward, G. Wheeler and E. Watkinson. Edmonton, AB: University of Albert Press: 11–25.

REID, G., J.M. DUNN and J. MCCLEMENTS. 1993. People with disabilities as subjects in research. *APAQ* 10: 346–58.

RESNIK, D. 1981. *The Ethics of Science*. London: Routledge.

SPINELLI, E. 2005. *The Interpreted World: An Introduction to Phenomenological Psychology*. London: Sage Publications, Inc.

STERN, D.N. 2000. *The Interpersonal World of the Infant*. New York: Basic Books.

STINEMAN, M.G. and D.W. MUSICK. 2001. Protection of human subjects with disability: guidelines for research. *Archives of Physical Medicine and Rehabilitation* 82: 9–14.

SWAIN, J., V. FINKELSTEIN, S. FRENCH and M. OLIVER. 1992. *Disabling Barriers – Enabling Environments*. London: Sage Publications.

TOLMAN, C. 1994. *Psychology, Society and Subjectivity: Introduction to German Critical Psychology*. London: Routledge.

TRANDA, V., I. BOIKOU, S. BATSIU et al. 1998. The exercises adaptation for the improvement of reaction time, as it concerns people with Down's Syndrome. Paper given at third European Conference in APA, Thessaloniki, Greece.

TRANØY, K.E. 1986. *Vitenskapen – Samfunnsmakt og Livsform* [Science—Society Power and Lifestyle]. Oslo: Universitetsforlaget.

TREGASKIS, C. and D. GOODLEY. 2005. Disability research by disabled and non-disabled people: Towards a relational methodology of research production. *International Journal of Social Research Methodology: Theory & Practice* 8 (5): 363–74.

TSAKLIS, P., G. AMBATZIDIS, K. BEIS and A. KITSIOS. 1998. The ideal relation of extensor and flexor muscles of the knee as the target of rehabilitation programs. Paper given at third European Conference in APA, Thessaloniki, Greece.

ULRICH, D.A., B.D. ULRICH, R.M. ANGULO-KINZLE and J. YUN. 2001. Treadmill training of infants with Down syndrome: Evidence based developmental outcomes. *Pediatrics* 108 (5): e84.

VAN MANEN, M. 1990. *Researching Lived Experience. Human Science for an Action Sensitive Pedagogy.* New York: State University of New York Press.

VEHMAS, S. 2004. Ethical analysis of the concept of disability. *Mental Retardation* 42 (3): 209–22.

Anne-Mette Bredahl, Department of Physical Education, Norwegian School of Sport Sciences, Postboks 4014, Ullevål stadion, 0806 Oslo, Norway.
E-mail: anne-mette.bredahl@nih.no

INDEX